Happy Christmas

Love Catherine x

CHAMPION

A donation from the proceeds of this book will go to Cancer Trials Ireland, a charity dedicated to providing every patient with cancer access to high-quality and potentially life-altering cancer trials.

'Clinical trials offer patients very real, tangible, important benefits – but they can also provide something as vital as it is intangible: hope. That is Pat's real gift to the people who come after him who are diagnosed with pancreatic cancer. Thank you, Pat.'

EIBHLÍN MULROE, CEO of Cancer Trials Ireland

CHAMPION

PAT SMULLEN

with Donn McClean

A MEMOIR

Gill Books

Gill Books
Hume Avenue
Park West
Dublin 12
www.gillbooks.ie

Gill Books is an imprint of M.H. Gill and Co.

978 07171 9365 3

Design and print origination by O'K Graphic Design, Dublin
Edited by Esther Ní Dhonnacha
Proofread by Ruairí Ó Brógáin

Printed by Clays Ltd, Suffolk
This book is typeset in 12/17 pt. Minion

The paper used in this book comes from the wood pulp of managed forests. For every tree felled, at least one tree is planted, thereby renewing natural resources.

A CIP catalogue record for this book is available from the British Library.

5 4 3 2 1

Dedicated with love to my children,
Hannah, Paddy and Sarah.

ACKNOWLEDGEMENTS

There are many people who made this book possible, who helped to bring it from concept to completion.

Big thanks to Brough Scott, who planted the idea in my head in the first place, and who convinced me that it would be a good thing to do. To all at Gill Books: to Teresa Daly and Laura King and my editor Rachel Thompson, and to Deirdre Nolan, whose belief in my story made this book a reality.

Thanks to everyone who helped me tell my story: to Dermot Weld, Kevin O'Ryan, Fran Berry, Joanna Morgan and Tom and Barry Lacy. To Mum, who was able to fill in some of the blanks in the story of my childhood; and to her and Dad, and my brothers, Sean, Ger and Brian, for being ever present in that story and in my life. To Donn McClean, who listened patiently and intently as I recounted episodes from my career and from my life, and who helped me put them all together. And to Frances, Hannah, Paddy and Sarah – not just for their help in writing my story, but for everything else too.

CONTENTS

PROLOGUE

The thoroughbred exists because its selection has depended, not on experts, technicians or zoologists, but on a piece of wood: the winning post of the Epsom Derby.

— FEDERICO TESIO

H arzand is nice and relaxed in the stalls. Stall nine, good draw, right in the middle. Colm O'Donoghue to my right, Seamie Heffernan to my left, but nobody is saying anything. Game faces. I give Harzand a little pat down the neck and I gather my reins. The starter shouts.

Inhale.

And they're off!

We're not that quickly away. That's Harzand's way. I don't expect to be up with the pace, but I don't want to get too far back in the field either. You don't win the Derby if you're too far back.

So the field leave the stalls for the Investec Derby of 2016. Port Douglas is hurried up to the lead with Deauville, also racing handily, and also moving forward in the early stages, Shogun. Ulysses up towards the inside as well as they make their way through the first furlong, with Port Douglas just taking them along.

I give him a little squeeze as we race uphill to the right-handed elbow. Colm O'Donoghue has gone forward ahead of me on Port Douglas; Seamie Heffernan is squeezing away beside me on Idaho, getting him to go forward too. I'm just nudging Harzand: get your position but don't expend too much energy.

1

Towards the outside of the field both Cloth Of Stars, racing in a handy position, in company as well with Massaat, who's racing a little keenly, as Port Douglas now crosses over and makes his way towards the running rail.

I'm happy enough as we round the elbow and start to move back to our left, back towards the inside running rail. I want to get as close to the rail as I can, as smoothly as I can. You want to have racing room, you don't want to be stuck behind horses with no way out, but you don't want to be too far wide racing towards Tattenham Corner: you don't want to be giving away too much ground. There are shouts and there is buffeting, but Harzand is strong. We ship a bump but he doesn't break stride. Somebody shouts for room to my left, Dougie Costello, I think, but I'm not giving away any space. It's race riding and this is the biggest race of them all.

In fourth place is Shogun, just ahead of Moonlight Magic, who's towards the inside at the moment, Moonlight Magic sitting in about fifth place as, settling just behind those, we have Idaho.

We're going a decent pace and Harzand is going as fast as he wants to go. Any faster and he's out of his comfort zone. But we're happy, seventh or eighth in a well-stretched-out field, plenty of racing room, three off the rail, Seamie Heffernan on Idaho just ahead of me, a danger. Andrea Atzeni to my inside on Ulysses, another danger. Dangers everywhere.

Ulysses drops into about midfield with Harzand at the moment, and also Across The Stars. US Army Ranger is given time towards the rear of the field, in company with Wings Of Desire, and having jumped from the outside stall, Red Verdon has been given time as well, crossing right behind the field along with Humphrey Bogart at the rear of the field.

It's the Derby but, really, when you are in it, it's just another race. You're trying to do the same thing that you are trying to do in a maiden at Roscommon: maximise your chance of winning. Conserve your horse's energy, get him settled, get him into a racing rhythm. Play to your horse's strengths. I have no doubt that Harzand will stay, so I'm determined that this will be a test of stamina more than a test of speed. But don't go for home too early.

So out in front and at a reasonable gallop, it is Port Douglas who tows the Derby field up the hill and continues the climb, from, in second place, the Godolphin blue jacket of Cloth Of Stars. Third for Moonlight Magic, racing on the inside of Massaat, with in fifth place the free-sweating Idaho, on the outside of Shogun and then Across The Stars.

There are people along the rails, but you don't see them. You see your horse's head, his ears, his mane. You remain motionless, allow him to stride on beneath you. No more effort than necessary, no more energy than you need to expend. I see the lads around me, Kieren Fallon, Kevin Manning, all threats, all dangers. We keep our rhythm, easy now.

Harzand midfield in company with Ulysses, then Biodynamic, who's just ahead of Deauville, Wings Of Desire in those maroon colours. US Army Ranger, the all dark blue, has Humphrey Bogart and Red Verdon behind. As now the field begin that trademark descent towards Tattenham Corner.

Freewheel down the hill. You maintain the metronome, soft hands, light touch, tell your horse that you don't need him. Not yet. You'll need him soon, all right. You'll need every ounce of energy that he has in his body soon.

And there is no hanging about for Port Douglas out in front; he has gone five or six lengths clear.

There's no urgency. I knew that Colm was probably going to go forward on Port Douglas, one of the Ballydoyle horses, stretch the field out. Make it a good test. I hope that he will come back to the field. I trust that he will weaken at some point in the home straight.

In second place Cloth Of Stars. Massaat, Biodynamic moves up on the outside. Then behind these we have Idaho. Just pushed along to give chase is Moonlight Magic.

I know that Ryan Moore is lurking somewhere in behind on US Army Ranger, the Ballydoyle favourite. I can't do anything about that, though. There are some variables that you can't control. Concentrate on the ones you can.

At this stage, Across The Stars with Harzand, Algometer comes next with Wings Of Desire. US Army Ranger still in no hurry, and right at the back of the field is Red Verdon.

Harzand is nicely balanced as we wing down the hill around Tattenham Corner. He's a well-balanced horse, and we're travelling well. That's crucial. If you are travelling and you are balanced, Tattenham Corner is not an issue. It's the horses who are under pressure who don't handle the downhill run. His foot doesn't seem to be ailing him at all, and that's a relief. I'd know if it was. Tattenham Corner would find it out.

Port Douglas leads the turn for home, but the pack are right at his heels. Cloth Of Stars poised to have first crack, then Massaat. Pulling out is Idaho, Harzand comes next.

We cross the path at the top of the home straight, about three and a half furlongs from home, and I'm looking for racing room. I want to go forward now. Seamie is to my right on Idaho, travelling well, keeping me in. Friends, eh? You don't have friends in the Derby; you don't ask for favours. Every square inch of racing room you get, you earn it. I let him pass and I pull out behind him.

Pulled towards the outside Wings Of Desire, US Army Ranger, Red Verdon getting a nice seam right up the inside rail. Port Douglas is taken on by Cloth Of Stars, now joining in down the outside is Idaho. Harzand comes next.

We get to the outside and into the clear. Seamie is rowing away on Idaho to my left, about a length and a half in front of me, and he's moving forward to join the leaders and rolling to his left with the camber of the track. I get lower in the saddle on Harzand, and he picks up. I give him a shout, give him a squeeze, give him one smack of the whip, and he picks up again.

Red Verdon ran out of room on the inside. Right down the outside Wings Of Desire and US Army Ranger.

We're not getting any closer to Seamie as the two-furlong marker flashes past. The masses are roaring but I don't hear them. I just see Seamie to my left and still in front of me, and the green baize that stretches down the hill and up the hill through the deep-packed crowds to the most famous winning post in racing.

Idaho, striped cap, and Harzand are the first to go for home. US Army Ranger is now in full cry towards the outside.

Harzand is strong. He's in full flight now and still going forward. I can see that Idaho is wilting. Slowly, we are inching closer. Eating into his lead. We get level with him on the run to the furlong pole. Harzand is rolling down the hill, in on top of Idaho, so I switch my whip, right hand to left hand, in order to keep him straight.

We're past Idaho now, we're a neck up, a half-a-length up, but there's that incline. Downhill for ages and now an uphill run to the line. It's a gruelling test, a true test. It saps all your energy. I can sense another horse closing in to my right. I can hear the hooves and I catch a glimpse of his white face.

They enter the final furlong. Harzand, US Army Ranger has got to the leader's girths, but has still got to get by.

US Army Ranger gets to Harzand's tail. He gets to the back of my saddle. He gets to my boot. I ask Harzand for one last effort. For all that he has. It's not fair – he has run his heart out for 11½ furlongs – but this is the Derby, and we just need one more lunge. One more lung-bursting effort for history.

And Harzand is pulling out more!

US Army Ranger doesn't get any closer. Harzand digs deeper than he has ever dug before. He finds the reserves of energy that we thought he had, that we hoped he had, and, actually, we are going away again inside the final 25 yards.

And it's Harzand, in the colours of the Aga Khan.

We hit the line. The Epsom Derby. Really? The Derby. Have we really won the Derby?

Exhale.

Sunday Night, March 2018

I wasn't feeling great on the Sunday night. Frances had been up with me all day, Dr Adrian McGoldrick had been up to see me; but now it was late, everybody had gone. It was my first night in a hospital bed on my own, knowing exactly what was happening, knowing that there was a juggernaut coming down the tracks to face me but not knowing exactly what form it would take. My mind was in turmoil: the uncertainty, the fear of the unknown. I was trying to put a brave face on things, but I wasn't really managing that too well.

I had never met Dee Swansea before, I had never seen her before, but suddenly she was there, in my room, sitting beside me, introducing herself, the head nurse in the Hawthorn Ward in St Vincent's Private Hospital. She talked me through everything, the processes, the timing, the details but, more importantly, she reassured me. These people knew exactly what they were doing. 'We'll get through this,' she said. 'We'll come out the other side.' It was *we* and *us*, not *you* and *them*. Like, that they were all in it with me. That I wasn't alone.

That conversation was a psychological tonic. It turned my frame of mind inside out. The fear had left me; I felt safe, reassured, comforted, up for the fight. We'll get through this, we'll come out the other side, all in it together.

I slept that night.

CHAPTER 1

'What do you want to be when you grow up?'

The headmaster was asking everybody.

There were nurses and teachers and doctors and farmers. To be honest, when you were growing up in Rhode in County Offaly in the 1980s, in rural Ireland, you didn't know much other than nurses and teachers and doctors and farmers. And the ESB, the Electricity Supply Board. Most of my classmates' parents worked for the ESB.

'A jockey,' I said.

There was a bit of a murmur around the classroom.

'A what?' asked the headmaster.

'A jockey,' I said again.

Some of my classmates laughed. They were behind me. I was up at the top of the class, so I couldn't see most of them – but some of them were laughing, all right. Most of them didn't know that a jockey was a thing, that it was possible to make a living out of riding horses.

The headmaster laughed too.

'Good man, Patrick.'

I didn't enjoy school, especially primary school: Scoil Mhuire Naofa in Rhode. I never enjoyed being in a classroom; I always preferred being outside, working with the animals, herding cattle or mending fences or even picking stones (and I wasn't a huge fan of picking stones), long before I was ever into horses. So I was starting off on a negative straight away, in a classroom, within four walls, behind a desk.

I found it hard work from the start. I was quiet enough as a kid. I didn't mess in class a lot and I didn't distract others, but I wouldn't have been the most academically gifted student in the school, and I was always playing catch-up.

As well as that, I don't think that the headmaster liked me very much. His wife taught in the school too, and I don't think she thought a lot of me either.

I wasn't encouraged at school; I was often just left there. I was rarely chosen to do anything in class, even read out loud. People would be taking it in turns to read a sentence from our reader; the teacher would be going through the class in order, by desk, by seat. You'd figure out when it was your turn to read, you'd be all geared up; then it would come to your turn, and he'd skip you. He'd go on to the next kid and you'd sit there, spurned, ignored.

It wasn't a healthy environment for me, and it certainly wasn't an environment in which I was encouraged to learn or develop.

Consequently, I downed tools early enough in my time at school. It was self-perpetuating then. I wasn't getting on, so I wasn't putting the effort in, so I wasn't getting on, so I wasn't putting the effort in. Chicken, egg.

I fought back a bit, and it spiralled as a result; the punishments were more frequently administered, but I couldn't really do anything about it. This was 1980s Ireland: teachers held a lofty position in rural communities, and I was just a kid. As well as that, my mother and father didn't like to rock the boat. You just put your head down and got on with things.

That was my father's attitude, and it was one that served him well all his life.

I used to have some epic battles with my mother in the mornings before school. Nearly every day. There was nothing enjoyable about school for me at all. I'm not saying that I would have ended up being a doctor or a rocket scientist or anything, and I would never have changed a thing about how my career as a jockey got going, but I could have achieved more at school if I had been in a different environment, if it hadn't been as difficult for me as it was.

I always regretted that I didn't receive a proper, good education. Not a master's or a PhD, but just a good education. It was something that was always in the back of my mind. It drove me on, though. It made me more determined to succeed than I might have been otherwise. I resolved that I would find something I was good at, and that I would make sure I succeeded in that, whatever it was going to be.

It's also why Frances and I were always adamant that our three children would get a good education. Thankfully, they took to school quite easily. (They take after their mother in that regard.)

I did enjoy secondary school more. I didn't hate going to secondary school like I hated going to primary school, but I suppose by then, academically, a lot of the damage was done. I realised how far behind I was in a lot of subjects when I got to secondary school, how hard I would have to work just to catch up, and I was only looking for an excuse to get out. I found one, too – a brilliant excuse.

I had a great upbringing. We were very much a working-class family. My mother was a stay-at-home mother, and my dad was a farm labourer.

They were both born in Rhode, they grew up in Rhode, and they raised us in Rhode. Four boys: Seán, Ger (Slugger), me and

Brian, in that order. The four of us shared the one bedroom. Two double beds in the same room. That was some craic. The fights we had, the fun. Our parents were very strict with us when we were in public – we had to behave ourselves when we were outside the house – but inside the house, they didn't seem to mind if we were messing or fighting or up late acting the maggot!

Rhode was a very rural village then, so we had loads of room, fields and space and open road. Even if we weren't out on the farm with Dad, we were out wandering the fields, or climbing trees or rolling around in the muck somewhere. During the holidays or on weekends, you went off in the morning, and you came back when you were hungry. We didn't have much, but we didn't want for anything.

Our house was an open house, too. That was the way my mother and father were. The door was always open at just about any time of the day or night. You could be there, in the sitting room, and one of the neighbours would just walk in. They wouldn't even knock on the door!

My mother and father welcomed everybody.

They weren't drinkers, there was never any drink in the house; but there was always food. I don't know how my mother did it. We didn't have a lot of money, but there was always food or dinner for anyone who wanted it. I would often be woken up at 11 or 12 o'clock at night by voices in the kitchen or in the sitting room: people having a discussion or an argument about football or politics!

My father worked for Trevor Cotton on his farm, and then for Seán Buckley when he bought most of the land from Mr Cotton. It was Seán Buckley's farm that supplied all the beef to the butcher's, FX Buckley. Dad and his brother-in-law Noel Hickey ran the farm between them and, after Noel sadly passed away, Dad ran it on his own.

Trevor Cotton was always very good to my father, as he was later on to me. When I got older and got going and managed to get a few quid together, he sold the 44 acres of land that he retained to me, and that is where Frances and I built our house and a few stables and settled down with our kids. The Brick Field. The field in which I worked with my father and my brothers when I was a kid. We called our house and our patch Brickfield Stud. Strange the way life works out.

Dad loved his work. He loved being out on the farm. He did go to work for the ESB in Rhode for a little while, just for a couple of months, but he didn't enjoy it. It was a really good job in the ESB – they were such a good employer: pensions and health benefits and everything – but he just didn't like being inside all day. He loved being out in the open.

We loved being out on the farm with Dad. I can't remember a time in my childhood when I wasn't out on the farm with my father. We probably weren't much help when we were very small. Back then, it was probably as much about getting us out from under our mother's feet as it was about getting us to help. But as we got older, we helped out, all right. We did a little bit of everything, herding cattle, scraping the yards, keeping it all clean, fixing gates, and we loved it. And we learned to drive in the fields. Tractors and cars and anything else that had an engine and wheels.

My father instilled in all of us the idea that you needed to work hard, and I had that work ethic throughout my whole career. I never thought that I was the most gifted rider, but I always thought that, if I worked hard at it, I had a chance.

Lambing season was crazy. Dad would drive back to the farm at around 12 o'clock every night to check the ewes, and at least one of us would go with him. I didn't love it every night. Like any child, you'd moan or give out that you had to go back out, especially if it was a cold night, but, in general, I always wanted to be on the farm and, from an early age, I always wanted to have a farm or land of some description.

For hard work, though, you didn't have to look beyond the bog. I never minded hard work, but the bog was something else. Everybody hated it, all the kids hated it, and yet everybody had to do it. If you lived in Rhode, you had to do your time on the bog.

During the summer, Dad would come home from work and have his dinner, and then we'd all be back out to the bog, cutting and heaping and footing turf. That was our fuel for the winter. There was no oil or gas in our house, no central heating: it was all turf from the bog. That's what kept every house in Rhode warm during the winter. You had a fairly short window within which you had to cut your turf for the winter, and it was all hands on deck then.

Thankfully, when we got a bit older, we got to a point where we were making a few quid, and my brothers and I clubbed together and bought in the turf for my mother and father, and that was the best money we ever spent!

Gaelic football was always a massive part of life in Rhode. People eat, sleep and drink Gaelic football, and the GAA has always played a huge role in the community. Rhode has always had great football teams: they are always competitive in the county championship, and they regularly win it.

Some of the great Offaly football players have come from Rhode. The most famous Rhode Gaelic football player, though, is undoubtedly Séamus Darby, who scored the winning goal for Offaly against Kerry in the 1982 All-Ireland Final. That was fairytale stuff.

There were some celebrations in Rhode that night, and they lasted for weeks. The Sam Maguire Cup did the rounds. It was in our school and it was in our house. It was probably in every house in the village at some point. I was only five at the time, but I remember all the excitement, and I remember sitting in the Sam Maguire Cup in our house!

Dad played for Rhode and he trained some of the underage teams. I played too when I was younger, but, unfortunately, I wasn't very good. I was small and I was light. I wasn't built for it.

I tried, though; I played until I was 11. I struggled away, I did my best, until one day my manager told me that I wasn't very good. It just confirmed what I knew myself deep down, but that was it for me.

I might have been looking for an excuse to give it up anyway, but that was the final straw. I came home that day. The washing machine was just in front of the back door at home when you came in, down the hall. I fired my bag along the ground towards the washing machine and I told my mother, 'I'm never playing football again.'

And I didn't.

I got a bit of stick for not playing football. Like, what are you at, off riding horses, off with your ponies? You should be playing football. That sickened me a bit against Gaelic football. So when I was a teenager, like 13, 14, 15, I was a little bit anti-GAA.

I came back full circle, though. Our kids played football: Hannah was always very good at Gaelic football, from the time that she started playing, and Paddy was always a great little guy to get stuck in, and Sarah seemed to have an innate talent for the game too, wherever she got it! They played with the club and they played with the school too.

We weren't allowed to hang out in the village when we were younger. Up to the shop and home again, or off to church and home, or up to the football pitch and home. Dad just didn't like us hanging around. Idle hands, he said. He wanted us all to be active. We fought with him about it a little bit; some of our friends would be hanging out in the village, but he didn't allow us to do that, and he was right. He wanted us to be doing things; he wanted us to be occupied.

I didn't know it at the time, but I would soon happen upon a pursuit that would occupy just about all my time.

CHAPTER 2

I t was Seán's fault, mainly. My involvement with horses was all down to my eldest brother.

Seán decided, after he did his Leaving Certificate, that he wanted to work with horses. It was out of the blue a bit; he had never really had anything to do with horses. All his work with animals – like mine and Gerard's and Brian's and Dad's – was with agricultural animals. But Seán took this notion into his head that he wanted to work with horses. So he went up to Greenhills Riding School in Kill in County Kildare after he finished school, and he did six months there, for no pay. Just so that he could ride and gain experience with horses. He was that determined. He was always clever, Seán; he could have gone on to do whatever he wanted to do, but all he wanted to do was work with horses.

Shortly after finishing in Greenhills, he started working for Joanna Morgan. He just saw an ad in *The Irish Field* looking for staff, so he wrote to Joanna and he got the job.

Joanna has always been an unbelievable person. She was a bit of a trailblazer. Originally from Wales, she rode point-to-pointers there, and she arrived in Ireland in 1974, just two years after female riders were first allowed a licence to ride. She was a pioneer. Riding for Séamus McGrath, Joanna set new landmarks for female riders all over the place. She was the first woman to ride in an Irish Classic, she was the first professional woman to ride at Royal Ascot, and she was the first female rider to ride a winner in Kenya! In fact, she rode over two hundred winners during her riding career, and she managed to combine riding with training before she retired from riding at the end of the 1997 season to concentrate on training and on buying and selling horses.

It was tough work for Seán at Joanna's, but he got on with it, and he loved it. He learned lots from Joanna and from her then-husband, Tommy McGivern. Seán would stay in Joanna's for the week and he'd come home at the weekends. I would usually go with Dad and Seán in the car on the Sunday evening. Joanna was very personable, very friendly; she would always be chatting to Dad when we'd go down. One Sunday evening she asked me and Dad if we would like to come in and have a look around the yard. It was all very exciting for me, seeing racehorses, a racing yard. Then Joanna asked me if I would like to go down some weekend and work with the horses. I went down the following weekend, and I loved it from the start.

Joanna had ponies, so she threw me up on a pony straight away. I had no experience of riding at all. There was this donkey that belonged to a neighbour of ours, and I used to hop up on him and ride him a bit, but to ride a pony was different.

I loved working with the horses, too. Joanna had about 30 horses at the time; she had horses in training and she had horses for the breeze-up sales, so there was a lot to be done.

It was some opportunity for me, learning how to ride from Joanna and Tommy. It was some education. Joanna was a brilliant jockey, and to have her taking an interest in you, teaching you how to ride, the subtleties and the nuances of riding a thoroughbred, was some head start for a young fellow. And Tommy was a top-class rider in his day. He had this really good, patient way with kids. He taught me an awful lot too.

I went from riding ponies to riding racehorses within about six months. It was a bit of a baptism of fire for sure, but I loved it. I was riding five or six horses out every morning, two-year-olds mainly, the breeze-up horses and the racehorses that were there at the time.

There must have been at least a little bit of ability in there, buried deep in me somewhere, but when you're young like that, you have no fear. I'd never say no to anything Joanna would ask me to do. Joanna was brave as well; she'd let me ride anything after a little while.

There were falls, of course. I wasn't a natural from day one, or anything like it. I got dropped and I got hurt, but I always picked myself up and got back up again. It was a great way for me to learn. In at the deep end.

I rode in the breeze-up sales at Newmarket when I was 13. It was some experience for a young fellow. I had never been out of Ireland before – I had never ventured too far from Rhode before. And here I was, on a ferry over to England.

Breeze-up sales are different from other sales, in that the horses 'breeze', or run, along a racecourse for two furlongs so that people can watch them or time them before they decide if they are going to buy them or bid for them. All the horses are unraced two-year-olds.

The horses used to come up two by two. With Joanna's horses, I'd ride one and Joanna would ride the other up beside me. Then we'd go back and do it again with the next two. That was some thrill, riding up the course at Newmarket, up the Rowley Mile, where they run the Craven Stakes and the Guineas and where they used to run the Champion Stakes.

About two years after I first went to Joanna's, Seán went to Canada. Joanna encouraged him to go; it was quiet enough at Joanna's during the summer and she said that he should go off and get some experience. So he went over to Roger Attfield, one of the top trainers in Canada, and he never came back. Seán went on to work for Frank Stronach's Stronach Group in Canada, where he still works today.

Seán's departure meant that it was very difficult for me to continue to go to Joanna's. I was very young, so I couldn't keep going on my own. I didn't have a car and it was too far for a bicycle, and I couldn't keep on asking my father to bring me every day. But I always appreciated all that Joanna did for me and, later on when I got going, I would ride for her whenever I could, and I would travel to the races with her sometimes. We have always had a very good relationship.

The only person who had horses within a distance of my home that was accessible for a 14-year-old on a bicycle was Tom Lacy. I got on to my father to get on to Tom to ask him if I could go in and work for him. I had Dad driven mad, plaguing him, so eventually he went up to Tom and asked him. Tom was great – he said, 'Yeah, sure send him in.' So I went in that first weekend and, again, I loved it. I just loved being around horses.

Tom had all types of horses: Flat horses, jumps horses, young horses, broodmares, a mixture of everything. It was a busier yard than Joanna's but, in many ways, the two yards were very similar. As in Joanna's, there was a lot to be done, so I got stuck in from early.

I went into Tom's any chance I got. School holidays, days off, everything. It was all I wanted to do. I was riding out and mucking out and working with the mares and breaking yearlings. Everything. And as soon as I turned 15, I applied for my apprentice's licence. I had the form filled in and ready to go so that, on my 15th birthday, all I had to do was send it in to the Turf Club.

Working with horses was brilliant, riding out and riding work. But the prospect of riding a real racehorse in a real horse race, on a real racecourse, against other horses and other riders, that would be dreamland.

BACK PAIN

The back pain started in the summer of 2017, and it drove me mad. You always had your aches and pains, they went with the territory, they went with the job, but you dealt with them and you moved on. This one felt different though. I couldn't shift this one.

I went to my physiotherapists as usual, Martha Kellaghan and John Butler. They tried to fix me, as they usually did, but there was no easing of the pain this time. It was so bad that I went for an MRI scan on my lower back, but it came back clear. I put it down to age. I had turned 40 the previous May. I had never been 40 before.

Turned out, if the MRI scan had been done on a different part of my back, a little bit higher, it would have revealed the source of the problem. But you have to be specific when you are going for your MRI scan, you have to focus on one area, and my pain was in my lower back, so that was the area that got the attention, not higher up, which is where the problem actually was.

That was a winter of discontent for me. I soldiered on, I said I would take it easy. My idea of taking it easy was riding one day a week. So I rode at Dundalk every Friday and I continued to get physio on my back. I hated taking painkillers, even paracetamol. I always preferred to allow my immune system to deal with any ailments if I could. That winter, though, I took painkillers, all right.

I went to South Africa for the International Jockeys' Challenge and, while it was a great trip, I was in agony with my back. The plane journey to South Africa was a nightmare; I was writhing around in my seat for the whole flight. I rode a winner there, but I almost passed out after crossing the winning line. I was in constant discomfort. People were saying that the humidity and the altitude were factors, so I put it down to that.

I went to Dubai as usual, and I went to Bahrain in February. I was riding there, but I also wanted to get some sun on my back, see if it would help with the pain. It didn't really. Then I was back to Ireland for the build up to the Flat season in February, back in Dermot's, riding out and riding work and getting to know the young horses. Looking forward to the 2018 season that was stretching out in front of me.

It was in the middle of March that I started to get a little bit of reflux, heartburn. I started to take Rennies, and they gave me a little bit of relief, but I was very concerned that something wasn't right. My dad had had severe heartburn before he was diagnosed with cancer, and I had never had heartburn before. Frances and I talked about it, and I mentioned it to Dr Adrian McGoldrick, the Senior Medical Officer at the Turf Club, who was a brilliant medical officer. I used to get regular blood tests, because of the history of cancer in the family – Dad died from cancer, Dad's father died from cancer – and my regular blood tests were all coming back fine, so I kicked on.

My weight was very good, unusually good. I put it down to the fact that I was older, that I had just turned 40 and that, finally, my body was starting to get the message! But actually, it was the cancer on the inside, busy working away.

On the Wednesday before the start of the turf Flat season, I came home from Dermot's and went to the toilet, and my urine was a really bad colour. When I told Frances, she tried to hide her concern, but she was straight with me and she was stern: directly up to Adrian's to get it checked out. My face had gone a bit of a jaundiced colour, too. Adrian took another urine sample and he sent me immediately to the Beacon Hospital in Dublin.

Adrian told me that it was probably gallstones, so I wasn't overly concerned initially. My main concern was the fact that I had told Mick Halford that I would ride work for him the following morning, on the Thursday morning, and, in my mind, there was no way I was missing that.

That was my thinking at the time. I just wanted to get the tests done and finished, boxes ticked, so that I could get back to doing what I always did. I had never missed a day's work, I had never missed a day's racing through ill-health, so there was no reason to start just because I had turned 40 and I had a bit of back pain. I just didn't really think of it as an option. I wasn't going to let Mick Halford down.

They wanted to keep me in overnight on Wednesday night so that they could do their tests on Thursday morning, but I just saw that as a waste of time. There was no need for me to stay in. If I stayed on Wednesday night, I would have had to miss riding work on Thursday morning, and that made no sense to me, so I checked myself out and went home.

It was an important piece of work, on a filly who was set to run on the Sunday at Naas, on the first day of the new turf Flat season. I actually rode two lots for Mick that morning before going back to the Beacon later on Thursday. Frances went back up to the Beacon with me on Thursday afternoon – I presume to make sure that I stayed there so that they could do their tests on Friday morning!

I had rides booked for Dundalk on Friday evening, and all I wanted was to be discharged so that I could go to Dundalk. It was so childish of me, and selfish. I had all these people trying to do the right thing for me, trying to look after me, trying to figure out what was wrong with me, and all I wanted was to go home so that I could ride at Dundalk. On Friday morning, Frances had had enough of me.

'Look,' she said, 'you're going to have to miss Dundalk.'

I rang my agent, Kevin O'Ryan.

'Kevin, they want to keep me here. I'm sorry but I can't make it to Dundalk this evening.'

'No problem,' said Kevin. 'Let them do what has to be done, and you'll be back out and ready for Naas on Sunday.'

Naas on Sunday was a big deal, the start of the turf Flat season, the first Flat racing on grass in Ireland since the previous November, the first two-year-olds' race, the Group 3 Park Express Stakes. So I was happy enough with that.

The tests started early on Friday and they went on all day, MRI and CT scans. Then Friday night rolled around, and I was settling in for another night in the Beacon Hospital, thinking of Naas on Sunday. I was just sitting there on the bed, Frances on the chair beside me, when the doctor came in and told us that they had found a tumour on the pancreas.

The world stopped for a second or two. A tumour on the pancreas. It was difficult to know what to do with that information. Difficult to know how to react. It was like an out-of-body experience, like the doctor was saying it about somebody else, to somebody else, like I was floating above the room, observing what was going on. Not like I was in the thick of it.

Suddenly, in an instant, everything changed. The things that I thought were important, all of a sudden, with the uttering of just a few words, didn't seem to be important anymore. Missing Dundalk on Friday, trying to get to Naas on Sunday, worrying about letting Mick Halford down, about letting Dermot Weld down, about letting owners down. Suddenly they weren't the most important things in the world.

It was all a bit of a haze, really, but we held it together. Frances and I talked about it and decided that we were just going to get stuck in, that we would do whatever we needed to do in order to get it sorted. Frances stayed with me for a little while but, in the end, obviously she had to go home to the kids.

I have to admit, I wasn't great after she had left. All my pragmatism, all my courage, all my bravery, it all went out the window. I felt lonely, lost, weak, helpless. And that night, that Friday night in the Beacon Hospital, lying in my bed, on my own, staring at the ceiling, unable to sleep, my mind in turmoil, that was the worst night of my life.

CHAPTER 3

When I watched racing, I mainly watched the jockeys, not the horses.

My father was a big sports man; he loved sport. He played Gaelic football to a high level with Rhode, and he obviously watched Gaelic football and hurling on television, but he watched other sports too, including soccer and golf and rugby. And racing. He'd have the Derby or the Guineas or the Grand National or the Galway Races on in the house when they were on. We only had two channels in those days, RTÉ1 and RTÉ2, so we were restricted in what we could watch, but the big race meetings were always on.

I was always fascinated by the jockeys, their different riding styles. I watched them closely, and I picked my favourites. Mick Kinane and Walter Swinburn, and Cash Asmussen. Cash brought the American style of riding with him, toes in the irons, whip in the air, and he had this swagger about him.

I watched Cash ride Suave Dancer to win the Irish Champion Stakes at Leopardstown in 1991, and I remember thinking how cool he was. And I watched Alan Munro riding Generous to beat Suave Dancer and Walter Swinburn in the Irish Derby earlier that year. Alan Munro adopted the American style too, whip up in the air like a periscope.

But Mick Kinane was my hero. I loved everything that he did. And it wasn't just his riding style: it was the way that he went about things. His demeanour, his professionalism, his concentration. I always thought that it meant something to him, every horse, every race. Get the job done. Be the best rider that you can be, give every horse that you ride the best chance of winning that you can give it.

I started off by trying to take different bits from different riders, different aspects of their individual styles, and by trying to combine all the bits together in order to create my own style. But the more time went on, the more I realised that I just wanted to be like Mick! I obviously adopted and adapted my own style over the years but, in the early stages for sure, it was very much based on Mick's style.

I was lucky that, when I started riding, I think that Mick took a bit of a shine to me. It was all very daunting at first, of course, going into the weigh room, being in there with Mick and Christy Roche and Stephen Craine, giants of the sport.

As a young rider, you were a child in an adult's world. In order to survive, you had to get up to that level very quickly. Seamie Heffernan and Declan McDonogh started off around the same time as me, Johnny Murtagh was a little bit ahead of us, but you had to be able to compete. It's why Irish jockeys have always been so good on a world stage. Because the standard of riding has always been so good in Ireland among the older jockeys, young jockeys coming through have always had to learn to be good very quickly if they are going to be able to compete and survive.

We respected the older riders – and I think that is lost a little bit in the weigh room now, the respect that the younger lads had for the senior riders – but they treated you with a bit of respect too, if you were good enough. It was a unique environment, the weigh room. You were all in there together, all changing, showering, talking together, and yet, when you went out to compete, you were all against each other. It was very different from a dressing room in other sports: all on the same team, all together on the field of play. On a racecourse, we were all against each other. And then you had the inherent danger that went with riding and horse racing as a backdrop to it all, with two ambulances following you around.

At festival meetings, when you'd be away for a couple of days, you'd find yourself at dinner one evening and Mick Kinane or Stephen Craine would be sitting beside you. A hero who, not 12 months previously, you were watching on the television, riding in the Derby, riding in the Champion Stakes, and wondering what it would be like to be out there with him. It would be like watching Cristiano Ronaldo playing in the Champions' League final on television, then a year later sharing a dressing room with him before a club match.

Strangely, I found it easy to go up to Mick and ask him questions. It was a little bit daunting, of course, but from the start, even as a young fellow, I didn't find him intimidating, and that surprised me in a way. I wouldn't have been the most confident person when I was young; I wouldn't have been comfortable standing up and talking in front of the class. But I never had a problem approaching Mick to ask him for his advice on something. He always made it easy for me.

I asked him everything, about horses and riding styles and tactics and racecourses. I even asked him about where he got his whips and his saddles and his boots. He always helped me out. He even got me whips. And even when he stopped riding, even when I stopped riding, he was always a person to whom I could turn if ever I needed anything. I numbered him among my very good friends.

I was obsessed about my weight. From a very early age, I was worried that I would grow too much, that I would be heavier than I needed to be in order to be a Flat jockey. On the morning of my 15th birthday, on the day that I applied for my apprentice's licence, I went for a run. I just figured that I needed to get into a way of doing things, into a routine, if I was going to keep my weight down low enough to allow me to ride on the Flat.

I could have ridden at 7st 11lb or 7st 12lb at my lightest. That was light, but you had a 10lb claim when you started riding, which reduced as you gained experience and rode more winners. That meant that, in most races, the horses that you were riding were allowed to carry 10lb less than their allotted weight. That was in order to compensate for the jockey's relative lack of experience, and in order to give owners and trainers an incentive to give opportunities to young inexperienced riders. But it meant that I couldn't claim the full 10lb off any horse that was set to carry anything less than 8st 7lb or 8st 8lb.

I struggled with my weight. All my career, I struggled with my weight. Nearly every jockey did. Nearly every jockey in the weigh room was riding at weights that were well below their natural body weight. I never made a big deal about it, I never really talked about it that much, it was just something that I wanted to do on my own without making a big fuss about it. But it was a big thing for me.

Your whole life is governed by what you can eat and when you can eat it. You are continually hungry and you are often cranky because of it. I suppose, when you have to be about a stone and a half lighter than your natural body weight, it's going to have an impact on you mentally.

Strangely, my biggest concern when I was starting to ride was about my weight. It was head and shoulders above everything else. I never really worried about injury, even though I knew that it was a part of it, and I never really worried that much about getting the opportunities, and I never really worried about not being good enough. I suppose I just figured that opportunities would come if I worked hard. But I always worried about my weight.

It didn't help that people would say it to me often. 'You need to keep your weight down.' 'You'll probably get too heavy.' I was determined that I wouldn't. But the most difficult time for me with my weight was not when I started riding, but more when I was in my early twenties, just at the time that I was starting to ride for Dermot Weld. You're transforming from a boy to a man at that stage in your life, and you start to develop physically. I found myself broadening across my shoulders, I could see physical changes in myself, and I tried to halt or stall those changes. That's when you are really battling against nature.

I became obsessed with it all, in a very unhealthy way. I was watching everything I ate and everything I drank – I was constantly thinking about food and drink. It became an obsession, and it became a huge battle, a daily battle, not just for me, but for most jockeys.

People generally didn't appreciate what jockeys had to go through in order to be able to ride at their racing weights. Even trainers probably didn't fully appreciate it. It was mental torture. You'd be thinking about food all the time. You'd be hungry, but you knew that you couldn't eat. Or drink. That was the killer, when you couldn't drink. The dehydration. When you were that light, anything you drank, tea, milk, soft drinks, even water, you put on weight. Your body was like a sponge when it was that light, it craved nutrition, any nutrition. You'd wring your body out in the morning in the sauna, bone dry, then any fluids it could get, it would soak them up and retain everything.

It took an awful lot of hard work, and it wasn't really until I met Frances that I started to get it under control. Not a lot of people would have known that I struggled with my weight. You knew the jockeys who struggled with their weight in general, their weight issues were well known. Mine weren't. People probably thought that I was fine with my weight, that it was easy for me to keep it under control, but it wasn't. I struggled badly. I just chose to keep it to myself.

It was always on my mind, though. First thing in the morning, every morning during my riding career, I would think about my weight. I would get out of bed and stand on the scales. Then I'd think, can I have a bit of breakfast, or can I have something to eat today? If you have 4lb or 5lb to take off before racing, that rules that out.

I probably went about it the wrong way in the early part of my career, before I became more educated on food and learned a little about nutrition and diets. Running and sauna, that was how I used to do it. Sweat it out of you. When I came on the scene 25 years ago, that was how it was done. You learned from the lads who were ahead of you, and that's how they did it.

I would usually go without breakfast, maybe have something small in the middle of the day, and then try to eat something healthy in the evening. I went through a phase of eating chocolate. I'd stop at a garage on the way to the races and get some chocolate. I felt that it gave me energy, it gave me a sugar-rush.

As time went on, I tried to develop a better diet and better eating habits, but it wasn't easy. I couldn't ride with food in my stomach. I just couldn't do it. I would feel unwell. I always liked to be a little bit hungry when I was riding. I always thought that I performed better if I was a little bit hungry.

I incorporated running and sweating into my routine. I built a little gym at home, and I built a sauna. I used to sweat every day, pretty much every day, all my life. Even if I didn't have to ride light on the day, I'd still have a sweat in the morning. It just became part of my routine.

My weight dominated everything. Even when we were away on holidays, I wouldn't be able to relax. Not fully. The first two or three days, I'd let my hair down a bit all right, have a bit of craic, have good food, have a drink, but after the first couple of days, I'd start thinking about my weight again. Even though we wouldn't be nearly at the end of the holiday, I'd be thinking, the heavier I get, the more difficult it's going to be to get the weight off. I would be able to feel my body getting heavier, and I didn't like it. So I'd even spend most of my holidays watching my weight – I'd go to the gym every day, too, for the last few days.

I just didn't have the mental strength to take off lots of weight. Other lads could do it no bother, you'd see them do it, take off 7lb or 8lb or 10lb when they'd get back from holidays. I just wouldn't have been able to do that, so the best thing for me was not to put it on in the first place.

I did get advice. I'd go through phases. I remember going to see a dietician in the Blackrock Clinic, and he put me on this programme that allowed me to eat three meals a day. I followed it initially, for a week, but I found myself putting on weight after a few days. I started to panic, so I reverted to my own way. Maybe I never really gave it a chance but, at the end of the day, you know your own body, you know what works for you. You end up finding your own way of doing things.

And you'd treat yourself every now and again. Everybody did it. You'd be on a night out and you'd have a nice meal, maybe a couple of drinks. Things that most people do as a matter of course, go out and have a nice meal. You'd be craving a good meal. It's a strange mindset. We might go out on a Saturday night or a Sunday night, depending on racing, and you'd know that you had to get back to your racing weight on Monday, but you'd treat yourself anyway. Then you're up on Monday morning and it's torture, getting the weight back off. Back to square one.

I was always 8st 9lb. That was always my racing weight. Fifty-five kilograms. I have ridden out at 60 kilograms, but when I was going racing, I would be 55 kilograms. Even if I was riding at 10 stone, I still went racing at 8st 9lb. I just figured that, in order to do things right, I needed to have some consistency in my weight, and my racing weight was 8st 9lb.

When I started my chemotherapy, the doctors and the nurses were all on to me about the importance of keeping weight on. We had a laugh about it. I told them that there would be no problem keeping weight on.

I gave up alcohol at the end of 2017, when I started to feel my back pain. I just figured that I wanted to give myself every chance of having as long a career in the saddle as I could have, and that giving up alcohol would be no harm. And I didn't really miss it at all. I never would have been a big drinker anyway, but I just wanted to give my body every opportunity. I didn't get heavy when I stopped riding, I didn't get fat, but I still put on a stone and a half after I stopped.

The weights that horses carry went up a couple of pounds between the time that I started riding and the time that I stopped, but I always thought that they should have gone up by more. When I was riding, I was very much of the mentality that, if you couldn't ride at nine stone, you shouldn't be riding. Just get on with it. But I changed my mind on that later.

It was an issue of health, in my eyes. Jockeys' health. People were getting progressively bigger. I felt that I was one of the bigger lads in the weigh room at the start of my career, but by the time I retired, I was one of the smaller jockeys.

Dr Adrian McGoldrick did a lot of research on the raising of riders' weights, and it was great stuff. Lots of horsemen, as they were known in America, would have been opposed to it; they argued that the risk of injury to horses is greater if the riders are heavier, but that was not scientifically proven. All that was proven was that race times would be slower, which makes sense. Horses carry bigger weights, that's going to slow them down. But it would be easy to cope with that if it meant that jockeys' health and wellbeing was going to be enhanced.

Horses have been exercised for years on a daily basis by riders who are much heavier than jockeys. And it was always more about being a good rider than being light. If you were able to distribute your weight evenly across a horse, not to be jumping up and down on them, that would always counteract any risk of injury to horses.

As well as the wellbeing issue, there was also the fact that, if you ran this forward to its nth degree, racing would run out of riders. We know that humans have been getting heavier for years, and soon there wouldn't be many people who would be able to ride at the lower weights.

There was always the option to be a National Hunt jockey, but I was never going to be a National Hunt jockey. It was never something that I wanted to do. The weights that horses carry in National Hunt racing are heavier than in Flat racing, so the jockeys can be a little bit heavier, but when I was growing up, it was Mick Kinane and Cash Asmussen and Walter Swinburn who were my idols, not the top National Hunt riders Richard Dunwoody and Charlie Swan.

I did ride a bit over jumps when I was getting going at first. Tom had National Hunt horses as well as Flat horses and young horses and mares, and we did everything with them. I was as likely to be schooling a young horse or breaking a yearling as I was to be riding work.

I had nine rides in total over hurdles, in 1993 and 1994. I rode a horse of Tom's called Plumbob in the Carroll Hurdle at Dundalk in May 1994. Dundalk is now an all-weather Flat track, but the Carroll Hurdle was one of the feature races there in the days when they raced on turf and over jumps. Plumbob wasn't a bad horse, but he just couldn't go the pace, and he got longer and longer at every hurdle. To be honest, it scared the life out of me! I was just glad that he and I both managed to get home in one piece.

I decided after that that jumping wasn't for me. That if I was going to make it as a jockey, I was going to make it on the Flat, and I was going to do everything that I could do in order to give myself every chance of making it. If that meant not eating for weeks at a time, then that was what I was going to do.

I started riding a bit on the pony racing circuit. Tommy and Paul Fahey shod horses for Tom Lacy at the time, and they were my introduction to pony racing. The Faheys were big in pony racing, and they used to bring me with them.

I got going quite quickly. They put me up on a mare, Last Chance, and she was dynamite. I won a whole heap of races on her. That got me noticed and it meant that I was in demand. As I found out later, when you are riding winners, in any discipline, under any code, you are usually in demand. I spent just one season on the pony racing circuit, and I was lucky enough to be champion southern rider that year. Pony racing was good for me in lots of ways. The biggest thing I got out of it was that it gave me a feel for the 'environment' of racing, of race day. Getting ready before a race, talking to the trainer or the owner after the race. So that, when I walked into the weigh room at a real race meeting as a jockey, or into the parade ring at a racecourse, it wasn't completely alien to me.

You could pick up bad habits from pony racing too, though. In pony racing, a lot of it was about going as fast as you could as early as you could and for as long as you could. The tracks were so tight. You couldn't really ride a race; you would never have learned about judgement of pace. A lot of very good jockeys have come from the pony racing circuit, but I always thought that you could learn more bad habits than good habits from pony racing.

I loved Dingle though. Dingle has always been the Royal Ascot of pony racing. It was more like a proper racecourse than any other pony racing track. You could ride a bit of a race there. It was seven furlongs around, right-handed, with a stand and white rails and everything. I had never seen white rails before at any other pony racing track. It was usually a rope and a fence.

Dingle was a three-day festival in the middle of August, and I went down with my mother and my father and my youngest brother, Brian. We went down for the week and made a proper holiday out of it, which was a real novelty for us. We didn't really do holidays when we were young, we couldn't afford them, but we made a holiday out of Dingle that year. We stayed in a bed and breakfast, we played games, and we rented bikes and went cycling. It's a beautiful part of the country.

To cap it all, I rode three winners over the course of the weekend, and I was leading rider for the meeting. That was brilliant. It was a special week for me.

I've always remembered my interview with the late Cahir O'Sullivan for my apprentice's licence. He was the Keeper of the Match Book at the Turf Club. He was a great man, a very fair man. He was a hugely popular man, liked by everybody, and he commanded so much respect.

He said to me, at my interview, 'You know that pony racing is finished for you now?' I just sat there in front of him and nodded. It was as if you didn't want to disappoint him. I was happy with that anyway. I was mad for the real thing.

CHAPTER 4

I knew about three weeks before my first ride on a racecourse that it was happening. September 1992, Listowel. That was massive. My first ride, in a real race, at the Listowel Festival.

You had to enter your horses three weeks in advance of the races in which you intended running them in those days, and Tom entered Power Source in the 10-furlong claiming race, the second race on the Monday of Listowel, the first day of the meeting.

Power Source wasn't a world-beater. He had run 18 times, 3 times over hurdles and 15 times on the Flat, and he had never won. He had been placed a couple of times, though, and I knew him well. I rode him lots at home. He used to carry his head low to the ground when he was galloping, which made him not the most comfortable horse to ride. His head was bowed so low, it was like you had nothing in front of you; you were perched up on his back. But he wasn't difficult, there was no malice in him and, actually, I didn't really think about that. I would have ridden a bucking bull.

I counted down the days. I couldn't sleep. I was as nervous as I was excited. My first ride in a race. Weight-wise, it was fine. I was claiming 10lb off nine stone, so he would be carrying 8st 4lb, which was perfect.

My mother and father both came down, all the way to Listowel, so it was a big day for them too. It was quite daunting, going into the racecourse, going into a real weigh room for the first time. Mick Kinane was there, and Christy Roche and Stephen Craine. They were all riding in the race. And John Egan and Niall McCullagh and Willie Supple. Paul Carberry was riding the favourite in the race, Legal Adviser for Declan Gillespie, in the famous black and white Tony O'Reilly colours. Paul was only getting going as a jockey at the time, but he had a little bit of experience, and he was from a racing dynasty, son of Tommy Carberry, grandson of Dan Moore.

For a young fellow from Rhode in County Offaly, son of Paddy and Mary Smullen, riding for Tom Lacy in the colours of Peig Lacy, it could have all been a bit overwhelming if I had allowed it to be.

I loved it, though. I loved being in the weigh room, being in there among those jockeys. Real jockeys. Great jockeys. I loved the smell of the weigh room, I loved getting my gear on, getting my silks on, weighing out. A jockey.

I was nervous as hell, but I was more excited than nervous. Meeting Tom in the parade ring before the race and getting legged up. I had two main concerns: getting to the start safely and getting out of the stalls. I was far more worried about getting to the start than I was about riding the actual race. In the race, you went at racing pace with all the other horses. As herding animals, most horses' natural instinct was to stay with the other horses. On the way to the start, though, you usually went down on your own, and you had to restrain your horse, conserve his energy, hold onto him, get him to stop at the start. My big fear was getting run away with on the way to the start.

I didn't. It helped that I knew Power Source well, and it helped that the 10-furlong start is close to the winning line at Listowel, so we didn't have far to go from the parade ring. I got into the stalls okay, and I got away well. No incidents, no dramatics. After that, it all went very quickly. It's amazing how quickly a race can go.

In truth, we didn't really get involved in the race as a contest, me and Power Source. We were never in with a chance of winning, and we ended up finishing ninth of the 11 runners. Even so, I came back in with a big smile on my face, exhausted, exhilarated. Rarely could a jockey have been so happy after finishing ninth!

I had to wait almost six weeks for my next ride. That was always going to be the way. I had to be patient. There wasn't as much racing in Ireland then as there is now, there weren't as many race meetings, and while Tom was giving me the opportunities that he could give me, he had to do as well as he could do for himself, too, and for his owners. A lot of the horses that he had were owned by him and his wife, so he could put me up on them, an unproven apprentice who needed experience, but he couldn't put me up on everything in the beginning. He had to get results himself.

My second ride was on a horse called Fairydel in a nursery at Naas at the back end of the 1992 Flat season, on the last day of October. He wasn't a bad horse, he had shown some promise in a couple of runs earlier in the season, and he would be a noteworthy horse for me the following season.

Fairydel ran well for me that day too. We were drawn in stall four, between Micky Fenton, who ended up winning the race on a filly of Austin Leahy's called Common Bond, and Warren O'Connor, and if you thought that it all happened quickly in a 10-furlong race at Listowel, it all happened twice as quickly in a five-furlong race at Naas. Literally! We finished fifth, and I came back in beaming again.

That was it for me for the season in terms of race riding. Going into the winter, I knew that it would be a long wait for my next ride. There was no winter racing on the Flat back then, there was no all-weather racing in Ireland, no all-weather track. So I put my head down and worked away at Tom's. I still loved the work, but I had got a taste for race riding, and I couldn't wait to have another go.

I learned lots at Tom's that winter. I was an apprentice and, back in those days, you served your apprenticeship in the true sense of the word. We did everything, from mucking out to riding out to cleaning yards to breaking yearlings. You got to experience all aspects of a racing yard. I counted down the days to the start of the Flat season though.

I got going quickly enough in 1993. Tom gave me opportunities from early in the year. I had a few rides in March and a few more in April and in May, and then, in June, on 11 June 1993 in an apprentices' handicap at Dundalk, me and Vicosa: dreamland!

Vicosa was a decent horse; he had been around the block. He ran lots the previous season as a three-year-old without winning, and he had run in a maiden hurdle at Killarney the previous month, when Tom's son, Tony, had ridden him.

I think Tom fancied him a bit that day at Dundalk, but I wasn't sure. I had only just turned 16 and, back then, you were a bit naïve about how good a chance you had or hadn't. It was another ride for me, it was only the 18th ride of my career and I had never ridden a winner, so everything was new to me. I was just delighted to be getting rides.

It lashed rain that day. Absolutely spilled down. But I didn't care. I would have ridden through a monsoon.

We only had one runner on the evening, and it was just a normal Friday evening, so there was never any talk of my mother and father going to the races. It was just me and Tom and Vicosa and Stephen Cox in the horse box going up. Stephen is from Rhode as well; he is now one of the stallion men at Ballylinch Stud, but he was with Tom at the time.

I left the weigh room and saw Tom in the parade ring. He legged me up and Stephen led me up and wished me luck as I left and cantered to the start. Nine furlongs in front of me at Dundalk, the Mountain Bay Apprentice Handicap, on the old turf track.

We got out and got a good position, we travelled around the home turn well and straightened up still going well. There was a ridge at the old Dundalk course that ran across the track, about a furlong out, and I remember getting over that in front and kicking for home. I probably didn't know it then, but I learned later that, if you could get over that ridge in front at Dundalk, it was always very difficult for the others to catch you.

I had Vicosa in a nice racing rhythm early on. I had a good sit on him, well balanced, keeping it together. When I hit the front and got over the ridge though, everything went to pot! I completely lost it, forgot everything, style and balance and poise out the window. I just wanted to get to the winning line by whatever means necessary. Get there as quickly as I could. I didn't care how I looked, and it never really occurred to me that I would be more of a hindrance than a help to the horse inside the final 200 yards, with me bouncing around all over the place.

Fortunately, all my flailing around didn't stop Vicosa. We got to the winning line with one and a half lengths to spare.

That was an unbelievable feeling. My first winner. On all previous 17 rides, there was something in front of me when I got to the winning line. That time, all my rivals were behind me. Back into the winner's enclosure, back to see Tom and Stephen, and all the back-slaps and well-dones.

I remember getting home late that evening too. There were no mobile phones or anything, I didn't stop to call home on the way, but my mother and father knew that I had won, all right. They were delighted, without going overboard. Dad would never go too high or too low about anything really. He was always very level-headed. It was just, well done, fair play, move on. But I knew that he was delighted for me.

It was some thrill for me but, like your first ride on a racecourse, once you have done it once, you just want to go and do it again. It's a bit like winning a football match. You've won, it's great, but you need to go on now and win the next one.

Thankfully, I didn't have to wait that long for my next winner. I rode my old friend Fairydel in another apprentices' race, a hands-and-heels race – that is, riding without using a whip – at Naas just six days after I had won on Vicosa at Dundalk.

That was a really good series of races, the hands-and-heels series, for young riders, sponsored by Derrinstown Stud. You couldn't use your whip, so you really had to get down and ride your horse. Definitely for me, I looked a lot more capable riding Fairydel in the hands-and-heels race than I did riding Vicosa in the apprentices' race at Dundalk when I could use my whip.

I felt that I had to use my stick on Vicosa, because that's what you did, but Vicosa probably lost more in terms of energy with me flapping around on him inside the final furlong than we gained in terms of distance covered. On Fairydel, I didn't have the option of using my stick, so I had to ride with my legs and my body. I tucked my stirrups up a little bit and, looking back at the video now, I looked an awful lot tidier on Fairydel than on Vicosa.

Tom bred Fairydel himself too; he was a proper little horse, and that was the horse's first win, so it was important to Tom. We just got home by a neck from the favourite, a filly named Reticent Bride, ridden by Wayne Smith and trained by Dermot Weld.

CHAPTER 5

The more rides I got, the more experience I got, and the more experience I got, the better I got. And the better I was getting, the more winners I was riding, and the more I was getting noticed.

Tom started to give me more opportunities as the 1993 season got going, and a couple of other trainers started to ring Tom to ask if I was available. Consequently, the number of rides that I was getting started to increase, from just three in April to five in May and in June, then 11 in July and 16 in August.

I probably went up a notch in Tom's eyes when I won a maiden on Bellissi at Tralee in August 1993. That was a really competitive maiden, a mile around Tralee, and a lot of the big trainers had runners in it – John Oxx and Con Collins and Jim Bolger and Paddy Mullins – with some of the top riders riding in it, Mick Kinane and Christy Roche and Johnny Murtagh and Stephen Craine. We won by half a length. My third winner.

I thought that Tom looked at me a little differently after that. 'This lad can ride.' I never thought that myself, though. I was always self-critical. I always doubted my ability. Even at the height of my career, when I was winning championships and riding top-class horses in top-class races, I never felt totally secure. I always thought that I had to be better. Improve, improve, improve. There was always that fear in my head, and it drove me mad sometimes. I never thought that I had arrived. I always felt that I had to work at it, to strive to be the best rider that I could be.

I ended up riding five winners in 1993 – Ferrycarrig Hotel in a 12-furlong handicap at Listowel in September and Kilmood Lass in a juvenile fillies' maiden at Down Royal in October, to add to Vicosa, Fairydel and Bellissi – and, as a result, I got a special recognition award from the Turf Club at the end of the season. Up-And-Coming Apprentice. There was no major prize for it or anything, but I got a trophy and it was nice to be recognised. And they arranged for me to go to Australia to get some more experience, but that didn't work out too well!

I had to pay for my own flights, so any money that I managed to get together during the season was mostly blown on that trip to Australia. It was all a bit surreal. I had only been out of Ireland once before, when I went to Newmarket to the breeze-up sales with Joanna, so it was all a bit daunting for me, as it probably would have been for any 16-year-old heading off to Australia on their own.

They arranged for me to go to a trainer in Randwick, Tiger Holland, but he didn't have many horses, so I didn't have that many opportunities. It was a good experience, to see how they did things on the other side of the world, but it was tough.

I lived in a little room over the stables, with a galvanised roof on it. I was supposed to be on my own, but I had to share it with a few mice and at least one rat. That was a bit of a nightmare.

I had five or six rides on the track at Randwick, but I never got close to having a winner. I was there for six weeks, but it was all a bit of a waste of time, really. I'm glad that I did it, but I was delighted to get home.

I came home heavy. I was homesick when I was in Australia, I wasn't eating the right foods, I wasn't watching my weight and

I wasn't race riding much. That all contributed to an increase in my weight. Tom could see it in me as soon as I got home, and he suggested that I might have to start thinking about being a National Hunt jockey. But, as I said before, all I wanted to do was ride on the Flat, so I set about getting my weight sorted.

In the early years of my career, I went very much on 'feel'. How I felt I should be riding races. I had my videos of Mick Kinane and Cash Asmussen and other top-class jockeys, and I'd watch them over and over again. For me in the beginning, it was all about style, and trying to get the technique of riding a horse right.

From a 'tactics' perspective, I had Tom telling me how he wanted his horses ridden. Where I should be in the early part of the race, when I should make my move, when I should kick for home. When I started riding for other trainers, though, I quickly learned that you had to think on your feet. You had to change plans if races didn't develop as you thought they would. And they rarely did. You had to make split-second decisions as you were hurtling along at 35 miles per hour, and getting those decisions right or wrong could be the difference between winning the race and losing it.

Declan Gillespie was one of the trainers who started to use me very early in my career. Declan was a top-class rider in his day: he rode Flame Of Tara to win the Coronation Stakes for Jim Bolger, and he rode Give Thanks to win the Irish Oaks, and he won the Irish 2000 Guineas on Prince Of Birds for Vincent O'Brien. He rode a lot of winners for Tom, too, in his day, so there was a relationship between the two of them before I ever came along.

Declan was a very astute trainer too. He was some judge of a horse and of a race. If he told you that a horse of his would win before you went out, it would invariably win, or go very close. And if it got beaten, it was invariably the jockey's fault!

'What were you thinking?' That was Declan's favourite line.

There were lots of instances of that with Declan. One that stands out was on Irish Derby day at the Curragh in 1996. I was riding a colt for him in the first race on the day, the seven-furlong maiden. He was a nice colt, Gunfire, owned by Tony O'Reilly, and I had ridden him on his racecourse debut two months earlier when he had finished fourth in a five-furlong maiden, also at the Curragh. I was just getting established, and it was great to have a ride in the opening maiden on Derby day.

I gave Gunfire a fine ride too, I thought, but we were just beaten in a photo finish by Mick Kinane on the favourite, a colt of Dermot Weld's and Moyglare Stud's, Beautiful Fire. Mick Kinane outrode me, but Mick Kinane was Mick Kinane, he was riding the odds-on favourite and he lifted him home. I was a 2lb-claiming apprentice who was riding a 12/1 shot, and we went down by a short head.

I didn't think that I had done an awful lot wrong. Declan had other ideas.

I had just dismounted, I had only just touched the ground in the unsaddling area that was reserved for the runner-up, when he let me have it. A real tirade. What he didn't call me! In front of everybody, Tony O'Reilly, Lady O'Reilly, everybody else who was there.

That shook me.

But I never thought of not riding for Declan. No matter how bad the bollockings were. If the devil himself had rung up wanting me to ride a horse for him, I would have been off. I just wanted to ride at every race meeting, in every race.

Declan didn't hold grudges either. Gunfire ran again a month later, in another seven-furlong race at the Curragh. Declan put me up on him again and we won easily.

Declan was great to me, and he was great for me, for my career.

For starters, it was some education. It made me work harder on race tactics. It got me looking back on races and thinking, What could I have done there? Was I right to do what I did?

Also, he gave me lots of opportunities, and he kept using me, so he obviously saw something in me. Other trainers saw it too. 'Well, if he's good enough for Declan Gillespie, he must be all right.'

Tom was happy to let me ride for other trainers. In the beginning, a couple of trainers would ring looking for me, and Tom would be happy to let me ride as long as he didn't have a horse for the race. As I got going a bit, though, he and his son Barry would ring around, looking for rides for me.

I was apprenticed to Tom, so he was getting a share of any prize money that I won. It was a 60–40 split, 60 per cent for Tom, 40 per cent for me. That was the Turf Club rule. I didn't care. It wasn't about money for me. I would have given away all of it in order to get the start that I got.

There were no jockeys' agents at the time, so I was very much dependent on Tom and Barry for outside rides. Barry was a great judge; he studied form and he knew what horses might be available and on what horses he wanted to get me rides.

Tom's mentality was to get up, get going, and if you were good enough, you'd make it. He didn't mind if I burned through my claim quickly. The more winners you rode, the more your claim reduced, until it got down to zero and you were competing on level terms with Mick Kinane and Christy Roche. It could be tough for apprentices in the initial stages after they lost their claim, but I was very much in tune with Tom's mentality at the time: if you were good enough, you'd make it.

I changed my attitude later, for other young apprentices. I liked to see the young up-and-coming apprentices protecting their claims, not burning through them too quickly. If they did that, they ate up their entire allowance before they really had a chance to become established. I didn't think there was any point in a good apprentice riding 10 or 15 winners during the winter and using up their claim when there were so many good and valuable and high-profile races during the summer.

I was very lucky in that I got myself into a privileged position relatively quickly. There I was, in a small yard, with the full support of Tom and Barry, riding just about all Tom's horses, and with the freedom to go and ride for other trainers as well. And in demand.

I got busy. The phone got busy. Trainers ringing up looking for me to ride, Barry or Tom or sometimes Peig ringing trainers, asking for rides for me. It got to a point where they were almost as busy booking rides for me as they were running the yard.

Tom instilled in me too the importance of loyalty. I would be loyal by nature, my father was loyal to the bone, but that was also driven home to me at Tom's in those early days. Because entries were three weeks before race days back then, you could be booked to ride a horse three weeks out. Once you gave your word that you would ride one, it was important not to deviate from that, not to jump off it even if a better ride came along.

I tried to keep that loyalty going throughout my career, and hopefully that stood to me. I always thought that it was the right thing to do, to keep your word, and I thought that people respected you for it. And loyalty engendered loyalty. If you were loyal to people, people would be loyal to you. I always thought that that was a thread that ran all the way through my career: my loyalty to others and others' loyalty to me.

Another thing that Tom taught me was the importance of showing respect to the owner. To take the time to speak to the owner. If you came in after finishing seventh, it was important that you got off the horse and took the time to tell the owner or the owners what happened, what you thought, how you thought the horse ran, how you thought the horse could improve. How to conduct yourself on and off the horse.

I learned an awful lot during my apprenticeship with Tom. It was some start for a young lad.

CHAPTER 6

I didn't set out to be champion apprentice in 1995. I didn't really think about it at the start of the season. To be honest, it was so far beyond my reality that it wasn't even on the horizon. To be champion apprentice, you had to be riding for one of the big yards. You couldn't win the title riding for a small yard in the middle of Offaly.

My mentality was to get out and get riding every day that you can, ride as many winners as you can. That was Tom's mentality too.

I got on a roll early in 1995, though. I rode five winners in May, two in June and five more in July, so that, at the start of August, I had 12 winners on the board and my momentum was up. Six more winners in August, and the possibility of winning the title came into view. Still, Tom and I didn't speak about it.

Whether the championship was a goal or not, it wasn't going to make any difference to what I was doing or how I was operating. I wasn't going to ride any better and I wasn't going to ride any more horses just because I decided that I was going to try to win the apprentices' championship. My goal remained the same: ride as many winners as I could. And if I ended up in front at the end of the year, that would just be a happy by-product.

I was riding for more trainers, I was riding better horses, and

I was riding more horses. I rode twice as many horses in 1995 as I did in 1994. Some stood out, like Misterio, a horse that Declan Gillespie trained for Lady O'Reilly, on whom I won twice in the space of three weeks in August, at Roscommon and Tralee, and Scene One, a filly of Kevin Prendergast's, on whom I won a handicap at Leopardstown.

It was great to get to ride for some of the top trainers, Kevin Prendergast and Dessie Hughes and Noel Meade and Edward O'Grady and Eddie Lynam. And Paddy Mullins. Paddy was some man, not just as a trainer of racehorses, but as a man. A gentleman.

He was always best known as a National Hunt trainer – he was champion National Hunt trainer 10 times after all – and as the trainer of Dawn Run, the mare who won the Champion Hurdle and the Cheltenham Gold Cup and who remains, to this day, the only horse in history to win both races. But he could train Flat horses too, as he proved with Hurry Harriet, whom he sent to Newmarket to win the Champion Stakes in 1973. Thirty years later he trained Vintage Tipple to win the Irish Oaks, with Frankie Dettori on board. That was some partnership: the bubbly, outgoing, effusive, effervescent Dettori with his crowd-pleasing antics and his flying dismounts, and the quiet, reserved, thoughtful, gentle Paddy Mullins. Geniuses both.

You'd expect, a trainer like Paddy Mullins, a legend of a man like that, that he would have lots of instructions for a young rider like me before sending me out to ride one of his horses, but not a bit of it. The more I rode and the more trainers I rode for, the more I realised that, in general, the better the trainer, the fewer instructions they had for you.

I rode a filly for Paddy Mullins at Tramore one day. She was a difficult filly, a talented but temperamental filly, and I knew that I couldn't be overly hard on her. She had to be coaxed rather than bullied. I remember going over to him in the parade ring and, just before I went to be legged up on her, he took my whip from me. He just reached over and gently lifted my whip out of my hand. 'You won't be needing this.' Just shows you the genius that Paddy Mullins was. I rode the filly hands-and-heels, and she won easily.

I started to ride a fair bit for Aidan O'Brien, too, in 1995. It was only two years since Aidan had taken over the trainer's licence from his wife, Annemarie, whose sister Frances – although obviously I didn't know it at the time – I would later marry. Aidan hadn't trained all the Group 1 winners then that he would go on to train, but, training on the Hill at Piltown in County Kilkenny (where Annemarie had trained and where Annemarie and Frances's father, Joe Crowley, had trained and would train again, and where Frances would later train, and where Aidan and Annemarie's son Joseph also set up as a trainer), he was starting to hit milestones all over the place.

A lot of those milestones were over jumps. Aidan had plenty of runners on the Flat in those days, but he had more runners over jumps. He had good National Hunt horses, like Hotel Minella and Double Symphony and Life Of A Lord, who led home an Aidan O'Brien-trained 1-2-3 in the Galway Plate in August 1995. Life Of A Lord was ridden to victory that day by Trevor Horgan, who later married Frances's sister Breda. And Aidan would have good National Hunt horses later too, like Urubande, his first Cheltenham Festival winner, and Istabraq, who broke the mould.

That said, Aidan was getting going on the Flat then too. Everything he was achieving, he was achieving on his own. He and Annemarie. This was a year before he moved to Ballydoyle to train from the establishment made famous by the legendary Dr Vincent O'Brien. Aidan had had his first listed race winner on the Flat in June 1994, when Wandering Thoughts won the Ballycorus

Stakes at Leopardstown, and he had his first Group race winner in August 1994 when Dancing Sunset won the Royal Whip Stakes at the Curragh. In 1995, he stepped up another notch on the Flat.

I didn't ride at all for Aidan in 1994, but in 1995, he used me quite a lot. Christy Roche was his stable jockey, but he was putting me up on a lot of the horses that Christy couldn't ride. I actually had more rides for Aidan in 1995 than I had for any other trainer that year. He put me up on some good winners too, like Lasting Peace, whom I rode to win a maiden at Gowran Park on her racecourse debut, and Steel Mirror, who went on to win over hurdles and over fences, and Archobello, an Archway filly on whom I won a juvenile maiden at Ballinrobe.

I started riding for Tommy Stack, too, in 1995. I only had three rides for Tommy that year, and I didn't manage to ride a winner for him, but he obviously saw something in me and he started to use me more. Tommy is the man who rode Red Rum to win his third and history-making Grand National in 1977, and he had made the transition very successfully from National Hunt jockey to Flat trainer.

So things were getting going for me a bit. It wasn't a conscious effort on my part – I didn't see the openings and go for them. I was just concentrating on riding as well as I could, on riding as many winners as I could, and with the help of Tom and Barry, it was happening for me. I was getting noticed, I was getting used by some very good trainers, and that was leading to more opportunities. I ended the 1995 season with 26 winners and the apprentices' championship title – nine more than Seamie Heffernan – and that took me into the top 10 in the overall championship, but still miles behind the champion that year, Johnny Murtagh, who had 86 winners.

It was great to win the apprentices' championship. As I said, it hadn't been a goal of mine at the start of the season but, as the season rolled on and the winners rolled in and the possibility of winning the title came onto my radar, I really wanted to win it.

It was important that I kicked on then, though. The road was paved with good apprentices who never made it further than that. You needed to have the talent for sure, but you needed the work ethic and you needed the opportunities and you needed the bounce of the ball.

There were decisions to be made. When you were just getting going, you took all that you were offered. You accepted everything willingly and gratefully and you did your best to maximise the opportunities that you had been given. It was great to be in demand but, when demand got to a point where it was greater than supply, you had decisions to make. You couldn't serve too many masters.

Tommy asked me if I would go down and ride work for him two mornings a week. That was brilliant. To go down and ride work in Tommy Stack's, to see the operation down there. That was a real eye-opener for me. It was a step up to the next level. Tommy and his wife, Liz, were brilliant to me, and the operation was very professional.

Tommy was big into times. He used to keep the workbook in the jeep so that he could record times and compare them. I remember the first serious piece of work that Tarascon did as a two-year-old – there was huge excitement because of the time that she clocked. And Tommy had top-class fillies like Las Meninas with whom to compare times. We knew from then that Tarascon was going to be top-class. She provided me with one of the highest highs of the early part of my career, but also one of the lowest lows.

Demand continued. John Oxx asked me if I would ride as second jockey for him, behind Johnny Murtagh. At the same time, Aidan O'Brien asked me if I would ride as second jockey to Christy Roche. I remember our conversation vividly. It was at Gowran Park one day; we were just chatting and he asked me if I could come down and ride for him. He was probably a bit surprised when I told him that I would have to think about it. Later, I realised that he probably expected that I would jump at the chance straight away. You could understand his surprise. He was breaking all these records, and he had just moved to Ballydoyle, where he would have the support of John Magnier and his team.

I was a bit blown away by it all. Aidan O'Brien and John Oxx both wanting me to ride for them, and this was while I was already riding for Tommy Stack.

I was lucky with the timing. My apprentices' title had come along at the right time. There were lots of opportunities with Tommy Stack and John Oxx, and Aidan O'Brien had just moved from Owning to Ballydoyle. There were positions to be filled. I had to decide, though: it was one or the other, Aidan O'Brien or John Oxx. I couldn't do both.

I gave it very careful consideration. I spoke to Tom at length about it, and I spoke to my father and I thought about it deeply. In the end, we decided that the John Oxx job was the right job for me at that stage of my career.

Of course, nobody knew at the time what Aidan O'Brien would go on to achieve. The recipe for success was there for sure – a young trainer who had achieved all that Aidan had achieved on the Flat and over jumps at every level, moving to Ballydoyle, with the training facilities that were there and with the might of Coolmore behind him.

It was a *Sliding Doors* moment. I never really thought too deeply about what would have happened if I had gone to Aidan's at the time but, if I had, I would have been there seven days a week. I wouldn't have been able to ride for Tommy Stack as well, and I obviously couldn't have ridden for John. Also, I wouldn't have formed the association with Dermot Weld that I formed in the early years, so I probably wouldn't have been in a position to take over as stable jockey with him when I did. I would have been riding as second jockey to Christy Roche at Aidan's, but I probably wouldn't have been able to take over as stable jockey when Christy retired. Mick Kinane probably still would have got that job. And would I have continued riding as second jockey to Mick then with Aidan? Probably.

So, when Mick moved to Ballydoyle, that was when I got the Dermot Weld job, which I obviously wouldn't have got if I had been second jockey for Aidan. And then, even after Mick left Ballydoyle, would I have got the stable jockey job? Ever? In front of Jamie Spencer? In front of Kieren Fallon? In front of Johnny Murtagh? I might have been promoted from second jockey to first jockey, but I might not have. And nobody knows, anyway, what would have happened in the interim.

When I thought about it later on in my career, I concluded that the steps that I took at that early stage brought me on to the career that I had, and I knew how lucky I was to have had the career that I had. I wouldn't have changed a thing about that decision.

I didn't ride for Aidan a lot after that. That was understandable too: I had gone in a different direction.

I never looked back, though. You were faced with important decisions in life. You took the time to make your decision, you weighed up all the factors, you spoke to the people you thought you should speak to who could help in your decision, and then, with the information that you had available to you at the time, you made your decision. Decision made, you don't look back.

I never regretted that decision. Not once. It was the right job for me at that stage of my career. John was brilliant, a complete gentleman. I never heard him raise his voice, never heard him use bad language. And he had some team of horses, he had some team of owners. To put on His Highness the Aga Khan's green-and-red colours, or Sheikh Mohammed's maroon-and-white colours, that was unbelievable.

Dermot Weld started to use me a little bit too in 1996. I rode a Theatrical colt called Troskie for him to win a maiden at Tramore that August, getting home by half a length from a mare ridden by multiple champion National Hunt jockey Charlie Swan in one of his relatively infrequent rides on the Flat, and I won a handicap at Dundalk in September on a horse called Fridolin for him. Dermot asked me if I could go in to him maybe one morning a week, so I jumped at that opportunity too.

So my week went something like this: Tom Lacy's on Monday, John Oxx's on Tuesday, Dermot Weld's on Wednesday, Tommy Stack's on Thursday, John Oxx's again on Friday, Tommy Stack's again on Saturday, and I loved every minute of it. It was very different, riding out on the Curragh, compared with riding out at Tom's. It was all very private at Tom's, a small country yard. You could show up in wellington boots if you wanted to. At the Curragh, though, you were on view. You felt that everyone was watching. All prim and proper, best sit, tuck up your stirrups, straighten your back, polish your boots. How you looked was as important as how you rode.

This was all with Tom's blessing. As I said before, the grounding that I got at Tom's was unbelievable. I couldn't have asked for a better apprenticeship. It was ideal, really. And I learned about values. A lot of the values that I learned from my parents were strengthened at Tom's. The value of commitment, the value of hard work, the value of loyalty.

Tom was never going to stand in my way, though, when opportunities arose. More than that, he encouraged me to take the opportunities, and he helped me in terms of choosing the right ones. I couldn't have asked for a better mentor in the early part of my career. It was the ideal foundation for what was to follow.

CHAPTER 7

The C.L. Weld Park Stakes was always a race that Dermot Weld liked to win. Sponsored by Dermot and named in memory of his late father, he always liked to have a nice two-year-old filly to aim at the race.

In 1996, he had two, Token Gesture and Absolute Glee, and, world-class rider though Mick Kinane was, he could only ride one of them. Dermot needed a rider for the other and, with Pat Shanahan out injured, and Daragh O'Donohoe just starting to ride for Godolphin at the time, there was always a chance that I would be close to the top of the pecking order.

It was Mick's choice, of course, but it wasn't easy for him. There wasn't much between the two fillies. They worked together the week before the race, and there was nothing in it. It was never easy when you had to choose between two stable companions, as I found out many times later on in my career. It was great to have the choice as stable jockey, it was a privileged position to be in, to be able to choose, but you still had to choose, and you could only choose one. Often, it was a marginal call and, when it was a marginal call, you often got it wrong.

I didn't know which filly Mick had chosen, and I didn't know for sure that I was riding the other one, until final declaration time. Then I saw my name down beside Token Gesture. That was nice to see: C.L. Weld Park Stakes (Group 3), Token Gesture, DK Weld, PJ Smullen. MJ Kinane was down beside Absolute Glee.

That was massive for me. A big ride in a big race, a Group race, for Dermot Weld, and wearing the famous black-and-white colours of Moyglare Stud. I knew that my filly had a chance too. She was a 10/1 shot, but she had won her maiden at Galway easily, and I knew that it hadn't been easy for Mick to choose between her and Absolute Glee, who was nearly favourite.

The plan was that I would let my filly stride on. She wasn't a pacemaker for Absolute Glee or anything like that, but we knew that she would get the seven-furlong trip well.

It was a good race, as you would have expected of a Group 3 contest at the Curragh. The favourite was Azra, a Danehill filly of Jim Bolger's who had won four times earlier in the season, and who had finished third behind Desert King in the Group 1 National Stakes on her previous run. And Aidan O'Brien had two in the race: Melleray, who had been impressive in winning her maiden at the Curragh in July, and Moon Flower, who had won her maiden at Gowran Park on her racecourse debut the previous month.

It was some thrill for me, putting on the Moyglare Stud colours. Those famous colours, synonymous with Dermot Weld and Mick Kinane, that had been carried to victory by iconic horses, horses like Go And Go and Trusted Partner and Brief Truce – horses that I had watched on the television and marvelled at. And there I was, going out to ride in the same colours.

I disputed the lead with Mick on Absolute Glee early on, matching strides, coming up the centre of the course, spearheading the group. I allowed my filly to stride on into the lead after a couple of furlongs, and Mick was happy to let his filly follow me.

I just let my filly go along at her own pace. She had a nice cruising speed, so I just dropped my hands on her and allowed her to bowl along at a pace at which she was comfortable.

It was slowish ground that day at the Curragh, and that suited Token Gesture well. I started to niggle her along at around the two-furlong marker. I could feel the challengers circling around me, and I was sure that my filly would find plenty for pressure. That's the type of filly that she was.

Mick arrived up on my left on Absolute Glee inside the final furlong, but Token Gesture dug deep to try to repel their challenge. Then Christy Roche arrived on my right on Melleray, and there was me, Pat Smullen from Rhode in County Offaly, in between Mick Kinane and Christy Roche, two of the best jockeys that Ireland had ever produced, going for the line in a Group race at the Curragh.

The three of us went past the line together. You couldn't tell for sure, but I thought that I had won all right. You usually knew. I didn't know which of the other two had finished second, it was that tight, but I thought that my filly's nose had hit the line first. She was so game. She just didn't want to lose.

And then they announced the result: first number six, Token Gesture.

That was some feeling.

Mick wasn't overly happy. He didn't say anything to me at all after the race. Not as we pulled up, not back in the weigh room. That was Mick, though, that was what made him the jockey that he was. That was one of the reasons why I admired him so much. That winning mentality. He was never a good loser. Show me a good loser and I'll show you a loser.

As the dust started to settle on the race, the magnitude of the win started to take hold in me. There was the initial adrenaline-fuelled exhilaration, the race, the competition, the driving finish. Mick Kinane on one side of me, Christy Roche on the other, and beating them both. That was the sportsperson in me. The competitor. Beating the best and winning my first Group race on my first attempt, at the Curragh, on one of the greatest stages in horse racing, for Dermot Weld and in the Moyglare Stud colours.

I wasn't getting above myself. Really I wasn't. I wasn't thinking, I've arrived now, I beat Mick Kinane and Christy Roche, I'm a real jockey. But I left the racecourse that evening with an immense sense of satisfaction in my gut.

I realised something else that day: Group races mattered. Sure, they were important from a jockey's perspective – the prize money was good and the profile was high. But from an owner's point of view, especially an owner/breeder like Moyglare, and especially with fillies, they were gold.

If a horse wins a Group race or a listed race, it is noted in bold, black type in a sales catalogue. You often hear about black-type races, a black-type winner. That's where the phrase comes from. From the sales catalogue, for a horse who has won or who has been placed in a Group race, a black-type race. And it stands out on a catalogue page.

So a Group race winner was big for Moyglare Stud, for mating plans for Token Gesture, for her prospects as a broodmare, for the quality and attractiveness of her progeny. And for me to ride her to that Group race win was massive. And she did become a successful broodmare, the best of her offspring, Relaxed Gesture, winning the Canadian International, a Grade 1 race at Woodbine.

It was a step forward for me in terms of my understanding of horse racing as a sport and as an industry. When I was with Tom, it was all about the horse and the race, winning a race with a horse. Riding as well as you could, maximising your chance of winning on every horse, riding as many winners as you could. I never really saw the bigger picture, the whole-industry picture.

I got a glimpse of the bigger picture, though, that day. I got an indication of how important a Group race win was, to the trainer, to the owner. About black-type winners and breeding and lineage and families, and how important all of that was to Dermot Weld and to Moyglare Stud.

I got home that evening, well content. There were no celebrations or anything, our house wouldn't be a house for wild celebrations, but I was happy for myself, and I could tell that my mother and father were happy for me. They knew that it was a big deal. I wore out the video of the race, I watched it so many times. Beating Mick Kinane and Christy Roche in a finish.

I didn't know it at the time, but that win probably had a greater positive impact on my career than any other winner that I rode. It was effectively the beginning of my relationship with Moyglare Stud and the Haefner family, and I think that Dermot Weld looked at me a little differently after that race.

The boss had obviously seen something in me before that – he wouldn't have put me on any of his horses if he hadn't, and he definitely wouldn't have asked me to come in to Rosewell House one day a week. But I thought that I went up a notch in his eyes that day. He never told me that, that wouldn't be his style, but I sensed it.

I loved going into Rosewell House, though, to ride out. The history of the place, the horses that were there at the time, all that the boss had achieved even at that point. Vintage Crop's Melbourne Cup win had only been three years earlier, the win that changed the face of international racing, and the boss had won the Irish Derby and the Irish Oaks earlier in the summer of 1996 with Zagreb and Dance Design respectively.

I loved going into John Oxx's, too, at Currabeg, and John had some team of horses as well. Three weeks after I had won the C.L. Weld Stakes on Token Gesture, I won the Listed Trigo Stakes at Leopardstown on Asmara for John. That was another big win for me. Again, the cards fell right for me. Again, the stable jockey had the choice, and chose wrongly. That time it was Johnny Murtagh, John's stable jockey, who chose John's other filly in the race, Oriane.

Oriane was the logical choice. She was the stable's first string. She had won her maiden easily at Listowel, and she had finished a close-up third in a listed race at Naas next time, getting closer to the winner (French Ballerina) than Asmara and I did next time at the Curragh. Also, Oriane was less exposed than Asmara. She had run just twice, she hadn't run as a two-year-old and she had more room for improvement than Asmara, who had run eight times and had never won.

That said, I was delighted to get to ride on Asmara again. She had given me a good ride against French Ballerina at the Curragh, and she was a really game and tough filly, typical of a filly of the Aga Khan's, and I knew that she stayed the 10-furlong trip well. I asked her for her effort early in the home straight, we hit the front halfway between the two-furlong pole and the furlong pole, and she ran all the way to the line.

Johnny wasn't too happy. Just like Mick at the Curragh three weeks earlier – that's the competitor in him. He just got checked a little on Oriane at the two-furlong marker, he had to switch outside and, by the time he got into the clear, we had flown. He was never going to catch us.

There was a painting of me winning the Trigo Stakes on Asmara hanging up in the house at home, my parents' house. My mother always loved that painting. When I was moving out of home a few years later, it was the one painting that she asked me to leave. I wasn't allowed take it with me!

That was another really good day, my first big winner for John Oxx, a listed race at Leopardstown, just three weeks after my first big winner for Dermot Weld. And, just like winning in the Moyglare Stud colours on Token Gesture, it was massive for me to win a good race in the Aga Khan colours, those famous green colours with the red epaulettes, colours that had been carried by so many famous horses, like Shahrastani and Doyoun and Kahyasi and, of course, Shergar. I would have more big days in those colours. Bigger days. The biggest days.

CHAPTER 8

In 1996 I was champion apprentice and, because I still had my claim at the start of the season, I was an apprentice again for the whole year. I wanted to win the championship again. I had momentum from 1995 and I wanted to keep it going in 1996.

Thankfully, I did. I got plenty of rides, more than in 1995, and I had a steady stream of winners. I rode winners for 14 different trainers in 1996, and I ended up with 29 winners, champion apprentice again and fifth in the overall jockeys' championship. Only Johnny Murtagh, Kevin Manning, Mick Kinane and Christy Roche finished in front of me.

I enjoyed the second apprentice' title more than the first one, probably because there was a level of expectation there. It was a goal. And I had the title in the bag from a fair way out as well in 1996, so I was able to enjoy the run-in a little bit more.

I was riding better horses, in better races. And I was riding for some of the top trainers in the country, and for some of the top owners in the world. You put on those colours, the Moyglare colours or the Aga Khan's colours or Sheikh Hamdan's colours or Sheikh Mohammed's colours. It was some feeling. For a young rider, it was some boost.

I always thought that I treated all owners the same, whether it was an owner with a horse in a maiden at Sligo or the Aga

Khan with a runner in the Derby. I always felt that I put the same amount of effort into giving the horse the best ride that I could give it, and that I gave as much time and as much information as I could to the owner. But there was something about riding in the famous colours, colours that had been worn by top-class jockeys and carried by top-class horses in the best races all over the world.

It was the same even later in my career. You would go into the weigh room and see the Moyglare colours, the Aga Khan colours, Prince Khalid Abdullah's colours, Sheikh Hamdan's colours, all hanging up on your peg, and you would grow a foot.

Strangely, even at the height of my career, I never thought that I was the best. I always looked up to other riders. I was always looking at others, thinking that I had to improve to be as good as them. When I started off, of course, there was Mick Kinane, and I never thought that I was as good as Mick, or that I could ever be as good as Mick. Then when I was getting going, Johnny Murtagh was champion jockey, and Johnny's international career was taking off. And I was looking at Mick and looking at Johnny, and looking at Christy Roche, and thinking that I had a long way to go to be as good as them.

Of course, I was very lucky to have the career than I had, but I always felt that I could have achieved more. I always felt that I could have ridden more Group 1 winners. And then, after I won my seventh championship, my eighth, my ninth, I started thinking, Mick Kinane won 13, so I had to win 14. I didn't get past nine. But that's the stuff that goes on in your head. You find reasons to tell yourself that you're not that good, that you have to keep working at it.

When I thought about it later, I concluded that it was down to a lack of confidence. I never thought that a lack of confidence came through in my riding, and maybe it wouldn't have shown on the outside, but inside, I lacked confidence. I was riddled with self-doubt throughout my career.

'Am I really good enough for this? To be riding for these people, to be riding the best horses, in the best races?'

Thoughts used to creep into my head.

'Am I really good enough to be in this position, or have I been lucky?'

I never thought that I was good enough to be able to relax.

'Am I just getting away with it?'

That spurred me on, and that was probably a good thing. It made me work hard throughout my entire career. I never felt that I had arrived; I never felt that I was as good as I could be as a jockey. I always thought that I could do better, that I could be more successful. I was always looking for ways in which I could improve. I was always seeking that security that success brings but, even after a victory, even after a big victory, that security didn't last very long. I was off on the hunt for the next win, the next piece of affirmation, the next victory that would tell me that maybe I was good enough.

There was the fear of failure, and that was massive. That was always there. Like, if it didn't work, if I didn't make it as a jockey, what were the alternatives? I was qualified to do nothing else. I didn't even have my Junior Certificate, never mind a Leaving Certificate or a college degree. It was back to being a labourer on a farm or in a stable yard or on a stud farm.

I always thought that there was a little bit of self-doubt in all sportspeople. Not just jockeys. All sportspeople. Even the most confident people, or the people who came across as being confident, if they were being true to themselves, they would probably admit that there was at least a degree of self-doubt.

I went on to spend most of my career riding for Dermot Weld, and that was significant. You were never allowed to get above yourself with the boss. Every day was important. He didn't measure you in seasons: he measured you in days. If you weren't getting up to the mark every day of every season, you wouldn't last. It's why Mick Kinane's relationship with the boss was so good and so fruitful and so long. Mick was at his best every day.

If I hadn't been hitting the mark every day, I would have been gone. I always thought that. It didn't matter whether the boss liked you or not; it was results that mattered. And performances. That was all. Just results and performances. If you hadn't been getting results in an operation like that, you would have been out the gate, that's for sure. So it gave me a bit of satisfaction that I was able to keep the job for as long as I did. And I got the results, I put up the performances, I kept the job because I worked at it. Every day, I worked at being as good as I could be, at being better than I had been.

We'd have our pep talk every year, at the start of every season. Ballydoyle are getting stronger, the boss would say to me. The competition is getting more intense. I have to be a better trainer than I was last year, and you have to be a better rider. And that's just to stand still. You have to be better than you were last year just to achieve the same results. If you want to do better, then you have to be much better. I got that talk every March, just before the season started, and I believed him. He was right. It made me work as hard as I could work in order to be better.

That's the type of person the boss has always been. He motivated everyone around him; he inspired every member of his team to strive to be better. He obviously played a massive role in my career, not only in providing me with the horses that carried me to all those victories, but also in motivating me to be the best jockey that I could be.

I got to know our horses very well, and I'd do my homework:

I'd study horses and races and opponents. So that, if the boss asked me anything about a horse or a race or tactics or what I was thinking of doing, how I was thinking of riding a particular horse, I'd have the answer. No hesitation. That was important.

Even so, it was tough sometimes, especially in the early days. The bollockings you'd get. You could get beaten on a horse at Ballinrobe on a Monday evening, and you could spend most of the four-hour drive home on the phone getting a bollocking from the boss!

You needed to be mentally strong, or a little bit naïve, or a mixture of both. If you were weak, you wouldn't last. I think I was more naïve than strong – I probably didn't really realise the magnitude of everything, the magnitude of the job, first jockey to Dermot Weld. Taking over from Mick Kinane.

I was never going to be the next Mick Kinane, but I was sure that I was going to be the best Pat Smullen that I could be. Even so, my mindset couldn't block out the noise. I remember going around the parade ring at the Curragh one day, and a punter shouting up to me, 'You'll never be Mick Kinane.'

I think my naïvety got me through the first couple of years with the boss. I had only just turned 21. If I had sat down and thought about it deeply enough, I could have cracked. Thankfully, I didn't crack, I kept it together, but I was riddled with doubt, riddled with fear. Fear that the boss would sack me, fear that I wouldn't be able to stick it. It was a pressure cooker, all day, every day. The boss was so results driven. If you got beaten on one, you knew about it, all right.

It was intense, right to the end of my time with him, right to the end of my career. As time went on, though, we developed a great understanding of each other. Importantly, I gradually figured out how he wanted his horses ridden. That's the advantage of being a stable jockey, of being around the trainer every day, of riding all the horses, of getting to understand the horses and the pedigrees and the families. It took me a while, but I got there.

We got to a point, too, at which he trusted me, and we got to enjoy each other. It took me about 10 years, but I got to figure out what he wanted. (I was a fast learner like that.) I knew all the horses, and it got to a point at which we didn't really need to discuss horses or races. I knew what he wanted and he knew what I was going to do.

I really enjoyed the last five years riding for the boss. Looking back on it, I probably didn't enjoy the early years so much. The last five or six years, though, I enjoyed them lots. It was just a pity that I couldn't have gone on for another five or ten years. We were only really getting going.

Serious

Dr Adrian McGoldrick was adamant that I needed to go to St Vincent's Private Hospital. He maintained that they had the best people there to deal with what needed to be dealt with, so I was more than happy to go with Adrian's advice.

It all happened very quickly. I was transferred from the Beacon to St Vincent's on Sunday afternoon, and that was the start of all the great work that the doctors and nurses and staff at St Vincent's did for me. I was under the care of Ray McDermott, who was renowned as one of the best oncologists in the world, and my surgeon was Justin Geoghegan, an amazing man.

Eva Haefner from Moyglare Stud was unbelievable; she told me that she would send me wherever I needed to go so that I could get the best care and attention that there was anywhere in the world. In the end, after doing all our research, we concluded that the best care that we could get anywhere in the world was on our doorstep, in St Vincent's.

There was a seriousness and an urgency to my situation. The seriousness was obvious – a tumour on your pancreas ticks that box. But the tumour was pressing on my bile duct, and it was preventing the bile from getting into my stomach, so the bile was going back through my body, poisoning me. That was what caused my urine to go a strange colour; that was what was causing my face to have this jaundiced look about it.

And it caused me to feel sick. I felt desperately sick, desperately nauseous. The bile was making me sick. So the urgency was in trying to fix that, to put in a stent which would open up the bile duct and allow the bile to flow back into my stomach. It was a complex procedure, and there were extensive preparations for that operation. It was Professor John Hegarty who performed it, and he was brilliant. I started to feel better immediately.

We were told that the tumour wasn't operable, because it was too close to the main artery, and that was fairly devastating news. Plan B had to be enacted: go through a programme of chemotherapy with the objective of reducing the tumour in size so that it could be operated on and removed.

I was in St Vincent's for five days. I had to go under general anaesthetic to get the stent in, and I recovered from that fairly quickly. Then I had to go under again to get the port for the chemotherapy put in, and I bounced out of that too. That was the upside of being a jockey, of being fit. They sent me home then. I had to wait two weeks, build up my strength again, before I could start the chemotherapy.

It was nice to get home, but it was also sad and frustrating and weird. My whole life turned upside down. I wasn't able to do my job, for starters. I wasn't able to go racing or to go riding out or to go down to Dermot's or to work with the young horses. I wasn't able to do what I had been doing my whole professional life. And then there was the longer-term stuff, like our family: how were we going to raise our family?

Frances was fantastic through all of that. She just kept reassuring me, telling me that everything was going to be all right, and that all the practical stuff was under control, insurance, security for the kids. Just shows you again the importance of having a great partner in your life.

The one thing that disappointed me on the insurance front was that I didn't get any payment from the Jockeys' Accident Fund. Not for me, really – I was lucky in that I had other insurance and I had a career that allowed me to cope financially with the juggernaut that had hit me. But because it wasn't an injury that I had suffered, because it was an illness, I wasn't entitled to anything from the Jockeys' Accident Fund. A fund that I had been paying into since its inception, a fund that I always thought would be there for me if I needed it. For other riders who weren't as fortunate as I was, that could have been devastating financially.

I managed to get that changed, to have a fund set up that jockeys could pay into, that would cover them for illness as well as injury. At the end of the day, if your career is ended because of some kind of debilitation, it doesn't matter whether it is an injury or an illness. The net result is the same: your career is over. It was crazy that there was no illness cover. Now there is cover for illness as well as cover for injury, and that is as it should be.

I knew that I had to concentrate on getting better. I knew that that was all I had to do. Just to get better. I had to channel all my energies into that. It was a new way of life for me. All the energy that I had devoted to racing, I now had to redirect into getting better. I had a new focus.

I took the challenge on board. I had dark days, of course. I had down days, days when I got depressed in myself. Days when it all got on top of me. Days when I was watching racing, watching one of Dermot's horses winning and knowing that, if things had been different, I would have been riding that horse. But in general, I was positive. I tried to make myself be positive, surround myself with positive people, think positive thoughts, and that was a big part of my road to recovery. On better days I would watch one of Dermot's horses winning and think that it was a horse that I would get to ride at some stage in the future.

I conditioned myself to a new way of life. Once I had accepted that my sole focus was on getting better, I had this weird sense of relief. I managed to get my head around that, that I could return to race riding in the future, but that my immediate and only focus was on getting myself healthy again. I decided that I had to give it everything I had; otherwise it would overtake me and consume me.

I was very lucky that I had great people around me, Frances and the kids for starters, Hannah and Sarah and Paddy, my mother, my brothers, my close friends. They were constantly ringing me, texting me, rallying around me the whole time.

I was lucky, too, that I was fit before I got sick. I was physically strong, and that allowed me to cope with the treatment better. Justin Geoghegan told me that, when he was doing the operation, he cut through skin straight into muscle. There was no body fat.

He said that I was the only person he knew who put on weight during a course of chemotherapy!

CHAPTER 9

Riding for John Oxx was very different from riding for Dermot Weld. Dermot pointed out the areas in which you had to improve, whereas John would inspire you with confidence. Both men were brilliant trainers and, for me, one complemented the other. I was lucky to be riding for the two of them at the same time, so early in my career, during a formative period. They had contrasting methods, and both methods worked for me.

Working for John was brilliant for me. I probably needed someone to be filling me with confidence at the time, someone telling me that I could ride. At the same time, Dermot's method kept me sharp. I always thought that I improved hugely as a rider for the guidance of both.

I didn't have a job with Dermot Weld at the start of the 1997 season. My jobs were with John, as second jockey to Johnny Murtagh, and with Tommy Stack, but Dermot was using me more and more, and I was going in to ride out for him whenever I could.

It was a great position for me to be in, as a young rider finding his way, but it couldn't last. Trainers might say that they were happy to share you with other trainers but, at the end of the day, they usually wanted you for themselves. They didn't really want you riding for other trainers. It made sense. If you spotted a good rider, if you thought that you had seen a rider who you thought was good enough to ride for you, you wanted him or her on your team. You wanted to keep them for yourself, and you definitely didn't want them riding against you, for your competitor. You wouldn't send a promising young football player out on loan to another club one week, and expect him to be playing for you the following week.

I got the opportunity to go to Japan in November that year, and that was a fantastic experience. I was invited out as champion apprentice in Ireland to take part in the international jockeys' competition, organised by the Japan Racing Association.

I was allowed to take someone with me and, as my mother and father didn't want to travel all the way to Japan, I took Barry Lacy. We were treated so well by the JRA – first-class flights to Japan, and treated like royalty when we got there. It was a real eye-opener for me, to see racing run in a jurisdiction like Japan. The crowds that went racing, the atmosphere, the noise. The facilities they had at the racecourses, for horses, for racegoers, for jockeys. The weigh room and the steam rooms and the saunas. Everything, really.

Jason Weaver was representing Britain, and Thierry Thulliez was representing France. Joe Bravo was there from America, and Johnny Velazquez. Yutaka Take was the Japanese star. The home crowd loved Take. He was like a movie star there. And me in the middle of all of this.

I didn't ride any winners, but I enjoyed every minute of it. Riding at Nakayama racecourse with the crowd cheering you on, and riding out at Miho Training Centre, and just experiencing a little bit of Japanese culture. Everybody was so nice to us, so polite. I was only there for a week, but it was a brilliant experience.

I rode in Japan four times in the years that followed, in the international jockeys' competition.

I loved going back to Japan. They are massive horse racing fans there, the prize money is phenomenal and their racing is top-class. And every time I went back, I was always made to feel very welcome by the Japanese people.

I was lucky enough that, during my career, I got to ride in lots of different countries, all over the world, from South Africa to Singapore, and they were all different. Hong Kong was sharp and tight, both tracks, Happy Valley and Sha Tin, with the city towering above you. The Japanese tracks were different – they were usually wide and galloping with sweeping turns – but they were different from each other too, right-handed and left-handed, turf and dirt.

I was lucky to ride in South Africa, too. I rode at Turffontein in an international jockeys' challenge there, and I was lucky to get to ride in Singapore, at Kranji. I rode Jammaal for Dermot in the Singapore Derby there in the summer of 2001, in the humidity. I had never experienced humidity like it before. Jammaal did well to finish third, but the humidity must have affected him too – it took him a fair while to recover from that trip, but he did come back and win the Diamond Stakes at the Curragh the following October.

The thing about riding abroad, though, was that you were usually in and out. You were there to do a job, you'd ride in your race or races, and then you were out of there. Usually, you didn't really get the chance to look around, to experience some of the culture. Japan was different, though: you had a little bit of time to take in some of the culture, and I loved that.

I loved riding in Dubai as well. I loved everything about Dubai. I got the opportunity to go to Dubai that winter, after coming back from Japan in November. Tony Lacy, Barry's brother, got a job with Erwan Charpy in Dubai. Willie Supple was riding as stable jockey to Erwan at the time, but he was looking for a second jockey, and Tony suggested me.

I met the late Michael Osborne in the car park at the Curragh one day after I had applied for the job in Dubai. Michael was such a great man, a brilliant ambassador for racing worldwide and for Irish racing in particular. He was very close to Sheikh Mohammed, and he was a key figure in getting racing in Dubai on the road, building up the quality of the racing there.

Michael was aware that I had applied for the job with Erwan Charpy and, once I knew that he knew that I had applied, and once he seemed so positive about it, I was very hopeful that I would get the job.

And so began my association with Dubai. I loved it from the moment I got there, and I have seen it develop as a nation and as a racing nation from year to year, every year that I went back. The change from Nad Al Sheba Racecourse to Meydan Racecourse, the development of the Carnival in the spring, the continual improvement in the quality of the horses and the quality of the racing. Progress was fantastic under the direction of Sheikh Mohammed and the Maktoum family.

I spent most winters in Dubai during my career. I spent eight full winters there riding, and even when I stopped going there for the full winter I would go out for some of the Carnival or for Dubai World Cup night, or even just on holiday. I rode for Erwan Charpy as second jockey to Willie initially, and then as stable jockey for three years after Willie moved to Dhruba Selvaratnam.

I learned an awful lot from Erwan in terms of times and judgement of pace. He is a Frenchman, but he served his time in America, where they were big on the clock long before race times ever really became a thing in Europe. So he taught me a lot about timing, about how important pace was, and that had a big influence on the way that I thought about races.

I rode for Dhruba Selvaratnam for a couple of years, another very good trainer – he trained for Sheikh Ahmed, who owned the other racetrack in Dubai at Jebel Ali – and then I went back to Erwan again. There was a great expat community there, and I made great friends there, lifelong friends.

And, of course, I would meet Frances in Dubai in 1998. Amazing. You travel halfway across the world to meet a girl who lives down the road.

I started off the 1997 season back home with no claim. Champion apprentice I may have been, dual champion apprentice, but that all counted for nothing when the 1997 season started. I was swimming in open waters, taking on Mick Kinane and Christy Roche and Johnny Murtagh on level terms. No claim. And it didn't even matter that I had finished fifth in the overall championship in 1996. For starters, that was with the help of a claim for most of the season. Also, all the scores were back to zero anyway at the start of the season.

But I was still in a great position. Riding for John Oxx, behind Johnny Murtagh, riding for Tommy Stack, riding a bit for Dermot Weld.

So it was riding out most mornings, racing most afternoons. It was busy, but I was exactly where I wanted to be. When I got a few quid together, I bought myself a car. When I got a few more quid together, I bought myself a bigger car.

Then you start to think that you're a real jockey. My career was on an upward curve, and I loved it. I loved getting ready to go racing, I loved going racing, I loved being in the weigh room, I loved race riding. I loved everything about it, except having to keep my weight in check. Apart from that negative, everything else was positive.

My career went up another gear in 1997. Most of my rides on the track were obviously for John Oxx and Tommy Stack, but Dermot was using me plenty too. Mick was riding a fair bit in Britain, riding a lot of good horses for Sir Michael Stoute, and for others, and he started to ride Aidan's horses in Britain. And he wasn't really going to the country tracks in Ireland during the week. So he would ride, say, at Leopardstown on a Wednesday evening, then he'd ride in England on Saturday and he'd be back in Ireland on Sunday. Unless there was a big meeting in Ireland on the Saturday, and Dermot would put his foot down a bit.

Pat Shanahan was second jockey, but there were still lots of rides going for Dermot, like if he had two in a race, or even going to some tracks that Pat wouldn't go to, like Tramore or Downpatrick. Usually, Dermot's horses at those tracks were steering jobs, so I used to love going off to ride them. And the more time went on and the more winners I rode for him, the more opportunities Dermot was giving me.

I was getting some nice outside rides as well. I rode Tout A Coup to win the Listed Glencairn Stakes at Leopardstown in June for Gerry Cusack, and I rode Burden Of Proof to win a listed race at the Curragh for Charles O'Brien. It was some thrill to wear Vincent O'Brien's colours, the red body with the white sleeves, the same colours that Lester Piggott had worn on Fatherland when he won the National Stakes in 1992, and on College Chapel when he won the Cork and Orrery Stakes at Royal Ascot the following year.

But the highlight of 1997 for me was Tommy Stack's filly Tarascon. Tommy loved Tarascon from the start. The times that she was doing on the gallops at home in Thomastown were comparable to the times that Las Meninas had been doing as a juvenile, and Las Meninas had won the 1000 Guineas three years earlier. I loved Tarascon too. I loved riding her work. The speed that she showed. I didn't know what a Group 1 horse was – I had never ridden one – but, even in my inexperienced eyes, she had something special. She oozed class.

She ran well on her racecourse debut at the Curragh in July

that year, finishing a close-up third in a big field behind a colt of Jim Bolger's called Dane River. She wasn't great at the gates – she got a bit worked up at the start, which wasn't ideal – but it was her first time to run in a race, so you could forgive her that. I wasn't overly hard on her, I held her up early and I let her finish off her race. It would have been nice to have won, but the most important thing was that she had a good experience, that she enjoyed herself so that she would look forward to going racing again.

She showed the benefit of that run next time, back at the Curragh two weeks later. We had a good tussle with Seamie Heffernan and Saratoga Springs through the final two furlongs, but Tarascon was strong in the finish, and we got the better of them on the run to the line with the two of us coming clear of the rest of the field. Time would tell that that was a seriously good performance, as Saratoga Springs won the Acomb Stakes at York on his next run, and went on to win the Group 1 Racing Post Trophy at Doncaster at the end of the season.

Tarascon came out of the race well, and Tommy targeted her at the Heinz 57 at Leopardstown. It was a big step up in grade for her, from a conditions race to a Group 1, but everybody thought that she was ready for the step up.

It was big for the filly, but it was big for me too, my first time riding in a Group 1 race. We thought that she had a real chance, but she was a little too keen through the early stages of the race and, when they quickened at the two-furlong marker, she just couldn't quicken past them. We finished fifth, and we weren't beaten that far by the winner, Princely Heir, a British challenger, trained by Mark Johnston and ridden by Jason Weaver.

Tommy wasn't too despondent. It had been a big ask for the filly, taking on the colts over six furlongs, and Tommy was still convinced that she was a Group 1 filly. I was hoping that she was.

I didn't know what a Group 1 filly was at that stage of my career, but I knew how highly Tommy regarded her, and I knew that she was the best filly that I had ever ridden.

The Moyglare Stud Stakes was the obvious race for Tarascon after that. A Group 1 race for two-year-old fillies over seven furlongs. The step back up to seven furlongs was always going to be a positive for her; she had stayed that distance well when she had beaten Saratoga Springs in July. Also, we knew that she handled the Curragh well; she had run well on both her visits there, and the fact that the Moyglare is restricted to fillies was another positive, after taking on colts in the Heinz.

It was exciting for me, going into another Group 1 race on a filly who had a chance. You're never thinking that you're going to win, you never allow yourself to think that, but I was excited at the prospect of riding in another Group 1 race, on a high-class filly with a chance.

Tarascon was a little bit temperamental, and she was tricky at the gates again that day, but she was away well and we were quickly into a good position, just behind the leaders. We moved in behind Willie Supple on Heed My Warning at the two-furlong pole, and I asked Tarascon for her effort at the furlong marker. She picked up well and we closed gradually on the leader, reduced the lead to a length, half a length, a neck. I always thought that, when I went for her, she would pick up, and I always thought that we were getting there. And we did. Just. She just put her head in front in the last strides to get home in a photo.

That was some feeling: a Moyglare Stud Stakes, a Group 1 win, my first Group 1 win. It was some feeling coming back into the winner's enclosure at the Curragh on the back of a Group 1 winner. Tommy was delighted, obviously; another Group 1 win for him, his first Moyglare Stud Stakes. I was delighted for him and his wife, Liz – they had been so good to me, giving me the opportunities that they had given me, allowing me to ride Tarascon in these Group 1 races. And the owner, Jane Rowlinson. I was delighted that I was able to deliver for them all.

It was a landmark win for me. I had only just turned 20, I was still living at home with my mother and father, I was only just making my way, so a Group 1 win was massive. I had proven that I could do it at the highest level, and I looked forward all winter to riding Tarascon in the Guineas the following spring. She was a Guineas filly, no question. With normal progress, a Moyglare Stud Stakes winner at two should make up into a Guineas filly at three. Irish Guineas or English Guineas or both.

There was talk about going for the Prix Marcel Boussac in France in October, but Tommy thought it best to leave Tarascon off for the rest of the season and bring her back fresh the following spring for the Guineas. It was a plan that made sense.

She wintered well, she grew and strengthened up nicely during the off-season. Tommy said that he wouldn't run her as a three-year-old before the Guineas. She didn't need a prep run. He had taken Las Meninas to Newmarket for the Guineas on her seasonal debut in 1994, and that worked out well, so why change a winning formula?

It was an exciting time for me. I was going to Newmarket with a filly who had a real chance of winning the 1000 Guineas. Her work in the lead up to the race was fantastic; we really thought that she would run a big race.

I hadn't been to Newmarket since I had been there with Joanna for the breeze-up sales back in 1991, riding up the Rowley Mile. I was back again, all set to ride up the Rowley Mile again, but this time it was for real, in the 1000 Guineas.

It was a disaster, though. From beginning to end. Tarascon's frailties at the start resurfaced. She got worked up at the stalls, she started lashing out, and she never settled in the race. It didn't help that we were drawn out in the middle of the track in stall two of 16 runners, 14 horses away from the stands rail – but, in truth, it wouldn't have mattered where we had been drawn. She had thrown it away before the race had even started.

We got away on terms, and I tried to get her to settle in behind horses out in the centre of the track, but she was always doing more than I wanted her to do. About half a mile out, the pace started to quicken, and she just couldn't go with them. I rode her along for a couple of furlongs, but we just got further and further behind. In the end, I just sat up on her and allowed her to come home in her own time, 16th of 16 and beaten a distance.

It was disappointing, but we knew that it just wasn't her running. There was consolation in the fact that we knew that it wasn't the real Tarascon. It would have been different if she had run her race and finished fifth or sixth, if she simply hadn't been good enough. In a way, that would have been more disappointing. The way it worked out, it was frustrating, it was a missed opportunity, but we still thought that she was a Guineas filly. We would have another chance in the Irish Guineas.

Alas, we wouldn't. Or at least I wouldn't.

CHAPTER 10

I t was never going to last, really, all those balls in the air. Riding for Tommy Stack, riding for John Oxx, riding for Dermot Weld. It was never sustainable in the long term. You couldn't keep all three plates spinning indefinitely.

You could do it for a little while, and it worked well for me for a little while. The three trainers' work mornings were on different days, two work mornings each – that was six days. There was even a day in the week left for me to go and ride out for Frank Dunne. But, in the end, something was going to have to give.

As I said before, trainers tend to want you for themselves. As you start to go up the ranks, it's very difficult to keep more than one trainer happy. Ruby Walsh did it with Willie Mullins and Paul Nicholls for 10 years. That was incredible, that Ruby was able to ride at the top level for the champion National Hunt trainer in Ireland and the champion National Hunt trainer in Britain for a decade. They probably had their difficult moments, but the fact that it worked so well for so long was obviously down to Ruby's immense talent as a jockey (and probably his diplomatic skills) and, obviously, the level of success that they all had. You can allow for a lot when you have the level and volume of success that those three had for all those years.

But that was rare, almost unique. Richard Dunwoody did it for a while with Nicky Henderson and David Nicholson too, before he joined Martin Pipe, but in general, it's almost impossible. You can't play for Liverpool on Saturday and for Manchester City on Sunday.

I was very happy to keep going as I was going, riding for all three trainers. It was an arrangement that was working well for me. But it was a delicate balance, and any change in the general ecology of the situation was always going to put the whole thing in jeopardy.

I was lucky in that it wasn't that difficult to avoid a clash between Tommy and John. It's just the way it worked out. It was down to circumstances rather than anything that I had cleverly figured out or orchestrated myself, but they tended to have different types of horses. Tommy had plenty of two-year-olds and three-year-olds: young horses, precocious types, sprinters and milers. John's horses tended to be slower burns. Not many sharp two-year-olds, more three-year-olds and older horses, and not so many sprinters and milers, more of the middle-distance and staying types that are typical of the Aga Khan's families.

The clashes were more between Tommy and Dermot. They had similar types of horses, and Dermot was asking me to go in to Rosewell House more and more. I think that Tommy was getting more and more annoyed about that, and he was starting to put more demands on me too. I couldn't do both; I couldn't commit more to both trainers. But I could be there for both trainers on work mornings, and I figured that I was okay as long as they had different work mornings.

Then Tommy decided that he wanted to work Tarascon on Tuesdays and Fridays, and that clashed with John's work mornings. That was the deal-breaker. I had to choose.

There was a lot to consider. Tommy had a nice bunch of horses, and he had a star horse in Tarascon. Okay, she had disappointed in the 1000 Guineas at Newmarket in early May, but we knew that that wasn't her true running, and she was on track for the Irish 1000 Guineas at the Curragh at the end of May.

But John Oxx was John Oxx. He had a stable full of talented horses. He always had. At the time he had Namid and Winona and Ebadiyla and Edabiya and Enzeli. Top-class horses for some of the best owner-breeders of thoroughbreds in the world. And I had committed to John. It was Tommy who had changed the goalposts. I had given John my word, and all my life, if I had committed to something, I always tried to honour that commitment. I always tried to keep my word.

Dermot was starting to use me more too. The day before I went over to Newmarket to ride Tarascon in the 1000 Guineas, I rode a treble for Dermot at the Curragh, Camargo in the two-year-olds' maiden, Stage Affair in the Mooresbridge Stakes and Two-Twenty-Two in the Tetrarch Stakes. A maiden, a listed race and a Group 3 race, all in one day.

Mick Kinane was at Newmarket that day – he was busy winning the 2000 Guineas on King Of Kings for Aidan O'Brien – so somebody had to ride Dermot's horses at the Curragh, but it was significant that he decided to allow me to ride them. Actually, he had three runners in the Mooresbridge Stakes: Pat Shanahan was on Sense Of Honour and Declan McDonogh was on Celtic Lore, both outsiders, while he put me on Stage Affair, the odds-on favourite and, ultimately, the easy winner.

They all won easily, too – they were just point-and-steer jobs. They won by an aggregate of 16 lengths. All I had to do was not mess it up.

In the end, it wasn't that difficult a decision, really. Not with an eye on the long term. Even as a wet-behind-the-ears 20-year-old who had the prospect of riding an Irish 1000 Guineas winner the following week, I could see the bigger picture. I could see the strength in depth that John Oxx and Dermot Weld had, that it was probable that they would have deep strength for the foreseeable future.

Tommy probably wanted a change anyway. Everything had gone pear-shaped at Newmarket with Tarascon. Maybe Tommy was thinking that it was my fault, or that, at the very least, a change of jockey might not be any harm. Also, I was riding more and more for John and Dermot, and maybe I wasn't giving Tommy the attention that I should have been giving him.

There wasn't really a decision to be made. I didn't really talk to anybody; I didn't really need advice on it. I didn't even tell John about it. John had this huge ship to run, and I had committed to being a part of it. The way I saw it, it was quite simple really: Tommy wanted me on Tuesdays and Fridays, but I was with John on Tuesdays and Fridays, so I couldn't go to Tommy's.

Even so, it doesn't mean that I wasn't gutted when I had to tell Tommy that I couldn't go down to ride work on Tarascon.

Maybe that was Tommy's plan all along. It's back to trainers generally wanting jockeys for themselves, not wanting to share them around. You could see it from Tommy's perspective. I was either riding for him or I wasn't. He could see that I was riding more and more for Dermot, and maybe he wanted to see where my long-term loyalties lay. Better to find out sooner rather than later.

By forcing the issue, at least he knew where he stood. And, if he was going to force the issue, best to do it before Tarascon ran in the Irish 1000 Guineas.

I was never bitter towards Tommy, though. He did what he had to do; he gave me the options and I made my decision. I was always hugely grateful to Tommy, for the opportunities that he gave me, and to Liz, for how welcome they made me feel down in Golden. And it's a long road that doesn't turn. Years later, in 2014, I rode Scream Blue Murder for Tommy to win the Group 3 Phoenix Sprint Stakes at the Curragh. Tommy and Liz's son Fozzy took over the licence in 2017, and he continued to have lots of success.

I could see all of that in later years, in the cold light of hindsight. At the time, though, I could only see it from my point of view, and I was desperately disappointed to lose the ride on Tarascon. Tarascon was my horse, my filly. I had ridden her in all her five races, including in the Moyglare Stud Stakes, my first Group 1 win. And I had been looking forward to my chance to right the wrong of the Newmarket Guineas by riding her at the Curragh. It was pretty gutting, knowing that somebody else was going to be riding her at the Curragh.

In the end, I didn't have a ride in the Irish 1000 Guineas, and that made it worse. I sat in the weigh room and watched it. At least if I had been out there, even on a 100/1 shot, out the back, I wouldn't have had to sit on my own and watch it on the television there.

And, human nature being what it is, I wanted Tarascon to be beaten. There was a small part of me that was delighted for the filly and for her connections, but the larger part of me was gutted that I wasn't riding her. I congratulated Tommy afterwards and all the team. I said and did all the right things at the time, but, deep down, I was in bits when Tarascon won the Irish 1000 Guineas.

In that situation, you'd hear jockeys say that they were delighted for the horse, delighted for connections, delighted for the team but, in reality, they were not. They were gutted for themselves. If you were out of commission through injury or suspension, or if you had just simply been jocked off, and you saw a horse that you could or should have been riding winning any race, you were disappointed. If that race was a Group 1 race, a Classic, you were devastated.

For me, at that stage of my career, just when I thought that I was starting to get going, I thought that it was the end of the world. I remember driving home that evening, back to my parents' house in Rhode, and thinking that that was it. That had been my big chance, my one chance at winning a Classic, and I had blown it.

But it is a long road. I had made my decision with an eye on the long term, on the future, and the future started happening in 1998. Mick was away more and more. He was riding more and more for Aidan O'Brien.

It didn't mean that he wasn't riding for Dermot in Ireland, though. He was still there on the big days and at the good meetings. But I was also getting lots of opportunities for Dermot, during the week and at the country tracks, and sometimes at the big tracks and on the big days, if big days in Ireland clashed with big days abroad, as happened with the Tetrarch Stakes at the Curragh and the 2000 Guineas at Newmarket. I was happy to travel the length of the country for a ride, for a potential winner. And it was great to be getting opportunities.

It was tricky to manage it all, though, and, surprisingly, I had fewer rides and fewer winners in 1998 than I had in 1997. The quality of my rides went up, but the quantity went down. It's never easy when you are second jockey. You have to wait to see what running plans are before you can commit to another ride. John Oxx might have had a couple of entries in a race, but he wouldn't know if he would be running one or two or three, or none, so you'd have to wait. Then only one of them might be declared at final declaration stage, but obviously Johnny Murtagh would be riding that, so you wouldn't have a ride. By then, all the good spare rides would have been booked up, so you'd be left without a ride in the race. And even if John ran two, you'd have to wait to see which one Johnny would be riding, and if you'd be riding the other one. And even then, you'd obviously be riding the lesser-fancied of the two John Oxx horses.

You'd also be keeping an eye on Dermot's entries, if there was the possibility that he would have more than one runner in a race, or if he would have runners at a meeting down the country to which Mick wouldn't be going, or at a meeting that was clashing with a big British meeting or a big international meeting, and you'd be hoping that Mick would be going there and that you'd get the call.

I also rode Access All Areas for John Mulhern to win the Listed Marble Hill Stakes at the Curragh on Irish Guineas weekend in 1998. Neither Dermot nor John had anything for the race. Mick rode a filly for Mark Johnston and Peter Savill, Acicula, and Johnny rode a filly for Noel Meade, Show Me The Money.

Access All Areas was a promising colt. He had won a big-field maiden at Leopardstown two weeks earlier at a big price under a young 5lb-claiming rider, Fran Berry. I thought that I gave him quite a good ride in the Marble Hill. I held him up at the back of the field early on, I asked him for his effort just inside the two-furlong marker, and he picked up well to get up and beat an Aidan O'Brien filly ridden by Walter Swinburn, Coralita, by a short head.

Access All Areas ran next in the Coventry Stakes at Royal Ascot; Mick rode him there and he ran well to finish third. Then he ran in the Heinz 57 at Leopardstown, and John booked Pat Eddery for the ride.

I wasn't too happy about that. Whatever about being replaced by Mick Kinane at Royal Ascot, it was different being replaced by Pat Eddery at Leopardstown, a track that I knew well. It didn't really register with me either that I was being replaced by Pat

Eddery, one of the best Flat jockeys of his era, a man who had ridden all those winners for Vincent O'Brien and Henry Cecil and Peter Walwyn, a man who had been champion jockey in Britain 11 times. In my eyes, I had done nothing wrong on Access All Areas in the Marble Hill, and I was disappointed that I was jocked off for the Heinz.

I saw John Mulhern in the parade ring at Leopardstown that day, so I took the opportunity to say it to him.

'Hello, Mr Mulhern,' I said politely. 'I was just wondering why you took me off Access All Areas?'

John Mulhern just looked at me blankly.

'I know it's Pat Eddery,' I continued, 'but I was just wondering, why did you take me off him?'

John Mulhern was probably shocked. He started to offer an explanation, he started to explain that it was Pat Eddery and that this was a Group 1 race and that Pat Eddery had the experience and that he was a world-class rider.

Suddenly he stopped talking. Suddenly he realised that he didn't owe this little upstart any explanation. His expression changed.

'Go away, you little pup!'

He was right. It was a bit cheeky of me. Of course he didn't owe me an explanation at all.

He was a great man, John Mulhern. He had this immense presence; he had a massive personality. He was a gentleman, he was a very generous man, and he was a seriously good judge.

Access All Areas finished second in the Heinz 57 under Pat Eddery, and I got back on him for his next race, in the Tattersalls Breeders Stakes at the Curragh, so John Mulhern obviously didn't hold my cheekiness against me.

There were rumours going around all year, too, about Mick moving to Ballydoyle full-time. Christy Roche was nearing retirement and Mick was riding all the big Aidan O'Brien horses in Britain and in France, so it seemed like a logical move. And if the rumours were right, if Mick was moving to Ballydoyle, somebody else was obviously going to have to take on the role as stable jockey to Dermot Weld.

Of course I was mentioned in the rumours as one of the contenders – there was lots of positive talk about me – but there was talk about others as well, so it wasn't a formality.

I never thought that I was definitely going to get the job. I never allowed myself to think that I was going to get it. Of course, I hoped that I would – I was desperate to get it – but I never said that to anyone. I just kept my head down and concentrated on riding as well as I could ride.

There was negative talk too, that I might not be experienced enough for such a big job. And it was legitimate talk. I had only turned 21 in May 1998, so I didn't have the years of experience that you would ideally have before you would take on a job like the Dermot Weld job, to be able to handle the pressures that a job like that would bring, to have the subtleties and nuances of race riding refined. John Oxx always said that a Flat jockey didn't reach his peak until he was in his mid-thirties.

I tried to block all the racecourse rumour out. None of it was helpful, neither the positive talk nor the negative talk.

Mick said it to me at the races one day, though: 'I think you might be the front-runner.' That got me thinking and hoping, although I tried not to do either. A couple of days later, I was riding at Naas, and Dermot asked me to call into him on the way home. There was something he wanted to talk to me about.

Of course, I knew that it was about the job. I knew that it was either that I had the job, or that I didn't have the job. One way or the other, I knew that I was going to find out.

I was nervous going into Dermot's that evening, but I didn't have long to be nervous. It was all very quick, really. He just asked me if I would like to be stable jockey. Mick was moving to Ballydoyle to ride for Aidan. I said that I would, and I thanked him lots.

That was it, really. I was back in the car and on my way home to Rhode, Dermot Weld's new stable jockey, floating on air.

CHAPTER 11

L ong before I ever had a ride for him, I knew who Dermot Weld was. Everybody knew who Dermot Weld was.

I was more into jockeys than trainers or horses when I was growing up and when my interest in racing was developing, but because Mick Kinane was the jockey to whom I looked most, and because Mick was Dermot Weld's jockey, a lot of the Dermot Weld horses had an extra resonance for me.

I was only 13 when Go And Go won the Belmont Stakes in America, but I remember it, all right. More for Mick Kinane riding the horse than for Dermot Weld training him. I didn't fully appreciate the scale of the achievement at the time, though. Go And Go was the first European-trained horse ever to win a leg of the American Triple Crown, and still no other European horse has managed to emulate that feat.

Dermot worked on the back stretch at Belmont Park as a teenager, and he always dreamed of one day taking a horse from Ireland back to New York and winning the Belmont Stakes. It was Dermot Weld all over. Just because something hasn't been done before, it doesn't mean that it can't be done.

Similarly, when he worked with Tommy Smith in Australia, he dreamed of one day taking a horse from Ireland to Australia and winning the Melbourne Cup. So he did. In 1993, he brought

Vintage Crop from one end of the world to the other and won the Melbourne Cup. Dermot was instrumental, too, in having the quarantine rules changed in order to make it possible. And once it was possible, and once Dermot had a horse with whom he thought he could do it, a plan was hatched and ultimately implemented.

I didn't see the race live, but I watched the recording, Mick Kinane punching Vintage Crop to victory in the Melbourne Cup and coming back into the winner's enclosure, all smiles, helmet off. Vintage Crop was obviously retired by the time I first walked into Rosewell House, but it was all still very fresh in people's memories. It was such a massive achievement in the world of thoroughbred racing. Groundbreaking. Before Vintage Crop, they said that no horse from the Northern Hemisphere could ever with the Melbourne Cup. David Phillips was still a big part of the Rosewell House team when I arrived, and it was David who had looked after Vintage Crop, and who had travelled with him all the way to Australia.

I cut my Dubai stint short in the winter of 1998/99. I didn't like doing that, and Dermot didn't ask me not to go to Dubai that year, but he did ask me to come back early in the spring of 1999.

It was understandable. The Flat season gets under way in Ireland in March, so preparations for the season start to warm up as soon as the calendar changes. Dermot always had a lot of young horses and he needed to get going with them early in the year, so it was never going to work if his new stable jockey would be missing most of the build-up to the season.

It wasn't ideal for me, though. I had my arrangements in Dubai, I had my contract with Dhruba Selvaratnam, and I hated breaking an agreement or getting out of a contract. Dhruba got it, I had a new job in Ireland, but he wasn't too happy about it, which was understandable. I felt really bad about it. As I said before, loyalty is a massive thing for me. If you gave your word, you needed to follow through. You couldn't go around breaking agreements. It's why, when I started off riding for Tom, if I was free and if I agreed to ride a horse for one trainer, I wouldn't go back on that agreement even if a better ride from another trainer came along.

But I was just after getting the job with Dermot, and the last thing I wanted to do was mess it up, or even get off on the wrong footing, before it even started. If Dermot wanted me back at Rosewell House in mid-February, then I was going to be back at Rosewell House in mid-February. It didn't sit well with me, though; Dubai has always been so good to me. It was always a home away from home for me, and Dhruba and Erwan Charpy were brilliant trainers to ride for. But all I could do was explain the situation as well as I could to Dhruba. After that, it got more and more difficult for me to go away for the winter.

I was only 21 in March 1999. I was very young, and there was a lot of pressure on me, taking over from Mick Kinane. On the one hand, you can argue that it was a lot of pressure to be heaping on young shoulders. On the other, however, I think that I benefitted from the fact that I was so young. I was so naïve. A lot of it passed me by.

Mick was a fantastic help to me at that time. He couldn't do enough for me. I was never afraid to go up to Mick to ask him for advice, and while his help when I was getting going as a jockey was huge, his help when I started riding for Dermot was even more valuable. I would often ask him how he thought I should handle a situation with Dermot. A horse or a ride or a particular state of affairs. Nobody understood Dermot Weld's modus operandi better than Mick Kinane, and it was brilliant that he was so approachable and so accessible to me at what was a crucial stage of my career. Mick's advice was instrumental in getting me through at certain times, in helping me to get my head around things and, importantly, in helping me keep my position as Dermot Weld's stable jockey.

I'd be careful not to be annoying Mick too much. I didn't want to be wrecking his head with inane questions. I chose my questions carefully and I chose my moments but, at the same time, I felt at ease when I approached him. I always got the feeling that he wanted to help. I think that he appreciated that I was asking for his advice. He could have easily told me where to go, not to be annoying him, but he didn't. As well as giving me advice on situations with the boss, Mick was also great with advice on other things, like insurance and pensions, life things which you wouldn't automatically think of as a 21-year-old jockey. He was always a proper man, a proper gentleman, and I appreciated every ounce of help that he gave me.

I loved being stable jockey at Dermot Weld's. I loved being part of the operation. As I got older and more experienced, and rode more horses for more people, I realised that I loved being part of a team. I loved going in to Rosewell House every day, riding the horses, slotting into the work routine, working with the lads, getting to know the horses.

It was a massive help, knowing the horses. When you were in the yard every day, you got to know horses' characteristics, their subtleties, the nuances about them, their personalities. As well as that, you knew how well they were going at home. You knew if they were in good form, if they were bouncing or just a little quiet, or if a run was going to bring them on, or if they were just one gallop away from absolute peak fitness. And you could ride them accordingly when they raced; you could try to give them a ride that would play to their strengths, or that would at least reduce the magnitude of their weaknesses. I won plenty of races that I might not have won if I hadn't known the horse as well as I did.

A lot of the really successful trainers in Ireland through the years had long-term stable jockeys, and I'm sure that both trainers and jockeys benefitted as a result. Vincent O'Brien and Lester Piggott, John Oxx and Johnny Murtagh, Jim Bolger and Kevin Manning, Dermot Weld and Mick Kinane, of course. It was the same in Britain: Michael Stoute and Walter Swinburn, Henry Cecil and Steve Cauthen, Peter Walwyn and Pat Eddery, Guy Harwood and Greville Starkey.

A fashion crept in a little while back for some owners to have their own jockeys. Several jockeys rode for owners, not trainers, and I didn't think that it worked as well, especially when an owner's horses were spread around different trainers. It was different when Frankie Dettori was riding for Sheikh Mohammed, or with Mick or Kieren Fallon or Johnny Murtagh or Ryan Moore riding for the Coolmore partners. That obviously worked well, with most or all of an owner's horses with one trainer. But when an owner had their horses scattered around among different trainers, it made it awkward for the owner's jockey.

It meant that the jockey was going around different trainers' yards, riding his owner's horses. He was not getting to know the horses as well as he would if he was in the same yard every day, he didn't see the horses every morning, he couldn't get the same feel for them. And then there was the fact that this owner's horses in every yard were always going to be ridden by the owner's jockey, not by the trainer's jockey. There was the danger that the sense of team might not be as strong as it should be.

Dermot was a tough taskmaster, but I was up for it, and I loved riding for him. I loved going to the races with a bucketful of fancied rides. I loved going into the weigh room and seeing the colours hanging up on my peg: the black and white of Moyglare, the blue and white of Sheikh Hamdan, the yellow and blue of Michael Smurfit. And later, the green and pink and white of

Prince Khalid Abdullah and the green and red of His Highness the Aga Khan. All iconic colours.

I loved going to Tramore or Downpatrick or Clonmel for steering jobs. I loved going out on horses that were expected to win. Anybody could have won on those horses, but I was the one who got to steer them around and who got to chalk up another winner. That brought with it its own pressure, of course, the pressure of expectation, but I loved it. The alternative was going out on horses that were not expected to win.

If you got it wrong, though, you heard about it from the boss. Sometimes, even if you got it right, you still heard about it from the boss. That was always tough, the postmortems were never easy, but I found them hardest to handle during the early part of my career. Those bollockings had quite a negative impact on me psychologically sometimes.

I was afraid of messing up a ride and incurring the wrath of the boss but, strangely, that spurred me on. I wasn't paralysed by fear as much as spurred on by a determination to get it right. It could have gone either way, of course. The pressure from the boss could have broken me. Nobody could have known how I would react to the pressure. Not the boss, not even me. I was just lucky that I happened to have the frame of mind to be able to deal with it. It may have been more naïvety than strength of mind, but I did manage to deal with it. Resolved that I would be better next time. Looking back on it later, I could see that it made me stronger, that it made me strive to become a better rider. Luckily, I grew for the pressure when I could have wilted.

I'd always state my case. Even in the early days, I'd state my case, defend myself, justify the ride that I had given a horse who had got beaten. I think Dermot respected that.

It was always easy to look at a race with the benefit of hindsight, to look at a loser and say, well, if you had done this you might have won, or if you hadn't done that then you would have finished closer than you did. There were hundreds of things, hundreds of variables in a race that a jockey could control.

Like, if you went inside, saving ground, and had your run blocked, of course you could look at that and say that, if you had gone outside and got a clear run, you might have done better. Or if you raced up with the pace and the pace was too fast. Or if you held your horse up and the pace was too slow. Or if you kicked at the two-furlong marker and got caught, you might have won if you had held onto your horse for longer. Or if you kicked at the two-furlong pole and didn't get there on time, you might have won if you had kicked earlier.

Sometimes, though, you just had to take your medicine.

I used to prefer it when Dermot was at the races. At least at the races, if something went wrong, he'd say it to you there and then, and he'd say it to you in private. You only had a limited amount of time between races, so at least the bollocking would be done and dusted after the race. If he wasn't at the races, though, you'd dread the phone calls on the way home.

I never felt like chucking it, though. I never felt like telling the boss where to go. Well, never except for once. You'd have your disagreements for sure, about rides, about horses, about tactics, and we did exchange words on occasion, but only once did we have a really bad, serious argument, and only once did I feel like walking away.

That was Vinnie Roe in the 2002 Melbourne Cup. Mick Kinane's advice was invaluable in dealing with that situation, because I felt strongly about it. I felt at the time that I couldn't continue in the job if I had been replaced for the Melbourne Cup. I had made up my mind that I would walk away. Maybe I wouldn't have had the balls to actually carry it through, but maybe I would have.

It would have been an untenable situation, in my eyes. You were stable jockey, but you were not riding one of the stable stars in the Melbourne Cup, the horse with whom you had formed such a strong association, on whom you had been so successful. And roll it forward: if you weren't good enough to ride in the Melbourne Cup, were you good enough to ride in the Derby? In the Prince of Wales's Stakes? In the 2000 Guineas? Where were you going to draw the line?

It would have punched a hole in the professional relationship that I had with Dermot, in the understanding that I would ride all the horses, and I had decided that I wouldn't be able to go on under those circumstances.

I had heard rumblings, I had heard that one of the part-owners, Michael Watts, was looking for an Australian rider to ride Vinnie Roe, but I tried to put it to the back of my mind. You hear so many things.

Then Dermot said it to me on the plane on the way home from France after Arc de Triomphe day. That was early October, about a month before the Melbourne Cup. I had been over to ride Agnetha in the Prix de l'Abbaye, and she had run a big race to finish fifth at a big price. That was clever of Dermot, to say it to me on the plane. I couldn't start throwing my toys out of the pram on the plane. He just told me that he was having difficulty keeping me on Vinnie Roe, that the owners were talking about getting a local jockey.

By the time we had landed, I had told Dermot that I didn't think I could continue as his stable jockey if I was jocked off Vinnie Roe. That probably wasn't a very clever thing to do. I told him that, if I wasn't good enough to ride Vinne Roe in the Melbourne Cup, then I mustn't be good enough to ride any of the horses in any of the races, and that that would be it for me. That I would walk away.

While it wasn't the cleverest thing that I ever did in my career, it was how I felt at the time, and I think that Dermot respected that too. It showed some grit, it showed a determination that I wasn't going to be a walkover. Some belief in my ability. And lots of stupidity.

Michael Watts obviously felt that I wasn't good enough to ride Vinnie in the Melbourne Cup, but Michael Watts wasn't Dermot Weld. Movie director Jim Sheridan, director of blockbuster films such as *In the Name of the Father*, *My Left Foot*, *The Boxer* and *In America* and, more importantly, Vinnie's main owner, was very supportive of me, and Dermot backed me. In the end, Dermot overruled Michael Watts and kept me on the horse. And Vinnie didn't let me down, as usual. He ran a cracking race to finish fourth behind Dermot's other horse, Media Puzzle.

But that's a whole other story.

CHAPTER 12

I met Frances in Dubai in the winter of 1997/98. I knew who she was, all right: Frances Crowley had been champion amateur rider twice, and she was just about to embark on her training career. She was working for the Emirates Racing Association in Dubai that winter, while at the same time riding out for Dhruba Selvaratnam, which is where I first encountered her. As I've said before, I have Dubai to thank for lots of things!

We decided to buy a house in Carlow in 1999. I was obviously riding for Dermot on the Curragh, I was in there every morning, and I was going racing all over the country, and Frances was training with her dad on the hill at Piltown in Kilkenny, so we figured that Carlow was about equidistant between Kilkenny and the Curragh. There was a lot of travelling involved and we were busy, but that was a great time. Ruby Walsh and Gillian Doran (now Gillian Walsh!) lived just a couple of doors down, and Niall Almond, Bubba, who is now head lad for Jessica Harrington, lived close by. We had lots of good neighbours.

Frances was a really good trainer, as you would expect, given that she learned about training racehorses from her late father, Joe Crowley. Joe was a gentleman, one of those people in whom you could only see good, and what he didn't know about horses wasn't worth knowing.

Frances had three winners from just 15 runners during her first month with a trainer's licence, June 1998, and she kicked on from there. She trained her first Grade 1 winner that November: she won the Drinmore Chase at Fairyhouse with Promalee, just six months after she had taken out her licence. She trained 42 National Hunt winners during her first full season, and the following season she sent out Moscow Express to win the Galway Plate, and provide Ruby Walsh with his first win in the race. She trained for just over 10 years, from 1998 to 2008.

We bought Noel Furlong's old place on the Curragh, Clifton Lodge, and moved there in June 2003. Dermot had been keen for me to move to the Curragh, so that I would be closer to Rosewell House. It made sense too – Hannah, our eldest, was just a baby then, so we were still fairly mobile.

We had a great time at Clifton Lodge, but it was a stressful time too. We were both very busy. Frances was busy training Flat horses and I was out riding every day. As well as that, we had a small baby in the house who also needed attention.

We were doing well professionally, but there was a huge amount of pressure on both of us, and that brought about plenty of stress. There just wasn't enough time in the day or in the week for us both to do everything that we needed to do, and it was impossible for us to find time for each other. That put a lot of stress on each of us as individuals, and on the two of us as a couple. It put our relationship under pressure.

As well as that, I wasn't great at dealing with disappointment. When a horse got beaten or when I had a bad day, or if the horses were off form or going through a quiet period, I wasn't very good at dealing with that, and that put us under more pressure.

It got tense; it was tough for a couple of years. I wasn't great company. I thought that my career was everything. It's not easy, living with a jockey. It just shows you the person that Frances is. How tough she is, how understanding. I'm not sure that too many people would have hung around with me during that time.

Something had to give and, in the end, it was Frances's career as a trainer that gave way. I feel bad about that, because Frances was a very, very good trainer. She has all the attributes that you need to be a good trainer. She could manage staff, she could manage owners, she could look after the business side. Frances is an intelligent person – she was well able for everything that went with training horses as a business. As well as that, and most importantly, she has always been great with horses; she has always had an intimate understanding of horses.

I was selfish about it at the time. All I could see was my career and the demands that were on me as Dermot Weld's stable jockey. How much pressure I was under every day. I felt that Frances should be there for me, that she should be there to make my life as easy as it could be. The routine things that go with running a house and looking after a young family, I felt that Frances should be doing all of them. But that wasn't fair – she was as busy as I was, and she was under at least as much pressure as a trainer as I was as a rider.

If things had been a little different, we could have been a great partnership in a racehorse-training operation. Frances as the trainer, holding the licence; me there with her, riding the horses. Bouncing ideas off each other. I think that our abilities would have complemented each other. One plus one equals three. She is strong where I am weak.

I always thought that training racehorses was more a way of life than a job. It was full-on, 24 hours a day, and you couldn't do it on your own. It was a team thing, a family thing. All in it together. You couldn't dip in and out.

If I hadn't been doing so well as a jockey, I could have easily envisioned a situation in which I could have stopped riding and rowed in with Frances, training the horses. If I had been a journeyman jockey, eking out a living and not getting any breaks, driving all over the country for one or two rides, I could have easily given it up, and we could have gone full-time into training. We could have given it a real go.

I never had a desire to train horses myself, I never thought that I would have been a good trainer, but I did think that I had a lot of knowledge and experience that would have been useful in the background. I knew horses well, and I always thought that I was pretty good at judging them in the mornings. So, with Frances on the front line, and all her skills and attributes, and me in the background, it could have worked very well. We could have been a really good team.

That was never really an option, though. I had a fantastic job with Dermot, one of the best jobs in the country. I was riding every day and I was riding good horses, high-class horses in high-class races. I was riding well and I was enjoying it. I couldn't have even considered giving it up. In the end, it came down to economics. I was making money riding horses and Frances was losing money training them. If something had to give – and we both agreed that something had to give – it made sense to give up the one that wasn't making money.

It wasn't easy for Frances, giving up training when she did, but she did. I'm hugely proud of all she achieved as a trainer: over 300 winners, five Grade 1 wins over jumps, and the first female trainer to send out a Classic winner, Saoire in 2005. She sent out her last runner in November 2008.

It was a positive for me that I wasn't living on the Curragh when I started as stable jockey for Dermot in the spring of 1999. I think it helped me to deal with the pressure. If I had been living on the

Curragh or in Newbridge, if I had been going racing with other jockeys, I'm sure that I would have been hearing all the talk. He's too young, he's too inexperienced, he's not good enough for such a big job. He's no Mick Kinane.

But I was doing my own thing. I was living at home with Mam and Dad, I was going to work on my own, going racing on my own. I wasn't hanging around in Newbridge in the evenings. And I was naïve. I heard some of the talk but, thankfully, a lot of it passed me by. I just put my head down and got on with it. If I had heard everything that everyone was saying, I'd say I would have crumbled.

In the beginning, I floated in and out of Rosewell House. I thought I was the bee's knees, stable jockey for Dermot Weld. But I quickly realised what was involved, the pressure that I was under. It was very different from riding for Tom, and it was very different from riding as second jockey to John Oxx or from picking up a few spare rides for Dermot. I was stable jockey for one of the most powerful yards in the country, and there was a pressure on that position that I hadn't fully appreciated before I got into it.

And that pressure was on every time you went out to ride in a race. Five days a week, six days a week. It was serious stuff. Every race, every day. Just because you won on the last one, it didn't mean that it would be okay if you didn't win on the next one.

There were days in the early years when the boss probably wondered if he had made the right decision in offering me the job. (There were probably days in the later years too ...) My approach to the job sharpened up very quickly in the early days with Dermot. Not just the job with him, but the job of being a jockey. If I hadn't sharpened up, I wouldn't have lasted very long.

I loved it and I hated it in the early years, probably in equal measure. I loved going racing every day with good rides, a real chance of riding a winner, two winners. But the pressure was fierce. When we were having a good run, it was brilliant. When things were going well, when the horses were running well and you were riding winners. Everybody was happy, I was happy, the boss was happy, the owners were happy. Success was so important. If you were having winners, it was all positive. You could get away with a poor ride as long as you won.

It's probably the same in all walks of life. In sport, in business, in politics. When things go well, it's all positive. But the converse is also true. When things go poorly, it's all negative. If there are cracks, a little bit of success can paper over them. Without success, though, the cracks are laid bare. The negativity gets in and they fester and widen.

And sometimes, even success wasn't enough. There was one day at Leopardstown at the end of my third year as Dermot's stable jockey, late October 2001. It was a Saturday afternoon at Leopardstown; it wasn't a bad card, but it was a big day internationally. It was Racing Post Trophy day at Doncaster, the year that subsequent Derby winner High Chaparral won that race, and it was Breeders' Cup day in America, at Belmont Park. Johannesburg won the Juvenile, Fantastic Light won the Turf and Tiznow just beat Sakhee in the Classic.

I had a very good afternoon at Leopardstown. I rode a four-timer, Free To Speak, Creux Noir, Tortue and Triple Try, three of them for Dermot and one of them, Tortue, for Noel Meade.

I was delighted. I had ridden a four-timer in Dubai before, but I had never before ridden four winners on the same day in Ireland. And I didn't do it again until two years later at Cork. It's a fair achievement for a jockey to have four winners on one card.

I was a bit disappointed with the ride that I had given one of the beaten horses, Luminous Beauty, in the Listed Silken Glider Stakes. I had gone for her on the run to the furlong pole and we had gone past Kevin Manning and a filly of Jim Bolger's called Marionnaud and hit the front just inside the furlong marker. But Kevin's filly rallied on the run up to the line and got back past us. My filly rallied again but, in the end, we failed by a short head to get back up.

I was very disappointed with that. I had only ridden one winner on the day before that race, and that would have been two with good strong rides still to come. But I rode three of the last four winners and walked out with four winners in the bag. Even so, the loser still stuck in my gut. I walked out thinking that, if the ball had hopped a little differently for me, I would have ridden five winners, and very few jockeys ever ride five winners in a day, on one card. That said, any day that you have four winners is a good day by any standards.

I was in the car about five minutes when the phone rang. The boss. I knew how he was, how fond he was of focusing on the losers as opposed to the winners, on the horses on whom you had got beaten as opposed to the horses who had won. Even so, I was sure that he was ringing to congratulate me on having four winners. But no. All he wanted to do was talk about the loser.

I was fairly incredulous initially. I had gone too early. If I had delivered her at the right time, Luminous Beauty would have won. And it was a listed race, a black-type race, a Moyglare filly.

'You know how important black-type races are for Moyglare fillies. Luminous Beauty was the best filly in the race. How can you get beaten on a filly when she is the best filly in the race?'

I quickly learned that if you were going to get beaten on a horse of Dermot Weld's, you didn't finish second. That was the worst finishing position of them all. Better to be out with the washing. Second is the first loser. If you finished second, if only one horse beat you, you could usually look back on the race and argue, with the benefit of hindsight, that if you had done something differently you might have won. And if you *were* going to finish second, don't get beaten by a short head.

I got off the phone in the car that day, halfway home, and thought, 'Well, there you go: you're never going to be good enough for this man.'

It was the boss's modus operandi, though. Never be happy with second. Second is not good enough. That was his winning mentality, and it quickly rubbed off on me. If you were happy with second, you were no good to anybody. If you were a good loser, you were not a winner.

There were ways of behaving, of course. You didn't behave badly when you lost, but you couldn't be happy either. Like Mick Kinane when I won the C.L. Weld Stakes on Token Gesture, beating him on Absolute Glee. He wasn't happy, he was born a winner, he was never going to be happy with not winning, but he didn't throw his toys out of the pram either.

It was probably part of a long-term plan by the boss, to get me into that frame of mind. To hone that winning mentality in me. To not be happy with having nearly won. He always had this great ability to get people to do what he wanted them to do, and it worked on me. It got me to focus. Winning wasn't important: it was everything.

As time went on, we figured each other out. I got to know what was important to the boss, but I always gave my point of view too. We had plenty of discussions about horses, about rides, some of them heated, but I was always respectful. Throughout my career, I always had complete respect for the boss. He commanded respect. But I was never afraid to put my point of view across, and I always thought that was a healthy thing. I thought he respected me for that, and that made for a strong relationship. He didn't want yes men around him; he wanted people who had opinions, and I would always give mine, whether it was right or wrong.

Of course, it was usually wrong.

I liked to think that I didn't change as a rider, though, for taking on the job as Dermot Weld's stable jockey. I didn't swan into the weigh room – 'Hey, I'm Dermot Weld's stable jockey.' I thought that I went into the weigh room at the start of 1999 just as I had left it at the end of 1998, with a very level head on me. I knew how lucky I was to have the job, and I knew that, if I didn't perform, I'd be gone. I never took the job for granted. From the moment that I started the job until the moment that I retired, I never thought that I owned the job. I always viewed it like that – if I didn't perform, I'd be out of there.

I developed a brilliant working relationship with the boss, but it was always at arm's length. He was the trainer, I was the jockey. It was a strong relationship that worked, but it was a professional relationship. We would never have gone for dinner together, we would never have socialised together. That kept me grounded too.

It was important that we hit the ground running in 1999, and we did. I rode 7 winners in April, 10 winners in May, 12 winners in June. I had never ridden 12 winners in a month before. This was at a time when Aidan O'Brien was building and building and building. The horses that he had! He had such strength in depth. Fasliyev and Giant's Causeway were two-year-olds that year, and he won the July Cup and the Nunthorpe Stakes with Stravinsky. It was getting more and more difficult to compete.

Dermot knew that. He knew that he had an opportunity to get out of the blocks early in the season, as the Ballydoyle horses were just getting going, and he had the team ready to go as soon as the season started. We had some good winners in the early part of the season, Two-Twenty-Two in the Gladness Stakes, Major Force in the Tetrarch Stakes, Immovable Option in the Cork Stakes, and that was important.

Those three were all Moyglare Stud-owned horses, and that was important too. It was great that I was able to consolidate my relationship with Stan Cosgrove and Fiona Craig, and with Mr Haefner and Moyglare Stud, reward the faith that they had shown in supporting me for the job, give them a reason to feel justified in batting for me. As well as that, Moyglare Stud were the main owner in Dermot's yard; they owned about half the horses that he trained at the time, I'd say.

I spoke to Mr Haefner on the phone a couple of times, and I saw him when he would go to the races, but he was based in Switzerland, and he didn't get to Ireland that often, so my relationship with Moyglare in the early years was essentially my relationship with Stan Cosgrove.

Stan Cosgrove was a remarkable man. A close friend of Mr Haefner's, he managed Moyglare from its inception as a thoroughbred breeding centre in the early 1970s through its emergence as one of the most successful breeding operations in the world of horse racing. Most people know him for his association with the Shergar story. He was Shergar's vet and, as a shareholder in the horse, he was one of the intermediaries through whom efforts were made to secure Shergar's safe return. Regrettably, those efforts were in vain.

But he was a seriously influential figure, too, in the bloodstock industry in Ireland. A hugely respected equine vet on the world stage, who broke new ground in his work on orthopaedic surgery and colic surgery on racehorses, he was one of the founding members of the Irish Thoroughbred Breeders' Association, and he was instrumental in the establishment of Troytown Veterinary Hospital and of RACE, the Racing Apprentice Centre of Education, for the training of young riders.

He was a true friend to me, a confidant, a mentor; he was instrumental in lots of the positive turns that my career took. He was a character, too. There was always a glint in his eye. He was just one of those people who enriched your life.

I was very lucky that I hit it off with Mr Cosgrove from the beginning. I was lucky that he seemed to like me as a person. Of course, if Mr Haefner hadn't wanted me to be stable jockey at Rosewell House, I wouldn't have been stable jockey at Rosewell House, but I knew that I had a big supporter in Mr Cosgrove. He stuck by me, too. Especially in the early years, during the periods when things were going poorly, when the horses weren't winning, and there were plenty of those periods. When I was feeling under pressure, if Mr Cosgrove hadn't been as supportive of me as he was, I was sure that I would have been out.

He would come in to Rosewell House twice a week, every Tuesday and every Friday, on the work mornings, to see the horses and to see the boss. He and the late Jimmy Feane, his right-hand man at Moyglare. And he would obviously go racing; I would see him in the parade ring before every ride I had for Moyglare.

It was great to have that relationship. It meant that, after one of those dreaded phone conversations with Dermot on the way back from the races, when you hung up feeling frustrated and useless, thinking that you didn't know how to ride a horse, you could call Mr Cosgrove and give your side of the story. That was a massive help to me in the early years, both in terms of having a relationship with the owner and in terms of my own mental wellbeing.

It was unusual for a stable jockey to have such a close relationship with the main owner in the yard. To speak to them regularly, almost every day. It was the same with Mick Kinane before me – he had a similar relationship with Moyglare Stud and with Mr Cosgrove.

He used to tell me to call him Stan. 'Give up that old "Mr Cosgrove", will you?' But I didn't. I wouldn't. He was always Mr

Cosgrove to me. He was just one of those special people, a unique individual, and I cherished the relationship that I had with him right up until the end. It was a sad day when he passed away in August 2019, just short of his 92nd birthday.

CHAPTER 13

I didn't win the jockeys' championship in 1999 – I finished second behind Mick Kinane – but I wasn't too despondent at the time.

I rode 72 winners in 1999, which was my best total by far in a year up until then; it was over twice the number of winners that I had ridden in 1998. But it was still 20 fewer than Mick rode in 1999, and I knew deep down that it left lots of room for improvement. Second was never good enough.

Mick was champion jockey multiple times when he was riding for Dermot, so I needed to set out to be champion jockey. Dermot never said it to me, but I knew that he wanted me to be champion too. It's a big deal for the trainer too, when his stable jockey is champion.

Even so, when we set off in 2000, I never set it as my goal to be champion jockey. I just concentrated on riding as well as I could ride, on minimising the mistakes. As the season went on and as I started riding winners, I gradually came to realise that it was possible, that I could be champion. I slowly became more aware, too, that Dermot wanted me to be champion. And I started trying harder. That was a mistake.

My riding style changed. It was a subtle change, but it was a change, and it wasn't for the better. I started trying too hard, trying to make things happen in a race instead of allowing them to happen. Sometimes you can't force things; you have to have the confidence to allow them to happen for you.

I started to ride more forcefully, too, and that wasn't me. I was trying to lift horses home instead of coaxing them home. I was trying to do the running for the horse. I was turning sideways trying to hit a horse, when I should have known that the horse was putting everything in without that. You can't make them run any faster than they can run. You're not helping them when you do that. Actually, you're hindering them: you're upsetting their equilibrium, causing them to become unbalanced. Slowing them down.

I went through a bad patch. I was getting pressure from the boss, I was trying too hard, and I was looking sloppy. I wanted to look stylish, but I wanted to be forceful, too: I didn't want a horse to be beaten through a lack of effort or force on my part. I wanted to get everything out of the horse, leave it all on the racecourse. I thought that, if we didn't win, it wouldn't be through lack of effort on my part.

That was the wrong way to be going about things. It wasn't the natural way for me to be doing things, but I thought that it was the right way. That that was how I needed to ride if I was going to get the best results.

My confidence took a knocking too. I knew that I wasn't riding well. I thought that it would come around. It's not easy, going out to ride when you know you're not riding well.

I should have talked to someone about it then, but I didn't. I thought that I had to figure it out for myself. Things have changed now, thankfully. Young riders have people to turn to if things are not going well. Back then, though, it was a sign of weakness if you spoke about it. Or I saw it as a sign of weakness, anyway.

Thankfully, I sorted it out. In truth, it took a couple of seasons before I got it sorted out properly, but I got there. I got my act together and it came back right. I did speak to people, Mick Kinane and Kevin Manning in particular. I spoke to them about riding, without admitting to them, or even fully to myself, that I wasn't riding well. I'm proud now, looking back, that I was able to sort it out, because it could have gone horribly wrong.

At its base level, it was a fairly easy problem to solve. It wasn't rocket science. It was nothing other than the fact that I was trying too hard. It was a frame of mind. I just needed to change my mentality – get back to thinking that my job was to get the horse to run as fast as it could, not to do the running for the horse. Encouraging the horse as opposed to forcing the horse. There's a difference. It's subtle, but it's significant. It was important that I got back to that, back to coaxing the horse, getting the horse to want to run for me, not bullying him into running for me.

It was down to confidence, too. Confidence is so important to jockeys. You make a hundred decisions during the course of a race, all of them made from the back of a horse while you are travelling at 35 miles an hour. The split-second decisions are easier to make when you are riding with confidence, when you are comfortable within your own mind that you are making the correct decisions. If you have to think about it, if you doubt it for a fraction of a second, the chance is gone and the decision is taken out of your hands.

I don't think that I really rode with confidence until the last few years of my career, maybe the last seven or eight years, and I think that I was at my very best during the last five years. I thought and felt that my next five years were going to be my best. Just shows you, you never know what life is going to throw at you. I do think, though, that if I had been able to keep going, and if

I had remained injury-free, the best years of my career were still ahead of me. I was only getting going!

Strangely, my confidence was lower during my second season with Dermot than it was during my first. The pressure was more intense. Ballydoyle were getting stronger and stronger, and we had to up our game just to be able to compete. I felt the pressure, and that affected my riding further. Ironically, I was riding plenty of winners, even though I felt that I wasn't riding very well, and I found myself in front in the jockeys' championship going into August, into September. Suddenly, the prospect of winning the championship was real but, instead of enhancing my level of confidence, I felt that that put more pressure on me.

I felt the pressure from Dermot too. We never discussed it, but it was there, all right. Mick was with Dermot for 16 years, and he was champion jockey in 11 of those years. There was a weight of expectation that went with the job. Towards the end of the 2000 season, he was inclined to let me off a horse of his if I could get on another horse in the same race, a horse that had a better chance of winning than his. That would never have happened earlier in the season.

I felt that I had to be champion, that I had to prove to myself that I was able to be champion. And the closer it got, the more the pressure mounted. I didn't enjoy the last couple of months at all. I struggled through them. It got to a point where I wasn't really thinking that it would be brilliant if I was champion; I was thinking more that it would be desperate if I wasn't.

It's like something you've always wanted, deep down. How brilliant it would be to get it. But then, when it gets so close that you can almost touch it, it changes to how awful it would be if you didn't get it. You don't enjoy the last stages of it. For me, the prospective disappointment of losing the championship took over from the prospective enjoyment of winning it. I just wanted it to happen. I just wanted it to be over.

That's the way it was for me through the latter stages of the 2000 season.

I got there. I got over the line. In the end, I had plenty in hand; I finished 15 clear of Mick, 81 to 66. I didn't relax, though, until it was mathematically impossible for Mick to catch me.

I still didn't enjoy it. From a fair way out, it was kind of expected that I would win it, or it was expected by everyone except me. I should have enjoyed it more at the time than I did. Champion jockey for the first time.

In hindsight, though, I have to admit that it is an achievement of which I am very proud. To be champion jockey in Ireland, one of the leading thoroughbred racing and breeding nations in the world. It's massive. And I was lucky enough to be champion a few more times, too. I'm very proud of that.

As the years went on, I always wanted to be champion. Every year. And I always said so. In interviews or anything, even at the start of the season, if I was asked, I always said yes, I want to be champion. Any jockey who says that they're not too bothered about being champion is talking through their hat. Everybody wants to be champion.

My agent, Kevin O'Ryan, was great during those latter stages of the 2000 season. Of course, it helped a lot that he got on well with the boss. Kevin was stable amateur for Dermot when I first started riding out at Rosewell House, and we hit it off straight away. He was looking to do something else then; he knew that he wasn't going to go on as an amateur rider forever, and he was looking for something else to combine with riding as an amateur, so I suggested that he operate as my agent. Ciaran O'Toole had been my agent up until that point, but I think that Dermot wanted someone who would concentrate on me and on me alone.

Kevin was the perfect fit. He knew Dermot well, and he was obviously completely familiar with the workings of Rosewell House. He knew his way around the industry well – his dad is the bloodstock agent Bobby O'Ryan, who would have bought lots of horses for Dermot through the years – and he was dying to give it a go.

As well as acting as my agent, Kevin was always a great friend. I could call Kevin whenever I wanted. If something was off or if things weren't going well, I could pick up the phone and vent my frustration to Kevin. He understood completely. He knew how the boss operated and he understood the pressures that I was under.

It was a great partnership, a three-way partnership, me and Kevin and Dermot. Kevin's understanding of Dermot was a huge contributor to the success of it all. I have Kevin to thank for the smoothness with which it all worked. And Kevin met his wife through me – Angela, Frances's sister – so I guess he has me to thank for that!

I went to Hong Kong that winter, the winter of 2000/01. It was my first time there, and it was a real eye-opener.

It's so different from Ireland. Everything about Hong Kong is different. They don't have a breeding industry, for starters: there are no indigenous horses – all their racehorses are imported – and there are very few fillies or mares. It's all very tight, too – two racetracks, Happy Valley and Sha Tin, and they race twice a week, Wednesday and Saturday. The racing is tight and hugely competitive, with the high-rise buildings towering above you and the wall of sound that the crowd generates.

It wasn't easy, getting over there in the middle of their season and trying to get going, but I didn't do badly. I rode four winners in the two months that I was there. That doesn't sound like a lot, but when you are there and trying to get going from a standing start, given the competitive nature of the racing and the fact that they only race twice a week, I was happy enough with that.

I got a three-month contract there for the winter of 2002/03, but it didn't work out very well. I found that I was putting in huge effort and getting nowhere. The winners I had ridden there the previous year counted for nothing. I was starting again. I wasn't riding for a specific trainer and I had no contacts. I knew nobody.

So you'd be sitting in the stable yard there, trying to get to ride work, putting your services out there for anyone who wanted to use you. And even if you did get to ride work, that was no guarantee of a ride in a race.

I picked up a few rides, but they were all outsiders, absolute no-hopers. They were rides that nobody else wanted. Even the horses that I got to ride work, a lot of them were unrideable. That's soul-destroying. You're going out there in races, knowing that you have next to no hope of being involved in the finish. You do it because you want to build up your contacts; you do it so that you might get a chance to ride the next one, and that the next one might have a chance.

It was a pity that Hong Kong didn't work out, but I don't think that it was down to a lack of ambition or a lack of ability or a lack of effort. I was working at least six days every week, often seven, trying to engineer opportunities for myself. It wasn't doing my confidence any good, and I would have been fragile enough in terms of confidence at that stage of my career anyway. I didn't need a prolonged period of scraping around for bad rides in an unfamiliar environment.

Hong Kong is an amazing place; it was great to experience it, and I have no doubt that I improved as a rider for the experience of riding around there. And I loved going back there to ride in the jockeys' challenges and at the international meetings, but going there in the middle of the season with no contacts just didn't work for me.

As well as that, Frances was expecting our first child, which was another reason why I was happy to come home. Hannah was born on 1 March 2003.

CHAPTER 14

Vinnie Roe was a bit of a boyo as a youngster. There was no malice in him; he was just a bit of a brat, like the young lad down at the back of the class who you needed to keep a bit of an eye on.

Paddy McLoughlin rode Vinnie in his work, and Paddy told me that he thought he could be all right. Vinnie was never a flashy worker; he wouldn't blow you away with what he did at home, but there was something about him. I rode him in a couple of pieces of work after Paddy had told me that he thought he could be good, and I agreed. There was obviously plenty of ability there.

Before Vinnie ever set foot on a racecourse, the boss asked me if I thought we should geld him. I said that I wouldn't be in a rush to do so. When you geld a horse, that can have the effect of calming him down, but it also obviously means that he can't be a stallion at the end of his racing career, and that is a shame if he happens to prove to be a horse of unusual ability. And, as it turned out, Vinnie Roe proved himself to be a horse of unusual ability.

The more he worked, the better he got. I never for a second thought back then that he would turn out to be the horse that he became, but I did think that he was a nice horse and that he would win races.

We didn't expect him to win on his racecourse debut at Leopardstown in June 2000, in a two-year-olds' maiden. I was hoping that he would run on up the home straight and finish third or fourth. I would have been happy with that.

It was a seven-furlong median auction race, and he was on his head the whole way. We know now that that distance was way short of his best but, once we levelled up in the home straight and he got himself organised, he finished off his race really strongly, getting up to beat Jim Bolger's filly Affianced by a head.

His work improved again after that. He did ony just as much as he had to do at home. That was him, from the first day we worked him until the day that he retired. If you worked him with a two-mile bumper horse, he'd work up alongside him. If you worked him with a good seven-furlong listed horse, he'd come up alongside him. He never killed himself at home but, on a racecourse, he always gave his all.

The film director Jim Sheridan was one of Vinnie's part-owners, and he raced in Jim's colours. I think he was the first racehorse that Jim owned, and that brought another level of excitement to the yard. That just added to the whole Vinnie Roe story. It was great to meet Jim at the races, to ride his horse. He was always gracious, in victory and in defeat. I think that he got great enjoyment out of Vinnie; he seemed to really appreciate all that the horse achieved.

The boss gave Vinnie a bit of a break after he won his maiden, with a view to targeting him at the Beresford Stakes in October. It was the obvious race for him, a juvenile who stayed seven furlongs so well in winning his maiden. It made sense to step him up in trip to a mile, and to step him up in grade to a Group 2 contest. See what we had.

He ran well in the Beresford. He wasn't that quickly away. I held him up early on and he kept on to finish third behind a hotpot of Aidan's, Turnberry Isle, who had finished second in the Royal Lodge Stakes at Ascot on his previous run.

Vinnie came forward again after that, and the boss decided that we would run him once more before the end of the season, in a listed race over nine furlongs at Leopardstown the following month, which he won. His stamina came through that day, soft ground at Leopardstown in November and nine furlongs. There are not many high-class juvenile races run over a distance in excess of a mile, but we knew that Vinnie stayed well, and he was strong in the finish that day, going on to win nicely.

Subsequent events proved that performance to be even better than we thought it was at the time, because the filly who finished second that day, Rebelline, had only won her maiden at that stage of her career. The following year, she won the Group 2 Pretty Polly Stakes, and she won the Group 1 Tattersalls Gold Cup as a four-year-old. She was a top-class filly for Kevin Prendergast and Lady O'Reilly, so it was a big performance by Vinnie to beat her as well as he did that day.

We spent the winter thinking that Vinnie could be a Derby horse, and he started off his three-year-old season by running in the Derby trials. He finished third in the Ballysax Stakes and fourth in the Derrinstown Stud Derby Trial.

That was Galileo's year. Galileo won the Ballysax Stakes and the Derrinstown, and went on to win the Derby and the Irish Derby and the King George, and became one of the most successful thoroughbred stallions there has ever been in the world. Second in that Ballysax Stakes was Milan, who won the St Leger at Doncaster that year. We finished third, a length behind Milan, and we were giving 3lb to both of them. Just shows you, Vinnie was carrying 3lb more than Galileo and trying to beat him! That was a hell of a race.

Vinnie was never going to Epsom; it was never likely that the contours of Epsom would play to his strengths. The Irish Derby was the race for him, but Dermot was also eyeing up the Italian Derby. Nobody knows the international racing programme like Dermot Weld. Even back then, when horses didn't travel as much as they do now, and when most Irish trainers generally didn't look too far beyond Ireland and Britain, he knew all the international races and he knew the types of horse that were required to win them. He was always looking for opportunities abroad.

Dermot had won the Italian Derby in 1992 with In A Tiff, and he was thinking about the race for Vinnie Roe even before he ran in the Ballysax Stakes. As bad luck would have it, the Italian Derby was on the same day as the Irish 1000 Guineas. I knew what I wanted to do. I wanted to go to Capannelle and ride Vinnie in the Italian Derby. I thought that he would win, and there was massive prize money for the Italian Derby then, about half a million euro for the winning owner. But I knew that the right thing to do was to stay at the Curragh. It's a Classic day at the Curragh, a dual Group 1 day, and I was down to ride Cool Clarity in the Irish 1000 Guineas and Muakaad in the Tattersalls Gold Cup, both trained by the boss, owned by Moyglare Stud and Sheikh Hamdan respectively. The boss wanted me to be at the Curragh, and I knew that it was the right thing to do. I wasn't going to let those owners down: they had done so much for me.

It wasn't a great day. Cool Clarity and Muakaad were well beaten behind Imagine and Fantastic Light respectively. As well as that, the boss had a winner, Caumshinaun, in the six-furlong handicap, but I didn't ride her.

Richard Quinn rode Vinnie Roe in the Derby Italiano, but they didn't win it. The ground was just too fast for Vinnie, and he couldn't let himself down and gallop. He finished fourth in the end behind a horse of Michael Jarvis's, Morshdi, who finished second in the Irish Derby next time.

Vinnie was sore when he came back from Italy. I was a bit concerned that the race might have jeopardised the rest of his season or that, even worse, it could have done some long-term damage. Luckily it didn't. He bounced back out of it and got going. You had to have a go, though. It was a good race for him, and there was so much prize money.

That was the first time that I didn't ride Vinnie Roe in a race, and it was the last time that I didn't ride Vinnie Roe in a race. He ran in 29 races, and I rode him in 28 of them.

His next race was the Irish Derby, only five weeks after the Italian Derby. He was a big price in the Irish Derby, and he ran accordingly. We finished well beaten behind Galileo and Morshdi.

After that, we realised that Vinnie didn't really possess the gears to be top-class over middle distances, that he probably needed to step up in trip, beyond a mile and a half, if he was going to be able to compete at Group 1 level. In the parade ring after the Irish Derby, I had only just taken the saddle off Vinnie's back when Dermot said that he was going to train him for the Irish St Leger.

The Irish St Leger is run over a mile and six furlongs, one and three-quarter miles. The difficulty with the Irish St Leger for a three-year-old, though, is that it is open to older horses. The Classics – the 1000 Guineas, the 2000 Guineas, the Derby, the Oaks and the St Leger – are traditionally for three-year-olds, and they're still that way in Britain. But in 1983 they opened the Irish St Leger to older horses. Consequently, it is difficult for three-year-olds to compete. In 2001, it had been 12 years since a three-year-old had won the Irish St Leger.

You would have thought that, therefore, the English St Leger would have been the race for Vinnie Roe. The English St Leger is still restricted to three-year-olds, so he would have been competing against his contemporaries. But that was to reckon without the mind of Dermot Weld. He has always had this intuition for horses, for races for horses. He has always had this rare ability to pick the right races for the right horses. He just thought that the Curragh would suit Vinnie better than Doncaster would. He had run twice at the Curragh, in the Beresford Stakes and in the Irish Derby, and he had been beaten on both occasions. Even so, the Curragh suited him. He loved to gallop and the Curragh, with its wide expanses, is a racecourse that suits horses who love to gallop. Call it instinct, call it intuition, call it genius – the boss was adamant that, even though he would be taking on older horses for the first time, the Irish St Leger was the race for him.

Vinnie improved again after the Irish Derby. He had worn blinkers for the first time in the Irish Derby, and he really came alive for them. He wore them again in a listed race at Leopardstown three weeks later over a mile and six furlongs, and we skated in. He wore them again in the Ballycullen Stakes at the Curragh at the end of August, and we got up and beat Pugin by a head. After that, it was all roads leading to the Irish St Leger.

That was a very good Irish St Leger, with four high-class British horses coming over. It was a prize that Irish trainers struggled to keep at home. The previous three renewals and seven of the previous 11 renewals had all been won by raiders from abroad, with six going to Britain and one to France.

Millenary was favourite for the 2001 renewal, John Dunlop's horse, ridden by Pat Eddery, who had won the St Leger at Doncaster the previous year. Marienbard was also in the race, the Godolphin horse who had won the Yorkshire Cup and who would win the Prix de l'Arc de Triomphe the following year, and Persian Punch, a top-class stayer who had won the Lonsdale Cup and the Goodwood Cup earlier in 2001, and who had only just been beaten in the Ascot Gold Cup.

Even so, we thought that Vinnie had a good chance. He was taking on hardened, older, high-class stayers, but we knew that he stayed the trip well too, and that he had a touch of class.

He could be a bit difficult in the parade ring before a race. He was a bit claustrophobic; he could be a bit anxious in the stalls. And going to the start, he used to carry his head between his knees. He could have had you over his head and on the ground in a heartbeat.

I was never anxious on him in a race. Once the race was under way, he was impeccably behaved. You could put him wherever you wanted to put him in a race, and he'd just travel along there, happy away, waiting for you to give him a squeeze. And when you did give him a squeeze, he just picked up. He was never flash but, over longer distances, he could quicken.

He was great that day at the Curragh. I settled him towards the back of the field as Richard Hughes and Persian Punch set a decent pace. We made some ground on the run around into the home straight, and I asked him for his effort at the two-furlong pole. When I did, he picked up for me, as he always did.

Pat Eddery and Millenary had taken over from Persian Punch inside the two-furlong marker, so we trained our sights on him and I asked Vinnie for everything. We caught Millenary just inside the furlong marker, and Vinnie stayed on strongly and willingly all the way to the line. When we got there, we had put two lengths between ourselves and Millenary.

That was some feeling. An Irish St Leger. An Irish Classic. My first Classic. It had been three and a half years since Tarascon had won the Irish 1000 Guineas without me, and I thought that I had blown my one chance of winning a Classic. Some contrast. And it was all that I thought it would be. The feeling of accomplishment, of fulfilment, of relief.

As well as that, it was my first Group 1 win for the boss. It was where I needed to be.

All the pressure that I was under, all the pressure that I was putting myself under, was eased that day. I was in desperate need of a good horse to come along and settle the whole thing down a bit, and Vinnie Roe was that horse. I owe him so much.

In the careers of most successful jockeys, in the careers of most sportspeople, you can usually point to a pivotal point in that career. A moment, an incident, that was a springboard, a catalyst for all that followed. For a jockey, it is usually one win, one race, one horse. For me it was Vinnie Roe. He picked me up and carried me into the racing public's consciousness. From that day, that win in the 2001 Irish St Leger, the questions about me being too young, too inexperienced, not up to the task, started to lose traction.

I wasn't a youngster who was punching above his weight any more. I wasn't a boy in a man's world, over-faced with a job that was too big for him.

I was up for the job, and I wanted more.

CHAPTER 15

My career moved to another level on Vinnie Roe's back. And it wasn't just his first Irish St Leger win. It was all that followed too.

I needed a top-class horse at that stage of my career. I needed a big win, a run of big wins, just to prove that, as a jockey, I belonged in the top flight. And riding for Dermot Weld, you needed to prove that you belonged in the top flight.

Vinnie Roe is probably the horse with whom I had the greatest affinity in my whole career. You try not to get too attached to horses. They are athletes, they are competitors and, coming from a farming background as I do, for me, animals are a way of life. Horses are a way of life. They are not pets. For a jockey, they are the tools of your profession.

But you get attached to some of them. You can't help yourself. They have their own personalities. They're like humans in lots of ways; they've got different ways of conducting themselves. Some of them are quiet, placid; some of them are not so nice. Some of them you like; some of them you don't like.

You form more of a relationship with some horses than you do with others, though, and, I have to admit, I got attached to Vinnie Roe. I'd say that I got more attached to Vinnie than to any other horse in my life. Not just because of what he did for me, for my career, for my confidence as a jockey, for my life. I am fairly sure that, if Vinnie Roe hadn't come along when he did, I wouldn't have achieved all that I achieved in my career. I am sure that I wouldn't have had the career that I had.

But also, he was a character. He had a great presence about himself. He was a bit of a dude, he had a strong personality, he was good and he knew that he was good. He was a bit of a star around the yard, and he acted like he was a bit of a star. He had this swagger, this self-confidence about him. Arrogance, even. Like a champion boxer. I loved that about him.

Vinnie wasn't finished for the 2001 season, either, after he won the Irish St Leger. He bounced out of the race, he was in great form, so Dermot decided that we would go to Longchamp at the end of October for the Prix Royal-Oak, the French St Leger.

Like the Irish St Leger, the Prix Royal-Oak had been opened up to older horses a good few years earlier, and Vinnie was one of just four three-year-olds in the race that year, in a field of 13. It didn't matter; he won again. He won well. He loved the heavy ground and we powered through the final furlong to come over two lengths clear of our rivals. He hung a little bit to his right, but he was inclined to do that a bit, and it didn't stop him going forward.

It was another big day for me. The Prix Royal-Oak doesn't usually have a huge profile in Ireland or in Britain, but it is a big race in France, a French Classic, and it was another Group 1. As well as that, it was a great training performance by Dermot, to have the horse in such good form again, at the end of a long season. That was Vinnie's eighth run of the 2001 season, and it was just six weeks after he had reached his peak and run his heart out to win the Irish St Leger. They're not machines. It was testament to Vinnie's talent and to his constitution and his willing attitude, and to the boss's ability as a trainer, that he was able to go back to the well again and again and continually deliver.

It was nice to be going into 2002 with a top-class horse. You had to be top-class to win an Irish St Leger as a three-year-old, and there was every chance that Vinnie would improve again as a stayer as a four-year-old, as he got even stronger.

All those top-class staying races were options: the Goodwood Cup, the Ascot Gold Cup, the Doncaster Cup. The Irish St Leger was definitely on his radar again too. Some of the top-class staying horses had won back-to-back renewals of the Irish St Leger – Kayf Tara, Oscar Schindler, and the boss had achieved the feat with Vintage Crop in 1993 and 1994 – and it was only right that Vinnie should be given the chance to emulate those horses.

And speaking of Vintage Crop, the goal that towered above all others was to go to Melbourne with Vinnie and win the Melbourne Cup. Dermot had done it with Vintage Crop in 1993, when they said that it couldn't be done. That no Northern Hemisphere horse could ever win the Melbourne Cup. No Northern Hemisphere horse had won the Melbourne Cup in the interim, so Dermot resolved that he would try to win it again.

Vinnie's programme in 2002 was not as busy as it had been in 2001. He had proven himself the previous year, so he didn't need to do that again. He didn't need to make his way up the ladder so that he could earn his place in the top-class races. Dermot could be more selective in his targets, the Ascot Gold Cup and the Irish St Leger, before getting on a plane for Australia.

There was a lot of confidence behind him going to Ascot. I was very hopeful. We knew that he had the ability, we just weren't certain that he could get the trip. We thought that he would stay all right – he had stayed two miles on heavy ground when he won the Prix Royal-Oak – but the Ascot Gold Cup is run over two and a half miles. That is an extreme trip for a racehorse on the

Flat. A lot of horses will get two miles, but when you go two and a half, when you go into the final two furlongs, then you have to dig deep; you have to go through the pain barrier, and not every horse will be able to do that.

On the first day of Royal Ascot 2002, I rode Pakhoes for the boss, and for Bert Firestone, to finish second in the Coventry Stakes. That was a little bit frustrating: we just failed by a neck to catch Mick Kinane on Statue Of Liberty, and we finished clear of the third horse.

The third day, Gold Cup day, started well, though. I won the Ribblesdale Stakes on Irresistible Jewel. She was a good filly, but she had only won her maiden at Naas two weeks earlier. Even so, Dermot decided that she was good enough to take her chance in the Ribblesdale Stakes at Royal Ascot, a Group 2 race that was full of high-class middle-distance three-year-old fillies.

That was brilliant. A winner at Royal Ascot, my first winner at Royal Ascot. And Irresistible Jewel was owned by Moyglare Stud, which made it all the better. And she was brave that day. They went fast and I held her up at the back of the field. She got a bit outpaced when they quickened in the home straight, but once I got her out and got her rolling, she stayed on strongly, and we just got up to lead close home.

I had no ride in the next race, the Norfolk Stakes, so I sat in the weigh room and I prepared myself mentally for the Gold Cup. My confidence was up after winning the Ribblesdale Stakes on Irresistible Jewel, and I was sure that Vinnie Roe was the best horse in the Gold Cup. I just needed to ride him like the best horse, keep it simple. He had never run over two and a half miles before, but I thought that he would stay all right, and I had to ride him like I was confident that he would stay.

Persian Punch led early and, actually, Johnny Murtagh had to ride Royal Rebel along early on just to get him up there, up on the outside of Persian Punch. I dropped Vinnie in where he was comfortable, about seventh or eighth and along the inside, nicely switched off, just going along at his own pace.

Vinnie was happy through the race, just lobbing away, happy with the pace he was going. They started to quicken as we raced out of Swinley Bottom with about seven furlongs to go, so I moved Vinnie off the rail a little. I didn't want to get caught in traffic behind horses who couldn't go the pace. Vinnie could go the pace, all right. I didn't have to do anything on him and he moved forward easily, up on the outside of Jamie Spencer and Hatha Anna.

We were still only sixth or seventh turning for home, but we were close, no more than three or four lengths off the leaders. I took Vinnie wide so that I could unleash him with one run down the outside, unchecked, without the added complication of having to negotiate traffic.

He picked up for me. Frankie Dettori picked up too in front of me on the Godolphin horse Wareed, just to my inside, and he was going forward, so I set my sights on him. We got to him before we got to the furlong pole, we drew level with him, both of us by now in the front rank.

We were still level with Wareed as we moved inside the final furlong, but I thought that we had him. I thought that Vinnie was stronger than the Godolphin horse, momentum up. The problem was that on the far side, though, Royal Rebel was battling back.

To this day I'm convinced that Vinnie couldn't see him. He was battling with Wareed; in his mind he was racing to beat the Godolphin horse. And he did. We beat Wareed. But he didn't see Royal Rebel on the far side until it was too late. When he did see him, he surged forward again, but he just didn't have enough time to catch him before the winning post arrived. We were past him 50 yards beyond the winning line.

It was a great ride by Johnny Murtagh. Royal Rebel was a difficult ride; he was a lazy horse who had to be cajoled into doing everything that he did. He had won the Ascot Gold Cup the previous year, too, but he had done nothing in the interim. He hadn't won a race. He hadn't gone close to winning a race. He had run seven times and he hadn't even been placed. He didn't win a race after that either. It was just bad luck that he decided to put it all in that day.

I was gutted. I'm still gutted. That is a race that I think we should have won. I was lucky enough in that I did win the Ascot Gold Cup a few years later, but I was as gutted for Vinnie Roe as I was for myself. He deserved to win an Ascot Gold Cup, and I'm convinced that we would have won if he had been able to see the other horse and engage him in battle.

I didn't think that I had done a lot wrong in the race, but even so, second is just the worst. To be beaten by a neck in the Ascot Gold Cup.

If I had stayed inside and ridden to beat Royal Rebel, you can argue that we would have won. But, at the time, given the information that we had, that wouldn't have been the correct move. Royal Rebel was a 16/1 shot, a lazy bugger who had been up there on the front end with Persian Punch the whole way. Wareed was second favourite, a progressive horse who had made his progress from the rear and was going forward. Who would you track? Wareed every time.

It was a good example of after-timing, of looking at things and thinking what you would have done differently, given how things panned out. But when you are there, in the moment, you don't have the 20/20 vision that hindsight provides. All you can do is plan for and react to the situation as you find it. Make the best decision that you can make given the information that you have available to you at the time.

I remember sitting on the steps going down to the old weigh room at Ascot afterwards, feeling sorry for myself. Frances was sitting on the steps with me, trying to console me, and Dermot walked past.

'You did nothing wrong,' he said.

That meant a lot to me. It wasn't like the boss, not to point out what you should have done or what you shouldn't have done. And I'm sure that he was just as gutted as I was, to have gone so close to winning the Ascot Gold Cup. We'd have to wait eight years before we could put that right.

It took me a little while to get over it, though. It's desperate – you win a Ribblesdale Stakes at Royal Ascot and you come home gutted. The Ribblesdale is a big race, a Group 2 race at Royal Ascot, but the Gold Cup is the Gold Cup. Group 1. I came home thinking that I had been beaten in the Gold Cup, not that I had won the Ribblesdale.

It took Vinnie a little while to get over it, too. Dermot gave him a little bit of a break, and then started preparing him for the Irish St Leger. The Ballyroan Stakes was a good prep race for him, a mile and a half at Leopardstown about four weeks before the Irish St Leger. It's only a listed race so, as a Group 1 winner, he was going to be conceding plenty of weight to his rivals, but he was the classiest horse in the race by far.

He wasn't fully fit for the Leopardstown race – he was a fair way off full fitness – but we still won. We only won by half a length, but I wasn't hard on him. I tried to give him as easy a race as I could while still winning. But the Ballyroan Stakes was not the objective. The objective was a second Irish St Leger, and then the Melbourne Cup.

His second Irish St Leger was different from his first. The pressure was on. In 2001, we had gone into the race as an underdog, the three-year-old taking on the older horses, the proven, classy stayers. In 2002, though, Vinnie was the proven, classy horse, the previous year's winner, the Ascot Gold Cup runner-up.

They made him favourite, odds-on, more likely to win than to lose. That brought with it added pressure. Everyone expected him to win. I expected him to win, too, but we had to go and do it. He was his usual boisterous self on the way to the start, and he was his usual anxious self around the stalls. He was just edgy. During the race, though, there was none of that. He just went around on the bridle in all those Irish St Legers.

He would always jump from the stalls well and get himself into a beautiful position. Then he'd sit and wait; he'd just travel away there lovely, waiting for me to tell him when I wanted him to pick up.

He travelled well for me in third place behind Pugin and Ballingarry. I asked him to get closer early in the home straight and he moved up nicely. We got past Seamie Heffernan and Ballingarry and we joined Johnny Murtagh and Pugin on the run to the furlong pole. From there, it was just a case of keeping him going all the way to the winning line. It was huge, another Irish Classic, another Group 1 win, but, in reality, it was more relief than elation for me.

Vinnie probably wasn't at absolute concert pitch for that Irish St Leger. The Melbourne Cup was a big target for him, and it was only seven weeks after the Irish St Leger, on the other side of the world. That was the genius of Dermot Weld again: have the horse well enough to win the Irish St Leger, but still leave a little bit there, so that he could come forward again for the Melbourne Cup.

It was nine years after Dermot had won the Melbourne Cup with Vintage Crop, and he obviously really wanted to win it again. He was sending two horses to Australia in 2002 – Vinnie Roe and Media Puzzle.

CHAPTER 16

Media Puzzle was a good horse. He ran in 17 races before he went to Australia in 2002, and I rode him in 16 of them.

I rode him when he won his maiden at the Curragh in 2000 and I rode him to win the Ulster Harp Derby at Down Royal later that year, and I rode him when he won at the Curragh on his debut in 2001. But he wasn't Vinnie Roe.

He didn't have Vinnie's class. They both went to Royal Ascot in 2002, but whereas Vinnie finished second in the Ascot Gold Cup, a Group 1 race, beaten by a neck in a race that I still think we should have won, Media Puzzle ran in the Duke of Edinburgh Stakes, a handicap, and finished eighth. And on Irish St Leger weekend that year, on the Sunday, the day after Vinnie had won his second Irish St Leger, Media Puzzle finished third in a two-mile handicap.

I was never going to ride Media Puzzle in the Melbourne Cup. I was never going to get off Vinnie. I wouldn't have been able to do the weight, anyway. Media Puzzle was set to carry 8st 4lb in the Melbourne Cup, and I would have had to have chopped off one of my legs, maybe both of them, to do 8st 4lb.

The two horses went into quarantine together and travelled to Australia together. The plan was always to run Media Puzzle in the Geelong Cup, two weeks before the Melbourne Cup, and for Vinnie to go straight to the Melbourne Cup.

Media Puzzle thrived when he got to Australia. He loved the sun on his back. Dermot booked one of the leading Australian riders, Damien Oliver, to ride Media Puzzle in the Geelong Cup, and they won it. Then the locals started to take him seriously as a real contender.

He came on for his Geelong Cup win too, and he thrived during the week leading up to the race. Every time I went in to ride Vinnie out, I could see how well Media Puzzle was doing. And they both benefitted from the presence of the other. I'm sure of it. A familiar presence in strange surroundings. Vinnie didn't melt, but he was always a little bit on edge. He didn't flourish like Media Puzzle flourished.

Six days before the Melbourne Cup, Damien Oliver's brother Jason was killed in a fall. It was heartbreaking, tragic beyond belief. Damien wasn't certain that he would ride in the Melbourne Cup after that but, in the end, decided that his brother would want him to ride in the race.

For my own part, I couldn't believe how big the Melbourne Cup was until I got there. I knew that it was big – I had read all about it and I had watched all the tapes – but until I got there a week before the race, I didn't truly appreciate the scale of it.

And how big Dermot was there. I travelled with him on the plane, and I couldn't believe the media attention that there was on him, immediately, even in the airport when we arrived. He was the man who had won the Melbourne Cup, the first foreigner to do so, and he was at the centre of a full-on media frenzy all week. The Australians recognised that he had two big contenders that year in Vinnie Roe and Media Puzzle.

It was unbelievable. The horses were at Sandown Racecourse, about 40 minutes from Flemington, so I went there every day to ride Vinnie out. And the media were there, all around Dermot.

It was in the papers all week, all over the media. We think that the Irish Derby is big in Ireland, or the Galway Festival, or the Grand National in England, but nothing that we have in racing in Europe compares with the Melbourne Cup. It was all that anybody was talking about all week, all the talk with everybody, all the talk in the media, and Dermot was at the centre of it. Could he win it again? Could Damien Oliver win it on Dermot's horse Media Puzzle? That would be the fairytale result.

Of course, nobody knew who I was, nobody recognised me, and that suited me fine. It meant that I could go about my business unhassled. It didn't mean that I didn't get criticism in the papers, though. A young rider, an inexperienced rider who wouldn't be able to cut it in the Melbourne Cup. The Aussie press were never shy about giving it to the visiting trainers and jockeys.

I didn't go to the parade. They have a parade through the streets the day before the race. It's massive. It's a big party. They get all the connections of every runner and parade them through Melbourne in open-top cars, and everybody stands and cheers and waves, but I didn't go to it. I probably regretted it afterwards, not going, not experiencing it, but at the time, that wasn't where my mind was. I wasn't into the razzamatazz. I was more into keeping my mind clear, focusing on the race. I had a job to do; that's why I was there. I wasn't there for a party.

I went to the gym.

You couldn't escape the razzamatazz, though. On the train to Flemington Racecourse, early in the morning, there were crowds everywhere. I was able to travel among them, unrecognised, which was nice. It just made the journey easier. I was able to get in early, get into the weigh room, get my head together.

I sat close to Damien Oliver in the weigh room. It must have been so difficult for him. There was a surreal feeling in the weigh room, eerie, even. His brother's funeral was the following day, and here he was, riding in the Melbourne Cup, at one of the biggest parties in the racing world.

Vinnie was a little boisterous when I got on him in the parade ring. That was just him, and you could forgive him that, with all the noise and all the partying that was going on around him. He was number one, he was top weight, so we led the parade, behind these two big grey horses. And as we walked out onto the track, I heard these Irish voices.

'Go on, Vinnie!'

And chanting: 'Vinnie Roe! Vinnie Roe! Vinnie Roe!'

The hairs stood up on the back of my neck. So far from home. Even the horse started to whinny!

And then we were off down to the start, away from the crowds, and that was nice. Then it was just me and Vinnie. The more we moved away from the grandstands, the quieter it got. Everything settled down, Vinnie relaxed, and I was able to concentrate on the job that lay ahead.

Dermot's whole theory was to keep momentum up in the race. Don't get stopped in your run. We had top weight in a Melbourne Cup, it wasn't going to be easy, but it was going to be even more difficult if we had to check and try to start our run again. So my priority was to try to get a clear run whenever we were going to start our run.

'All right, riders?'

The stalls crashed open and Vinnie was quickly into his stride. Drawn seven, towards the inside, I got a nice position just behind the leading group, about tenth or eleventh and three off the rail.

You could hear the noise from the stands as we raced up past the winning post first time with a circuit to go. We started down the back straight, and I let Vinnie move up a little on the outside.

Richard Hills was up in front, disputing the lead on Hatha Anna. Mick and Frankie were just ahead of me on Daliapour and Pugin, stride for stride, in third and fourth. I was happy to be close to wherever they were.

We moved further forward as we went to the end of the back straight. I was very happy with Vinnie. He was travelling well for me, doing everything easily, lots of energy, waiting for his instruction to go.

We moved up around the sweeping home turn, up on the outside of Frankie and into fourth place, just half a length behind him. I was happy that I was in the right place, fourth place in the Melbourne Cup turning for home, with nothing on my outside, so it was unlikely that we were going to be stopped in our run.

Frankie started to niggle away beside me and I allowed Vinnie to move up past him. Still I hadn't moved. I sensed another horse coming up on my outside as we straightened up for home, so I gave Vinnie a squeeze. I didn't want anything getting past us on the outside and coming across us. Suddenly we were in front but, as I got lower in the saddle and started to squeeze, I could see a noseband coming up beside me. I recognised that noseband, Media Puzzle's noseband, Media Puzzle's head, and Damien Oliver in the yellow Michael Smurfit colours.

He moved up on my outside and went a neck in front. In a split second, I went from thinking we might win the Melbourne Cup to knowing we wouldn't. Media Puzzle moved over to the rail and ran away from us. Vinnie got on galloping all the way to the line, but he was tired, under his big weight, 9st 4lb, with Media Puzzle carrying just 8st 4lb. Two other horses came past us on the outside before we got to the winning line, and we pulled up fourth, deflated, exhausted.

I could say that I was delighted for Dermot, delighted for Damien Oliver, the tragedy that he had been through, the fairytale ending, and I got to appreciate all of that in time, but, honestly, in the moment, I was gutted. Absolutely devastated. There's no point in saying anything else. Dermot's horse after winning the Melbourne Cup and me not on it. You're selfish. You want to win everything. That's how I felt. Distraught.

I could never have ridden the horse, I could never have done the weight and, as I said, there was no way I ever would have chosen to ride Media Puzzle in front of Vinnie Roe. But you don't see the rational side of it at the time. You just see Dermot Weld winning the Melbourne Cup with a horse you had ridden in almost all of his races previously, and you're not on him on the biggest day.

Vinnie Roe ran his heart out, but fourth place is no good to anybody.

I nodded and smiled and said that it was great that Dermot won it, it was great for the yard. And it was. Brilliant for the lads in the yard, for the team. And with the passage of time, I felt that. Genuinely. But when you're riding, you're selfish. It was all about me. Dermot had won the Melbourne Cup before. I had never won the Melbourne Cup.

It's not a nice personality trait in the broad scheme of things, but as a rider, as a competitor, I think you need to have that selfish streak in you if you are going to be successful. All successful sportspeople have it. If you don't have that, you're no use to anybody. I think that Dermot understood that. I think that he'd be the first to understand that. He knew that I wanted to win every race. Good for the team, for sure, but good for me too.

The Melbourne Cup took a lot out of Vinnie Roe. He came home a tired horse, and Dermot gave him all the time that he needed.

The plan in 2003 was the Irish St Leger again. Obviously. It was his race. No horse had ever won it three times. Dermot had won it twice with Vintage Crop, and Oscar Schindler had won it twice, and Kayf Tara had won it twice, but no horse had ever completed the hat-trick.

Vinnie started off in the Ballyroan Stakes again, conceding lumps of weight to all his rivals again, and he won it again. We just got up to beat Mick Kinane and Carpanetto by a head. Then it was back to the the Curragh.

He wasn't favourite for the 2003 Irish St Leger. That surprised me. Maybe the thinking was that the good to firm ground would be faster than ideal for him, and that, as a five-year-old, he wasn't as good as he had been. We won again, though. Vinnie was brilliant again. He was his usual self. He travelled well for me there, just behind the leaders, settled lovely, just waiting for me to ask him to go. And when I did ask him to go, at the two-furlong marker, he picked up as usual, hit the front and went on to win the Irish St Leger. As usual. A third Irish St Leger. History.

He had three objectives the following year, the Ascot Gold Cup, another Irish St Leger and the Melbourne Cup.

He started off in the Saval Beg Stakes, a race in which Johnny Murtagh went a sprinter's pace from early on Ted Walsh's horse Windermere, who was race-fit from hurdling in the spring. He went about a furlong clear, and we couldn't catch him. The stewards had me and the four other beaten riders in after the race to explain our rides, but I was happy with the ride that I gave Vinnie. I was never going to send him on at a sprint pace after the leader, on his first run of the year on fast ground and carrying 10st 2lb. I was happy with his run too; he stayed on well to take second place.

Dermot gave him a nice break and brought him back to Leopardstown for the Ballyroan Stakes again. He ran well there too, but we just couldn't catch the English raider Foreign Affairs, Sir Mark Prescott's horse, to whom he was conceding 4lb. The one-and-a-half-mile trip and the fast ground probably made it more of a test of speed than was ideal for him at that stage, as a six-year-old, but he stayed on well to take second place, going down by just a neck.

That race brought him forward nicely, though, for his main objective that season, a fourth Irish St Leger. He was great in the build-up to the race, he felt great. I was a little worried that, as a six-year-old, he wouldn't have the ability that he had as a younger horse, but we needn't have been worried at all.

It rained at the Curragh on Irish St Leger day 2004, and Vinnie Roe loved rain. It rained during the race, and he lapped it up. Every drop of rain eased the ground further, and Vinnie loved to get his toe in. He was electric when I asked him to pick up. He was deadly that day. He just took me clear. He did it easily.

I could hear the applause from the stands when we got inside the final furlong, victory assured. I took the time to enjoy that. People appreciated him. They may have backed him or they may not have backed him, but they gave him a great reception, not only as he raced to the winning line but also when we came back into the winner's enclosure afterwards.

That's the thing about Irish racegoers: they appreciate good horses. Irish people are like that. They appreciate sporting achievement, and they love it when it's one of their own.

That was amazing: a fourth Irish St Leger and Vinnie Roe's place in Irish racing history secure. And, at six years of age, that performance was up there with the best performances of his career.

There was talk of the Arc again, and of the Prix Royal-Oak again, but I think that, as long as Vinnie showed that he was up for it, in Dermot's mind, he was always going back to Melbourne. Vinnie had unfinished business in the Melbourne Cup.

I didn't go down to Australia as early this time as I had done two years previously. I knew what to expect and I didn't need to be down there for a week, reading all the negative press. Even when I got there, I very much kept to myself. I tried to focus.

But we weren't the centre of attention. The spotlight was reserved for Makybe Diva, the Australian supermare. She had won the Melbourne Cup in 2003, and the Aussies couldn't see her being beaten in 2004. The media was all about Makybe Diva, so we were able to stay under the radar to an extent.

Vinnie had top weight again, 9st 2lb. We had to concede 5lb to Makybe Diva, and that was never going to be easy. He was in great form, though. He had travelled down great, again with Media Puzzle, and all his pre-race training had gone perfectly. Dermot couldn't have had him in better form. And the ground was on the easy side.

I thought we had a real chance of winning the Melbourne Cup that year. It was just a shame that we had to run into a mare of the calibre of Makybe Diva on the day.

We were slowly enough away, but I didn't mind that. My priority through the early stages of the race was to get Vinnie settled. He was a little keen with me through the first furlong or furlong and a half, but he dropped the bridle nicely as we raced up past the stands with a circuit to go.

We were about tenth or twelfth as we raced around the turn away from the stands, up on the outside. We were four horses wide, but I didn't mind that too much – it meant that I had clear sailing, that I should be able to move when I wanted to move.

He travelled well for me down the back straight, and he moved nicely as the pace picked up in front. The field stretched out as we started to turn out of the back straight, but I was happy to sit. It's a long way from the end of the back straight at Flemington to the winning line.

We started to get closer as we started to round the final turn into the home straight. We were still wide, but Vinnie was doing everything easily. He was getting closer to the leaders without me asking him to do anything.

It wasn't until the 400-metre mark went past that I asked him to pick up and, when I did, he changed gear.

The leader, Zazzman, was two lengths in front of me towards my left, but we were closing on him and I knew that we would catch him. Then I saw the blue silks of Glen Boss on Makybe Diva getting this dream run up the inside, between Zazzman and the inside rail, where there was hardly a gap. He had got his racing room, he had got his gaps. I'm not sure, if I was in a similar situation, a foreign rider, that I would have got the same gaps.

Vinnie was picking up, but so was the mare. She shot through on the inside and went on. Vinnie was going forward, we were coming away from the others, but I felt it slipping away as she went on ahead of us. We managed to close her down a little close to home, but when we got to the winning line, we were still just over a length behind her.

That was gutting. Devastating. To have gone so close. To have come so far to go so close. Second place is just the worst.

Vinnie had run his heart out. I'd say that that was the best performance of his life, and it was in defeat. Trying to give 5lb to Makybe Diva was probably impossible. She was a brilliant mare. She won a third Melbourne Cup, too, the following year, as well as a Cox Plate and an Australian Cup and a BMW Classic. She is the only horse to win the Melbourne Cup three times in the history of the race.

It was such a shame for Vinnie Roe that he came up against a mare who was as good as she was, on a day on which everything was right for him. I'm sure that he would have won most Melbourne Cups that day. He deserved to win a Melbourne Cup.

Vinnie raced on the following season as a seven-year-old. He won the Saval Beg Stakes on his seasonal return, but he didn't manage to win again. The Ascot Gold Cup was run at York that year, as Ascot was being refurbished, and he ran well in it to finish third behind Westerner and Distinction. The ground was a little faster than ideal for him, but he was beaten on merit.

We went for a fifth Irish St Leger, but he came up just short. And we went back to Melbourne in November 2005 for one more shot at the Melbourne Cup, but Vinnie just wasn't as good as he had been the previous year. We finished eighth behind Makybe Diva.

Before Vinnie ran his last race in that Melbourne Cup, Coolmore Stud bought him to stand as a National Hunt stallion at their Grange Stud. So the decision all those years ago not to geld him paid dividends in the end!

He was massive for me, though, for my career. I needed a big horse at that stage of my career, and Vinnie Roe came along. I needed a Group 1 horse, and Vinnie Roe was a Group 1 horse. And as well as being a special racehorse for my career, he was a special horse to me. He was a character. He was a dude. He was just an amazing horse.

WORKING

The chemotherapy was once every two weeks. I'd go up to St Vincent's on Wednesday morning and have my treatment, and I'd be back home on Wednesday evening and fit for nothing for a week.

So it was week up, week down. It wouldn't really be until the Wednesday of the following week that I would start to feel a little bit normal again, but then I knew that I had to go up again the following Wednesday, and I would be right back down on the floor again.

Strangely, I didn't dread those Wednesdays. I knew how I would feel afterwards, I knew what was involved, I knew how sick I would feel, but I also knew that every session was bringing me closer to being well again.

And I could feel that the chemotherapy was working. Maybe it was my imagination, maybe it was me trying to be positive, but I thought that I could feel that the treatment was having an impact on the tumour. Always in the back of my mind, I was thinking that it had to work. There was no other option. It had to have the impact that it was designed to have; it had to succeed in reducing the size of the tumour, enough so that they could operate on it and take it out.

There were six sessions of chemotherapy, one session every two weeks, so I spent 12 weeks on a seesaw, one week good, when I felt like a normal person, one week bad, when I was on the floor and couldn't do anything. After 12 weeks I went for a scan, to check whether the chemotherapy had had any effect on the tumour. That was fairly nerve-wracking, getting the result of that scan. If the chemo had had no effect, if the tumour hadn't been reduced in size, then we really had no options. Thankfully, it did have the desired effect: the tumour had got smaller, which left me as a candidate for surgery.

I couldn't wait to have the surgery then. I counted down the days. Every day that passed was a day that took me closer to surgery. I had

With Dad and the lads: my brothers Sean, Ger and Brian… plus a red panda and a smurf!

In the stables with Joanna Morgan's daughters Katie and Maggie, Joanna's mother, Margaret, and the pony I learned to ride on.

Holding my trophy for leading rider in Dingle, 1992.

With Mam and Dad at the old Tralee Racecourse. (© *Healy Racing Photographers*)

Recording my first Group race win on Token Gesture for Dermot Weld in the CL Weld Park Stakes at the Curragh in 1996. I was always certain that this win was a key factor in the boss's decision to make me his number one rider in 1999. (© *Healy Racing Photographers*)

In the winner's enclosure at the Curragh with Tarascon and her trainer, Tommy Stack, after winning the Moyglare Stud Stakes in 1997 – my first Group 1 win. (© *Caroline Norris*)

Dubai in the early days: (L–R) Declan McDonogh, me, Willie Supple, jockeys' agent Heather Deane, Shane Kelly and Ted Durcan.

Coming down the outside on Refuse To Bend (with the noseband), on our way to victory in the 2000 Guineas at Newmarket in 2003. (© *Julian Herbert/Getty Images*)

Punching the air as I hit the winning line in the 2004 Irish Derby on Grey Swallow, half a length in front of the Epsom Derby winner North Light and Kieren Fallon. (© *PA Images/Alamy stock photo*)

With Frances and the great Stan Cosgrove at the Moyglare dinner in 2005. Frances received a surprise award that night for winning the Irish 1000 Guineas with Saoire earlier that year. (© *Caroline Norris*)

Benbaun and I come clear of Kingsgate Native to land the Prix de l'Abbaye at Longchamp in 2007. (© *Alan Crowhurtst/Getty Images*)

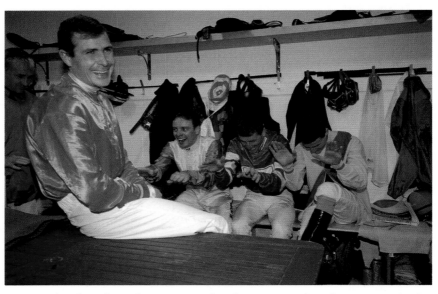

Having a laugh with Declan McDonogh, Johnny Murtagh and Fran Berry in the weigh room. (© *Healy Racing Photographers*)

Taking a hit from (former boxer) Johnny Murtagh at Leopardstown. I was just glad that he had gloves on! (© *Caroline Norris*)

Jumping from the stalls at Dundalk in 2009: me, Mick Kinane and Johnny Murtagh. (© *Healy Racing Photographers*)

The 2010 Ascot Gold Cup, when Rite Of Passage and I just got the better of Age Of Aquarius and Johnny Murtagh in a thrilling finish, the end of a battle that lasted the length of Ascot's home straight. (© *Caroline Norris*)

In the winner's enclosure with Joanna Morgan, the trainer who put me up on a racehorse for the first time. (© *Caroline Norris*)

With Joseph O'Brien and the championship trophy at Dundalk in 2012. That championship went all the way to the wire, with Joseph ultimately beating me by three: 87 winners to 84. (© *Healy Racing Photographers*)

Winning the Royal Whip Stakes at the Curragh on Famous Name in 2012 – the 19th of Famous Name's 21 wins. He was a remarkably talented, consistent and sound racehorse. The lads called him my ATM! (© *PA Images/Alamy stock photo*)

With my agent, brother-in-law and true friend, Kevin O'Ryan. (© *Healy Racing Photographers*)

Going for home on Free Eagle in the Prince of Wales's Stakes at Royal Ascot in 2015. We are being chased down by The Grey Gatsby and Jamie Spencer, but we had enough in hand to get home by a short head. (© *Charlie Crowhurst/Getty Images*)

An indescribable feeling: winning the Epsom Derby in 2016 on Harzand. (© *Alan Crowhurst/Getty Images*)

Receiving my trophy from Queen Elizabeth II after my Epsom Derby win. (© *Danny Martindale/Getty Images*)

In the car on the way back to the airport from Epsom, with a feeling of deep satisfaction after winning the Derby on Harzand. (© *Healy Racing Photographers*)

All smiles with the boss, Dermot Weld, after another Derby win on Harzand – this time the Irish Derby in 2016. (© *Cody Glenn/Sportsfile via Getty Images*)

With the family at Leopardstown in 2016 after being crowned champion jockey for the ninth time: my mum, Mary, Frances, Hannah, Sarah, Paddy and my niece Aoife. (© *Healy Racing Photographers*)

Reading the *Racing Post* in my hospital bed during chemotherapy.

With Frances at the Irish Racehorse Trainers' Awards in 2016.

With my great friends and travelling companions Declan McDonogh, Kevin Manning and Fran Berry in Fallon's of Kilcullen.

Champions, all: a roll call of champion jockeys for the Pat Smullen Champions Race for Cancer Trials Ireland at the Curragh in September 2019. (Back row, L–R:) Johnny Murtagh, Joseph O'Brien, Paul Carberry, me, Charlie Swan, Richard Hughes, Kieren Fallon; (front row, L–R:) Ted Durcan, Ruby Walsh, AP McCoy. It was a regret to me that I couldn't ride in the race, but the lads all made me feel like I was a part of it. It was a special race, a special day. (© *Seb Daly/Sportsfile via Getty Images*)

With AP McCoy after he won the Pat Smullen Champions Race for Cancer Trials Ireland on Quizical, trained by Sheila Lavery – a day on which I experienced just about every emotion on the spectrum. (© *PA Images/Alamy stock photo*)

With Frances at Ruby and Gillian Walsh's house during Royal Ascot 2020.

The Smullen family – Mary, Frances, Sarah, Hannah and Paddy – at the Pat Smullen mural outside the weigh room at the Curragh.

an idea of what lay ahead; I knew how tricky and how complicated and risky the surgery was going to be, but at the same time, I just wanted it to happen. The objective of the surgery was to get the tumour out of me, and I couldn't wait for that.

I developed my faith in God again very quickly. We were very much a Catholic family when I was growing up; we used to go to Mass every week and say the Rosary every night, but when you're young and busy, flying from A to B, you don't think about God or religion very much. That said, while I was never a great Mass-goer, I always had my faith. And when my back was to the wall, it didn't take me long to think about God again. I prayed lots during that time.

Justin Geoghegan came in to me the night before the surgery. He went through everything with me and Frances – consent forms, the details of the surgery, what was involved, what we could expect. He was going to be carrying out a procedure called the Whipple procedure. I told him that I didn't need to know too much about it, that I had complete faith in him, that I knew that he would do the best job that he could possibly do for me. Even so, he insisted on telling Frances and me the details of the surgery, the risks, the possible downsides. He told me that we needed to know. He was right, we did, but it scared me a little bit. I went to sleep that night a little bit concerned, but equally I was looking forward to getting up the next morning and getting going.

One of the things he told me was that there was a chance that, when they opened me up, they wouldn't be able to operate. If the tumour had wrapped itself around my spinal cord, they wouldn't be able to do anything about it. We'll just have to back out, he said, and that will be that. And they wouldn't know that until they opened me up. They couldn't tell that on the scan. So I knew that the longer the operation went on, the more successful it was going to be.

The operation lasted seven hours. When I woke up and was told that it had lasted hours, and that everything had gone as well as they could have hoped, I had a huge sense of relief. I was overcome, to be honest. Joyous, even.

That was just the start of the road, though. Under the Whipple procedure, they take out some of your stomach, your gallbladder, some of your bile duct and some of your lymph nodes. Then they reconnect the parts of your stomach and your bile duct that are left to your small intestine. Effectively, you are completely re-plumbed!

It takes time for everything to start working again. All I could do was wait for it to happen, for what's called stomach-emptying, to see if everything would go through the kidneys and the bowel and start working again.

They put a tube down my nose into my stomach, which was horrific. The only thing I could eat was jelly, and if it didn't pass, they would suck it back up out through my nose. That was really horrendous. After a while I got an infection in my stomach, which made me desperately ill, more ill than I had been from anything else.

The recovery from that surgery was the toughest physical challenge that I ever had to face in my life. It was horrible, the physical side. I was so weak I could hardly lift my hand to my face. I felt sick all the time. I couldn't go to the toilet. I got to a point where I thought that I would never be able to go to the toilet again. Getting out of bed to get to the bathroom, which was literally five steps away, was like climbing Mount Everest. One day, my nose was itchy. I was on my own in my room, and I literally couldn't lift my hand up to scratch my nose. I didn't have the strength.

After four weeks, they concluded that my stomach wasn't working, that the re-plumbing wasn't working, so they put a scope down and realised that I had a twisted gut. So, when everything had been settling down after they had closed me back up again, they had to open me up again.

The last thing I wanted was another operation, but I was thinking that at least it would be quite a straightforward procedure: open me up again, straighten out the gut, close me up. Done. It wasn't. It was another long and complicated operation, which took four hours.

It was worth it, though. That operation was a complete success. After that second operation, thank God, things started to happen reasonably quickly. My stomach started to work, and I started to get my strength back. This was November, so I said that I'd definitely get out of there before Christmas. That was my next target.

With every day that passed, I was getting stronger, and I pushed myself forward. Get to the wall and back to bed, get to the door, get out into the hall. I got to a point where I was able to do laps of the ward. You'd be passing different rooms, and you'd happen to look in the doors and see the people, and I thought, Jesus, there are lots of sick people here. I didn't think for a second that maybe I was the sickest of them all.

My sickness changed me, no question. When you are running around the country riding horses, trying to ride winners, trying to be champion jockey, trying to get on the next big horse, trying to win the next big race, you can forget about the important things in life. You can get stuck on the hamster wheel and you can just flick through the things that should be central to your life.

When I stopped riding, I also stopped stressing about riding. I wouldn't have chosen the path that I found myself on, of course I wouldn't have chosen it, but it did make me stop and think about what was important in my life. Frances, the kids, my mum, my brothers, my friends. I was so lucky in life that, for whatever reason, I found myself surrounded by brilliant people.

When I was riding, I was short with people. Cranky, grumpy. Frances got most of that. I was a much better husband after I got sick than I was before I got sick. I was a better father. A better person.

We decided to make the news public very early. We figured people would get to find out anyway, the news would seep out, the rumours would start, so we just thought that we would be straight up with everybody from the beginning, call it as it was. That way, we weren't hiding anything and, we figured, it might help us cope with it better.

It was all so tough on the kids, though. Hannah, our eldest, was 15 when I got sick. She was always a clever girl, she knew exactly what was going on, and it was tough on her. She was doing her Junior Cert that year, so that was so difficult for her.

I was told not to go on Google, not to try to find out on Google what was going to happen to me because all you get there is the bad stuff. So I didn't. But Hannah was on Google, all right. She was reading all the doom and gloom, and she was trying to cope with it all herself.

Paddy was always one of those quiet kids. He didn't say too much, but he was always a deep thinker and I could see that all of this was weighing heavily on his mind. He was sad a lot of the time. All I wanted to do was to make it better for him, for all of them, which made it more difficult because I knew that I was the reason why they were sad.

Sarah was young enough that a lot of it went over her head, thankfully. But it was still tough on her, on all of them, coming up to see me in the hospital, seeing me in the bed, and me not able to get out of the bed to give them a hug or anything. They were amazingly resilient, though. I learned that. Kids can cope with lots of things. They were like little rubber balls, three little rubber balls that just kept bouncing back.

The saddest part of my day, every day, was when they went home. No matter how bad I felt physically during the day, I knew that Frances and the kids would be coming to see me in the evening, and it was great to know that. And when they arrived, they always gave me a massive lift. No matter how bad I was feeling, mentally or physically, I always got a great boost when they arrived.

We'd have our time together, just catching up on everything, mundane things, everyday stuff. But it was magical for me, just to have them there, just to listen to them as they told me all the things that had been going on with them in the previous 24 hours. Then they would leave, and that was always difficult, the darkest part of every day. I'd have about an hour after they left when I would feel down in myself, before I'd get to sleep. Then I'd wake up the following morning and look forward to them coming to see me that evening.

I got out of hospital in December. I got home before Christmas, and that was brilliant. That was a very special Christmas.

CHAPTER 17

I used to watch the Galway Races on television when I was a kid. Dad would be watching Galway, so I would watch it in passing when I was small, without any major interest. Galway was unusual, because it was racing in the evening during the week. Any other racing that was on television, it was on in the afternoon, on a Saturday afternoon. That made Galway a bit special, that and the stone walls and the rural feel about the place.

Even back then, Dermot Weld and Mick Kinane were always big at Galway, with the green-and-white Bert Firestone colours or the black-and-white Moyglare colours. As I got older and started going into Joanna's and then on to Tom's, and started to ride as an apprentice, I started to appreciate what Galway was, and how dominant Dermot was there. Of course, I didn't know then how big a role the Galway Races would play in my life.

It was always an unbelievable meeting; it was an amazing week, Galway week. What it grew into. How the manager John Maloney and the committee built it up to be what it became, and John's son Michael after John retired. And seven days long.

The atmosphere was unreal. All week, it was like a carnival. And the racing was ordinary in the main. You had the Galway Plate and the Galway Hurdle, the two big National Hunt races, but the Flat racing was generally ordinary enough.

Even so, everybody wanted to have winners there. The quality of racing was always secondary; it was the profile of the event. It was one of the few race meetings that made the front pages in the Irish newspapers, and the first four days were live on RTÉ. If you had a winner there, it was big news.

I got to appreciate Galway more after I stopped riding. The mixture of racing, Flat, hurdles, chases, bumpers, amateur riders' races. The mixture of people. The number of people who watched it from around the world, who came home to Ireland for the week, to go to Galway. It was just a unique race meeting, a unique week.

I dreaded Galway week as a rider, though. Dermot always wanted winners, he wanted winners everywhere, but Galway was different. He had to have winners at Galway. Galway was his week. The King of Galway, they called him. The King of Ballybrit. Everything was more intense; winners were expected and their importance was heightened. There were horses at Rosewell House that had been trained all year for Galway.

You'd be riding in low grade handicaps at Galway, and every one of them would be like the Derby. There was so much pressure, not just from Dermot, but from everybody, from racegoers, from the public. Everything I rode was expected to win. I felt that the pressure was on all the time, maybe some of it coming from myself. And even if I had a winner, it didn't really relieve the pressure, because the next one would be expected to win too. No matter how many winners you rode, it wasn't enough. You had to win on the next one too.

You'd wake up in the morning and get the paper; you'd have four or five rides, and every one of them would be favourite in the paper! You'd know that there would be three or four that should be big prices, you would need everything to go right for them if they were going to win, but because they were trained by Dermot

Weld, and because it was Galway, they were all favourites. So there was huge pressure there, especially in the early days.

And Galway is a really difficult track to ride. It's tight and it's undulating and it's stiff. That's an unusual combination. It's a unique track. You need to be fast early in order to get a good position, but you don't want to use up your horse too early, because of the stiff finish, and you don't want to be too wide, because it's so tight.

I think that I learned to ride it well. Maybe I was on the best horse a lot of the time, and that was obviously very helpful, but, with experience, I figured the track out a little bit. I got the hang of getting horses into positions from which they could win. That was the key.

And not to move too soon. If you moved too soon at Galway, you didn't win. People didn't realise how stiff the climb was to the winning line. You couldn't really appreciate it from the television pictures, or even from the stands. You needed to go down to the home turn and look up to the winning line. Or, better still, be sitting on a tiring horse at the home turn and look up the hill. How many times did you see horses leading around the home turn at Galway and finishing out of the first three?

I always thought that getting momentum down off the hill and into the dip was important. Then you could get your horse prepared for the hill, ideally one off the rail, one or two off the rail. Then you could use the bend as a kind of slingshot move, propel yourself off the turn and up the hill. You didn't want to be too wide, but you didn't really want to be on the rail either. If you were on the rail and you were stopped in your run, you had no chance. You couldn't recover the momentum.

A wide draw over seven furlongs or a mile made things tricky. It depended on the horse, but in maidens, I used to try and go forward and get over towards the inside before the bend and get a position. You generally wouldn't have full fields in maidens, 10 or 12 maybe, so a wide draw wasn't as wide as in a 17-runner handicap. You'd have to use your horse up early in order to get a position, but you'd be hopeful that you could conserve enough energy during the race to be able for the final climb. If they were good enough, they were able for that.

A wide draw in a big handicap was different, though – because, in theory, all horses are given an equal chance of winning, with the better horses carrying more weight than those that are less good. There was always fierce competition for the early lead, so I used to take back and tuck in and ride for luck. If you went forward and you got trapped wide going around the first turn, you might as well be at home.

Galway was different in those days, in that most days were mixed; there were Flat and National Hunt races on the same day. That made it a bit of a stop-start meeting for the jockeys. So, on the Monday evening, there were seven races, but there were two hurdle races, a bumper and a qualified riders' race. That meant that there were only three races in which professional Flat jockeys could ride.

I enjoyed that in a way. I enjoyed the craic with the jumps boys, sharing the weigh room with them. And I was always interested in National Hunt racing, so I enjoyed watching the jumps races. I was never sitting around. And Dermot would have had runners in the National Hunt races, so I would be rooting for them. But it made for a bit of a patchwork week. These days, they have Flat days and National Hunt days during the week, and that makes more sense.

Galway has been very, very good to us as a track. I had lots of success there. Frances had plenty of winners there; she won the Galway Plate in 1999 with Moscow Express – so we have lots of good memories of Galway. It's just that, from my own perspective, in my own little bubble, it wasn't enjoyable when I was in the middle of it. It was all pressure: pressure to perform, pressure to win. The pressure that expectation brings. I'd go home on Sunday night, exhausted and relieved that it was all over.

If we had had a good week, that sense of relief would be accompanied by a sense of accomplishment. Galway over, job done, Dermot happy, owners happy, and it would propel you into the rest of the season. After Galway, you could have a look at the jockeys' championship and see where you were, see how good a chance you had of winning it.

CHAPTER 18

We always liked Dress To Thrill. She was a lovely filly, bred and owned by Moyglare Stud, by Danehill out of their mare Trusted Partner, who had won the Irish 1000 Guineas in 1988.

Dress To Thrill was a two-year-old in 2001. She won the Listed Flame Of Tara Stakes on just her second run, and she finished second in the Moyglare Stud Stakes.

In 2002, she missed the first part of the season, but she made up for it in the second part. She won her first four races, including the Matron Stakes at the Curragh and the Sun Chariot Stakes at Newmarket. Neither of those races were Group 1 races then, but they are both Group 1 races now, so she should have been a dual Group 1 winner.

I rode her in the Breeders' Cup Mile at Arlington Park that October, when it just didn't happen for her. She was the only three-year-old filly in the race. But we went back to America in December, to Hollywood Park. And, back against her own sex, we won the Matriarch Stakes.

She had this turn of foot. My God, she was explosive. She used to sit just off the pace, third or fourth, and then, just in the last furlong, she'd unleash this turbo. I think she was at her best that day in the Matriarch Stakes; I think that it was the best performance of her life. She beat Golden Apples, who had won the Beverley D Stakes and the Yellow Ribbon Stakes, and Banks Hill, then trained by Bobby Frankel, who had won the Prix Jacques le Marois for Andre Fabre earlier in the year. They were both brilliant mares; they were both a year older than Dress To Thrill, and she beat them both that day.

I got some kick out of that. Pat Valenzuela was riding Golden Apples. For me, to beat Pat Valenzuela in a driving finish in a Grade 1 race at Hollywood Park, that was dreamland. There was some line-up of jockeys in that race. It was only a six-horse race, but the jockeys: Jerry Bailey, Laffit Pincay, Kent Desormeaux and Victor Espinoza, as well as Pat Valenzuela. All brilliant jockeys. Hall of Fame jockeys. And me, Pat Smullen from Rhode in County Offaly.

I always loved American racing. I was always really interested in the style of riding in America. I could have spent all evening every evening watching American racing if I had been allowed!

I was fascinated by American jockeys, Jerry Bailey and Pat Valenzuela and Garrett Gomez in particular. So to be riding against them was massive for me. But it wasn't daunting. I didn't feel overwhelmed; I didn't feel like I didn't belong. I was after having a good year and my confidence was high.

As well as that, I had a lot of confidence in my filly. It was the perfect race for her, fast ground, sharp track, nine furlongs. And it was the perfect race for me. It was December, and the Flat season was over in Ireland, so there wasn't much attention on the Matriarch Stakes that was being run on the other side of the world. I must admit, I went into that race feeling very relaxed.

In America, it was all about speed: speed out of the gates, speed down the back straight, speed in the finish. You had to be sharp. I couldn't believe how tight the track was. You'd be going down the back straight and looking at the bend at the end of it, this hairpin bend that you wouldn't see in Shelbourne Park, and thinking that you wouldn't be able to get around it, going the speed you were going.

I loved it, though. Dress To Thrill loved it too. She was fast. American racing suited her well, and she made it very easy for me. I loved that, getting up to win by a head.

I didn't stay and enjoy it, though. I thought later that I should have stayed and enjoyed that, spent a few days in America, but all I could think of was not missing the flight home, not missing the next ride, not missing the next winner.

I really enjoyed riding in America, all my American trips. I often thought, if I had been a stone lighter, and if things had gone a bit quiet for me in Ireland, I would have loved to have gone to America and given it a go. That never happened. I never rode in America for a prolonged period of time.

Four days after Dress To Thrill won the Group 3 Desmond Stakes at Leopardstown in August 2002, Refuse To Bend made his racecourse debut at Gowran Park, and he won by four lengths. And a week after Dress To Thrill won the Matron Stakes, Refuse To Bend won the Group 1 National Stakes.

We liked Refuse To Bend a lot from the start, too. He was another Moyglare horse, bred and owned, by Sadler's Wells out of the Moyglare mare Market Slide, Media Puzzle's dam. He worked well from day one, we expected him to win on his racecourse debut at Gowran Park, and we hoped that he would win the National Stakes after that, so it was great when that plan all came together.

The plan the following season was the Derby. The Guineas first if we could, but we thought that he was a Derby horse. With his breeding, a half-brother to Media Puzzle (who had just won the Melbourne Cup the previous November), there was every chance that he would stay a mile and a half. With the pace that he had to win a National Stakes over seven furlongs, we thought that, if he stayed a mile and a half, he could be a Derby horse all right.

We had a good run with him in the spring, so Dermot decided to run him in the Guineas Trial at Leopardstown in April. That wasn't an easy assignment. He was a Group 1 winner and that was a Group 3 race, so he had to carry a Group 1 penalty; he had to give 7lb and more to all his rivals, but he was well able for it. He kept on well for me and won nicely.

After that, we were thinking 2000 Guineas. It was important to get a run into him if he was going to go to Newmarket for the Guineas. He was a big, gross horse; he needed plenty of work. He was bred to be a Derby horse, but he was showing the pace of a Guineas horse. Dermot could have gone the Derby trials route, Ballysax Stakes, Derrinstown Stud Derby Trial, then on to Epsom, but he thought that there was a chance that he would have the pace to win a Guineas, which is why he ran in the Guineas Trial over a mile, not in the Ballysax Stakes over 10 furlongs. There's the genius of Dermot Weld again.

I remember the piece of work that Refuse To Bend did on the Tuesday during the week leading up to the Guineas in the spring of 2003. Up Walsh's Hill. Pat Shanahan rode the lead horse and I rode Refuse To Bend. I remember pulling up at the top of the gallop, and Pat looking over at me.

'He'll win the Guineas,' he said.

I didn't know what type of horse was required to win the 2000 Guineas, but I just knew that this fellow was very, very good. In the back of my mind, I have to admit, I was thinking more Derby than Guineas. On pedigree, he was bred to get a mile and a half. So I was thinking going to Newmarket, if he could run a nice race and finish third or fourth in the Guineas, that would leave you thinking that he would have a right chance in the Derby. Pat Shanahan thought differently, though. He was such a good judge.

It was an emotional time for me, the whole build-up to the Guineas in 2003. Dad had just been diagnosed with cancer. Dad was never fazed by anything – he would always play everything down – but it was a sledgehammer blow. To my mother, to my brothers, to me. And to him as well, even though he didn't let on.

My head was all over the place. I was trying to come to terms with the fact that Dad was sick while at the same time preparing to ride a horse with a chance in the 2000 Guineas at Newmarket. I tried to focus on my preparation for the race. The last thing that Dad would have wanted was for him to cause me to give anything less than 100 per cent to the race.

I didn't have huge experience of riding at Newmarket, but I had ridden there a bit. I had ridden Dress To Thrill to win the Sun Chariot Stakes there the previous October, and I was never worried about the track. I remember walking the track on the morning of the 2000 Guineas and thinking, This is fine. I was never concerned about how to ride the track. I was more concerned about getting my position, getting the right run, getting my tactics right.

Newmarket is a tricky track to ride. There is a dip about a furlong and a half out: you run downhill into it and uphill out of it. Races can be won and lost in the dip. You're stepping on the gas at the time, you're putting the pressure on, a furlong and a half from home. Horses can get unbalanced if you put them under too much pressure on the run down into the dip, and you can blow it, so you have to try to use the dip to get fluency down into it, then try to propel yourself home for the last furlong. But it's the old story: a good horse is well balanced and, if you are travelling well, you'll handle the dip all right. If you are travelling well, you'll handle most things.

I was a bit concerned about our draw, stall 3 of 20, right over on the far side. But, as it turned out, we gravitated towards the left, towards the stands rail. That suited us well, because there was some congestion over towards the rail, whereas we were able to sit easily on the outside of the field, away from most of the traffic.

It helped, too, that Refuse To Bend was an uncomplicated horse. He settled well wherever you happened to end up in a race; he didn't need cover. He just travelled wherever you put him, and then you could unleash his turn of foot. And it had rained the day before the Guineas. Everything was coming right.

The race could hardly have gone any better for me. We broke well and we got a nice early position, in the second wave just behind the leaders and up on the outside, so that I could ask him to go whenever I wanted, with no traffic problems. I gave him a bit of a squeeze as we passed the three-furlong pole and he went forward. Steve Carson started to scrub away on Tout Seul beside me as we moved up on his outside.

I rode him down into the dip, just hands and heels, and he picked up again. Then we hit the rising ground and he felt strong. We got past Tout Seul just inside the furlong marker, and suddenly we were in front and driving up the hill to the line. I asked Refuse To Bend for all he had, and he gave it. He stretched his neck out and grabbed the ground as we raced up the hill. We were only about a length in front, I could hear them snapping at our heels, but I knew that my horse was strong. He powered all the way up the hill and hit the line.

A 2000 Guineas. Mad.

I stood up in the saddle and punched the air. It was just a reaction. Ask me beforehand what I would do if I won the 2000 Guineas, and I wouldn't have known. I didn't think about it. I focused on the race. The 1760 yards between the stalls and the winning line, not the 10 yards after the winning line. Standing up in the irons and punching the air? Okay, if you must.

Paul Scallan, who was riding Monsieur Bond for Bryan Smart, reached over and shook my hand. He held it for a couple of seconds, a couple of strides.

I pulled up, game over, job done, adrenaline rush abating, and thought of Dad. In an instant, I went from all smiles, winning the Guineas, to thoughts of Dad. I knew that he was watching at home. I choked back the tears. Mark Weld, Dermot's son, came running towards me as we walked back down the course towards the exit to the paddocks, then Kris Weld, Mark's brother, then commentator Derek Thompson with a microphone.

Derek asked me about the horse, the race, how it felt. All I could think of was Dad. 'I'd just like to say, Derek, my father hasn't been feeling very well for the past while, so hopefully this will give him a great boost.'

Dad wouldn't have been at Newmarket anyway. He didn't like to travel too far from Ireland. He and Mum drove me everywhere in Ireland, all over the country to go pony racing in the early years, and when I started riding on the track as an apprentice, when I was too young to drive. If I ever needed a lift anywhere, he'd drive me. No questions. He just would. I only had to ask. But he was never one to get on a plane and go over to England to watch me ride there. Actually, he was never really one to go too far in Ireland to watch me ride, if I didn't need him to drive me. He was always much happier watching on the television from home. The furthest he'd go otherwise would have been to the Curragh.

He never tried to tell me how to ride. His advice to me was always simple: do your best. And do all that you need to do in order to enable you to do your best. Put the effort in. Work hard, give it 100 per cent. That's all that you can do. And then, once you have given it 100 per cent, what will happen will happen, but you are comfortable in the knowledge that you have done as much as you can.

That's what he did, in everything that he did. He gave it his all; he did everything to the best of his ability. It was his philosophy on life, it served him well, and it was a philosophy that he tried to impart to us. I think he did.

He was very much a GAA man, a Gaelic football man, but he was also a sports man. He always loved watching racing, good racing, and his interest obviously started to grow after I started riding. His knowledge of racing grew too, but he would never try to advise me about horses or tactics or how to ride a horse or a race. Never ever.

Even when I messed up, and he knew that I had messed up, and he knew that I knew that I had messed up, he wouldn't mention it. He'd never say, 'Well, how did you get on today?' He would always know how I did, winners and losers, and he'd know by me when I got home, when I was living at home, if I was happy with how the day had gone, or otherwise. (It was usually otherwise.)

He'd never sit me down and try to discuss it with me. That was never his way. He knew that I wouldn't have wanted that. He'd always look to tomorrow. Look forward to tomorrow. Do all that you need to do in order to ensure that you give it 100 per cent tomorrow.

He was always there for advice, though, when you wanted it, when you weren't too proud to ask for it. He was a great reader of people, a great judge of character. He was brilliant at sorting out the good people from the others. If he ever said something about somebody, like, 'Be careful of this person,' or, 'Maybe don't be having too much to do with that person,' I always took note, and he was rarely wrong.

I spoke to him about big choices, big decisions I had to make, career choices, jobs to accept and jobs to pass. He'd never tell you what to do, though; he'd never interfere. He'd listen, a sounding board, and he'd just help you figure it out for yourself.

He was a great man, such a practical, honest man. He was just very practical about everything in life, and I think that when you go about life with that mindset it's very helpful.

The saddest thing, though, was the timing of his death. We had just bought the land in Rhode, including the Brick Field, where he used to work, where we all used to work together. He loved that, and he loved that we had bought the place and intended to settle there. He had just finished working for the Buckleys, with whom he had worked all his life, and had started to work on our little farm there.

We hadn't built the house at that time; we were still living on the Curragh and Frances was training, but the horses would come back to our place in Rhode when they were on a break, and he'd mind them. He loved that. We were buying and selling a few horses, too, and he was very much a part of what we were doing.

We were looking forward to him being a part of it all going forward. We were looking forward to moving back, beside him and Mum. It was great to be close to Mum when we moved back, but Dad would have loved to have had us close too. He would have loved us building the house and moving there.

He loved Frances. I think that he had a better relationship with Frances than he had with me! They got on great. He used to open up to her. She'd tell me stuff about my father that I didn't know. They'd talk about the horses, horses that had problems or issues, and they'd keep it from me because they figured I was under enough pressure with the job. They'd sort out the issue, the two of them, and I wouldn't know that there had been a problem until after it had been solved.

And he loved Hannah, our eldest daughter. He was gone before the other two arrived, but he adored Hannah. He would have loved to have been around for Sarah and Paddy too, watching them growing up. And he would have loved to have been a part of what we were doing, buying and selling horses, living in Rhode, just down the road from him and Mum, working there with us. It would have been a lovely way of life for him. It was sad that he didn't get to experience that. He was taken from us far too early.

CHAPTER 19

started to ride a little bit for Brian Meehan in Britain in 2001. Brian didn't really have a stable jockey at the time – Pat Eddery was riding a bit for him when his other commitments allowed – but the connection was made through Kevin O'Ryan and he asked me if I would go over and ride for him a little, when I was free, obviously.

I had two rides for him at Newbury late in the season, in the autumn of 2001, Oases and Top Prize, and they both won, so it grew from there. I rode for Brian a bit in 2002, when my commitments to Dermot allowed, and I got a few rides for a few other trainers in Britain too, Neville Callaghan and Ed Dunlop and Eric Alston. When I won the 2000 Guineas in 2003, obviously my profile in Britain got a little bit higher.

I noticed, too, that there appeared to be more interest in me in Britain than there had been – media interest, requests for interviews. I had a few rides for Sir Michael Stoute and I had a few rides for other British trainers, like Alan King and Charlie Cyzer.

I won the Group 2 Duke of York Stakes for Brian on Twilight Blues just 10 days after the Guineas in 2003. He was a big price, but he was tough; he kept on strongly and we got home by half a length. It was great to win another big race in Britain, a Group

2 race just 10 days after winning the Guineas. Twilight Blues was owned by Paul Roy, who would take over as chairperson of the British Horseracing Authority (BHA) a couple of years later.

I enjoyed all of that. I liked being in demand, and I liked going over to Britain to ride horses with chances in decent races. It wasn't that I was an international rider or anything, but it was my first sense that I was being noticed outside of my own little circle, that I was in demand outside of Ireland.

In July 2003 I won the American Derby at Arlington Park on Evolving Tactics, and I loved that. America is all about speed, and Evolving Tactics was brilliant that day. That was a race at which Dermot liked to target a horse, if he had a suitable horse for it. He had won it with Pine Dance a couple of years earlier, and we won it again with Simple Exchange the following year.

All the while, Grey Swallow was going well at home. He was a really nice colt, a son of Daylami, bred by Mrs Weld from her mare Style Of Life (who had won a couple of times over six and seven furlongs as a three-year-old).

Dermot had the seven-furlong juveniles' race on Irish Derby weekend pencilled in for Grey Swallow for a little while, and we fancied him out of the way. The race was on the Friday night of Derby weekend, and I thought he was a certainty. I thought that it was just a case of going down to the start and coming back up.

The start was where it all went wrong, though. Grey Swallow was always a little bit nervous, always a little bit edgy in the stalls. So they put us into the stalls late, but when we went in, the horse beside us, Chestnut Gallinule, started to act up and that set my horse off. Grey Swallow reared up and came down on his backside.

Thankfully, he was okay, we were both okay, but he had to be withdrawn. We weren't going to take a chance with a horse that could be as good as we thought Grey Swallow could be. There would always be another day. Even so, my perfect start to Derby weekend was ruined!

You can understand why horses sometimes get upset in the stalls. Some horses are claustrophobic, and it's quite a confined space. People don't realise how confined an area it is. Then, obviously, there's the anticipation of jumping out to race. Their adrenaline is pumping. It's a dangerous place, and it's a dangerous position to be in when a horse starts to get upset in the stalls.

It's surprising that there aren't more accidents in the stalls than there actually are, but I never really worried too much about the stalls. If you start worrying about what might go wrong in the stalls, you're finished anyway. Strangely, you should be okay if a horse goes backwards. You either fall back behind them out of the stalls, or you can step off them onto the step in the stalls.

It's when a horse goes down in front of the stalls, that's when it's dangerous. They can drag you under very, very quickly if you don't react. It happened to me in the Nunthorpe Stakes at York in 2015. I was riding Take Cover for David Griffiths and, for whatever reason, he just took it into his head to dive down under the stalls. It was out of the blue, he caught me completely unawares. One minute he was there, I was sitting on him, ready for the stalls to open; the next minute he was gone, disappeared from under me. He took me with him, of course, and my foot got caught between him and the bottom of the gate. It was just by the luck of God that I managed to free myself; otherwise he would have dragged me under with him.

I broke a few bones in my foot, but it was fine. I was riding a filly for Dermot and Prince Khalid, Palmetto Dunes, in the next race, and I was riding a horse for Sir Michael Stoute, Grand Inquisitor, in the concluding handicap, and I was fine to ride both of those. My biggest problem was getting my boot on over my swollen foot!

It's so different in America. Admittedly, the stalls in America are a little different: they're a little wider and the gates are lower, and every horse has a handler in the stalls, but they do so much work with them in America, that there is rarely an incident at the stalls. I did have words with a few trainers I rode for. I just thought that some European trainers should have done more work with the stalls than they did. It was always a bugbear of mine.

Anyway, Grey Swallow was none the worse for his mishap at the stalls on Irish Derby weekend, so we headed for Galway. Dermot aimed Grey Swallow at the two-year-olds' maiden on the opening evening, the Monday evening.

They made a horse of Aidan O'Brien's, Rock Of Cashel, favourite, and he had had the benefit of a run beforehand but, to be honest, I was very confident about our horse. I thought that Rock Of Cashel was going to have to be very good to beat Grey Swallow.

Grey Swallow was fine in the stalls. We put him in last. He was starting to get a bit anxious but he was literally only in for a couple of seconds before we were off, so that was perfect. After that, it was all very smooth. When I gave him a squeeze, he just took off. He won doing handsprings. As easily as he liked. We know how steep the Galway hill is, but on Grey Swallow that evening it felt as if there was no hill there at all. He did it so effortlessly. I'd say that during that race he was the easiest winner that I ever rode, not just at Galway, but anywhere. We knew that he was good, but we realised that day that he was a special horse.

Dermot gave Grey Swallow a nice break after that, and brought him back in October for the Killavullan Stakes at Leopardstown. It was only a four-horse race in the end, and Grey Swallow was very good in winning it. I couldn't have been happier with him, so we went into the winter dreaming of winning the Guineas again.

That was always the plan, to go for the 2000 Guineas at Newmarket, and I thought that he had at least as good a chance of winning the Guineas as Refuse To Bend had the previous year. Dermot decided that he should run in the Guineas Trial at Leopardstown, and we won that. He wasn't impressive in winning it – we only got home by a head from Meath, a horse of Aidan O'Brien's – but the ground was very soft at Leopardstown that day, which wouldn't have suited him. As well as that, he had to give 5lb to all his rivals, and it was his first run of the season; Dermot had left plenty to work on. In the end, I was happy with the way that he battled, I was happy that he won, and I was sure that he would improve for the run, with the Guineas as his target.

We only finished fourth in the Guineas and, I have to admit, I was a bit disappointed with that. He didn't quicken like I thought he would, he just kind of kept on. He didn't show the turn of foot that I thought he had. Not at that level. And it was a very good Guineas that year. Haafhd won it, Barry Hills' horse, and he won the Champion Stakes at the end of the season. Azamour was third, for John Oxx and the Aga Khan under Mick Kinane, and he went on to win the St James's Palace Stakes and the Irish Champion Stakes later that season, as well as the King George the following year.

We came back to the Curragh with Grey Swallow for the Irish 2000 Guineas and, again, he just didn't show that turn of foot at that level that you need to have if you are going to win a Classic over a mile. I thought that it was going to be between us and Azamour, but Bachelor Duke came down the outside and beat the pair of us, which was a bit of a shock to me. Azamour was second; we were third.

I knew then that Grey Swallow had to step up in trip. He just didn't have the pace that you need if you are going to win a Group 1 race over a mile. In the Irish Guineas, he rode like a horse who would get a trip, who could do better if he stepped up in trip. So where do you go then? The Eclipse at Sandown, a mile and a quarter? But you are travelling and you are taking on the older horses. The Irish Derby? But you are stepping up to a mile and a half. That's a big step up in trip, going 50 per cent further than you have ever gone before.

Dermot had no doubt: the Irish Derby was the obvious target. The Curragh is just across the road from Rosewell House – it was the right race for him. If he didn't stay, he didn't stay, and you could always drop back in trip. And if he did stay, he would have a massive chance of winning the Irish Derby.

It was shaping up to be a good Irish Derby, though. North Light, the Epsom Derby winner, was coming over, Sir Michael Stoute's horse, Kieren Fallon riding, and it was going to be very difficult to beat him. The second, third and fourth from Epsom, Rule Of Law, Let The Lion Roar and Percussionist, were also coming over from Britain, and Aidan was going to run four or five. It was shaping up to be a deep race.

In the end, it was a ten-horse race: four from Britain – the first four home in the Epsom Derby – five of Aidan's, and us. Dermot and me and Grey Swallow in among them. I wasn't fazed, though. I knew that my horse had the class.

I remember Ted Walsh had no doubt that he would stay. He was covering the race with RTÉ, and he came up to me beforehand to tell me to ride the horse as if he would stay. Don't be worried about his stamina, he said to me. He'll stay all right.

Grey Swallow worked really well in the lead-up to the race, and I went into the race with a lot of confidence. And, as it turned out, it was one of those rare races that I could enjoy. It doesn't happen very often, but everything went right for me in the race.

From the word go, from the stalls, he landed in the right position out of the gate, just where I wanted to be, fifth or sixth and along the inside with North Light in my sights. He was the only horse that I wanted to follow, the Epsom Derby winner.

I remember going up to the top of the hill, and it was like everything was in slow motion. Everything was happening the way I wanted it to happen, I could see everything, and I had time to think. We moved up on the inside of Jamie Spencer on Cobra and we sat in fifth place, just behind Mick Kinane on Let The Lion Roar and Kieren Fallon on the favourite, North Light. And my main thought at that stage was, don't hit the front too early!

I knew that I was travelling better than Kieren was. He was on the Derby winner; we knew that North Light stayed a mile and a half and we didn't know that Grey Swallow did, but my horse was travelling so well: he was giving me such a good feel and he felt like he had buckets of energy left. So from very early in the race, from fully five or six furlongs from home, I thought that we would win.

Grey Swallow was so relaxed, he was just travelling away there for me, easily, smoothly. And he did whatever I wanted him to do; he went wherever I wanted to go, effortlessly, expending no energy. I never thought that he wouldn't stay. He was so relaxed. I was just thinking, Don't move too soon, don't get there too soon, don't give Kieren's horse a chance to get back at you. Just fecking get this right!

It's a common trait with Dermot's horses, how relaxed they are. They nearly all relax through their races: they don't over-race. It's the way he trains them, the staff he has, the atmosphere that there is around the place. He trains them to relax. That means that you can put them where you want to put them in their races, depending on the race, depending on the opposition. You don't have to lead and you don't have to have cover, and that's brilliant for a jockey.

I always thought that I was okay at getting horses to relax, I always thought that I had good hands, and that was probably a part of it too. But it was only a part of it. You can have the best hands in the world, the softest hands, but if a horse is very aggressive, he's going to be keen with you. I was blessed throughout my career that I was riding horses who were relaxed, uncomplicated, good rides. Dermot's horses. It meant that I could nearly always ride the race that I wanted to ride.

Kieren started to ride North Light along as we passed the four-furlong marker. That was Kieren's style as a rider; he was a busy rider, he liked to rev horses up, build them up gradually. And I knew that North Light would find lots for pressure. He had come under pressure early enough at Epsom too, he had led at the top of the home straight and he had stayed on well to win nicely. Even so, that day at the Curragh, at the top of the home straight in the Irish Derby, I knew that I was travelling far better than he was.

I didn't really ask Grey Swallow to pick up until we were on the run to the two-furlong marker. By then, Fallon was in full flow on North Light, and he was staying on. He challenged Rule Of Law for the lead as we moved inside the two-furlong marker, but I always had him in my sights.

I gave my horse a smack of the whip, and he picked up. He had that really willing way of going; he stretched his neck out and went forward. We got up level with North Light by the time we reached the furlong marker, and I asked him for all that he had. We got past North Light as we raced inside the final furlong and set sail for home. That was some feeling. I never thought that we wouldn't get there but, even so, to be in full flight, inside the final furlong at the Curragh, in the Irish Derby, still moving forward and your main danger just behind you to your right, beaten, nothing but green grass in front of you and no danger of anything coming from behind you – I thought that I was going to explode.

I punched the air as we went past the line. An Irish Derby. I couldn't stop smiling. I looked to my left: Colm O'Donoghue came up behind me on Tycoon. I looked to my right: Kieren Fallon had gone past me again on North Light. I punched the air again. We got to the end of the track, to the pull-up, the white fence with the Budweiser logo on it, and we slowed. Mick Kinane shouted over to me as he pulled up on Let The Lion Roar. He grabbed my right hand with his left hand, held it aloft for a second or two, then let go of my hand and put his arm around my shoulder. I hugged him back, both of us still on horseback.

It was a massive win. I knew it even at the time, as I pulled up there, just beyond the winning post. It wasn't that it took time to sink in. I knew the magnitude of it straight away. I remember thinking at the time, It doesn't get any better than this. The race, the history of the race. The Irish Derby. To win the Irish Derby! The atmosphere. There were huge crowds there on the day, at the height of Budweiser's sponsorship of the race.

Frances and Hannah were there, which was really nice. I was delighted that they were there. Hannah was only two at the time, but Frances packed her up and the two of them hung out for the day. Mam and Dad weren't there. Dad was obviously going through his treatment for cancer at the time, but he wouldn't have been there anyway. A first cousin of mine was getting married down in Killarney and they were both down at the wedding. There was huge excitement at the wedding, apparently. My brothers told me that it made the day, that Mam and Dad and everybody there got a great kick out of me winning the Irish Derby, so that was really nice.

It was great for Dermot. He had won the Irish Derby before, but only once, eight years earlier with Zagreb, and this was different.

The fact that it was with Grey Swallow, a horse in whom he had always had huge faith, bred and part-owned by his mother. It was a special day for him.

It was a special day for me, too, on a personal level. One of the highlights of my career, no question. The Irish Derby was one of the pinnacles for me as a young boy growing up. The Irish Derby and the Epsom Derby, they were the two races that I had the greatest regard for, more than any other races. As a young boy, starting out as a jockey, wanting to win the Irish Derby, in front of my home crowd. That was the pinnacle of my career then, and it remained the pinnacle until 12 years later, when it went just a little higher.

CHAPTER 20

Life was all about horses for Frances Crowley growing up.
Our kids have always been into their horses and their
ponies for sure, but they have also always had lots of other
interests. Music and reading and football and rugby and other
sports. But for Frances, it was 100 per cent horses.

Frances's mother, Sarah, insisted that her six daughters all got
a third-level education, so Frances studied Commerce in UCD
before doing a postgrad in Equine Studies in the Veterinary
College. She always felt that it was a bit of a waste of time, given
what she went on to do, but I was always envious of her education.
I would have loved to have had the same opportunities.

The only other advice Sarah Crowley gave her daughters was
to avoid a career with either horses or art. Annemarie, Breda,
Frances and Angela all ended up working in racing, while Teresa
and Monika both entered the art world, so obviously that advice
fell on deaf ears!

Annemarie started to take over the training of the horses a little
from her dad when she was about 17 or 18. She was champion
lady rider in Ireland, too; she was a very good amateur rider. She
rode over hurdles and over fences too, not just in bumpers.

Frances would have loved to have been a Flat jockey, and she
did have a few rides as an apprentice on the Flat when she was

15, before she took out her amateur licence. But realistically, in a mainly National Hunt yard, the only way she was going to get rides was to ride as an amateur.

She wanted to emulate Annemarie, but she had to fight for rides. Even in her own yard. She just used to pester her dad, Joe, keep asking him for rides, until he agreed to put her up.

Annemarie was still riding at the time, and Frances was snapping at her heels. Her dad encouraged the rivalry. He must have thought that it heightened their enthusiasm, that they would spur each other on, and he was probably right. It led to some almighty fights, though, the type of fights that only siblings can have!

Annemarie took over the trainer's licence from Joe in 1990/91, and she was champion National Hunt trainer in 1992/93, the first and still the only female trainer to be crowned champion. Annemarie's now husband, Aidan O'Brien – whom she had met as they circled at the start before a bumper at Galway – had started riding for Joe Crowley by then. He was champion amateur in 1993/94, the same year that he took over the licence, and was also champion National Hunt trainer, taking the first steps on the road that would lead to him becoming Ireland's most successful racehorse trainer of all time.

The operation grew, Aidan on one side of the hill, Joe running the yard for him on the other side. Aidan would have had about 70 or 80 horses on one side of the hill and Joe would have had about the same number on the other side. They all raced in Aidan's name, but it was a big team effort.

Joe told Frances that, if she worked hard and if things went her way, she could emulate Annemarie and be champion lady rider. Frances wanted to go higher, though: she thought that she could be champion amateur rider, and she told her dad as much. Joe dismissed it out of hand at first – no woman had ever been champion amateur rider in Ireland before – but he warmed to the idea. By the time the 1994/95 season was in full flow, he was almost as consumed by the idea as Frances was.

The problem with that was that Ger Ryan had his eye on the amateurs' title as well, and he was riding for Aidan too, for the yard on the other side of the hill. So, one of the features of the 1994/95 National Hunt season was the battle between Frances and Ger Ryan for the amateur riders' championship. In the end, Frances won the title with 23 winners, four more than Tony Martin and five more than Ger Ryan.

Frances won the title the following year too. Well, she shared it with Willie Mullins. She was happy to share it, though. Willie Mullins drew level with her on 21 winners, and he went up to her and said, 'Look, I don't want to ride another horse.' Willie was hanging up his boots as a rider – he was going to concentrate on training – so he asked Frances if she would share it with him, draw stumps on the season. Frances did a quick calculation and figured that, if they both continued riding, Willie would ride more winners than she would between then and the end of the season, so she said yes to Willie. Of course. Share it. That's fair!

Frances took out an apprentices' licence the following year. She rode on the Flat and she spent a season in Australia, where she rode two winners. I actually beat her by a head in a race at Tramore in 1997. I was riding a filly called Molly Coates and she was on a filly called Amidancing. She never let me forget that one either – I think she would have lost her claim if she had won that. That was the first time that I encountered Frances, and I beat her in a photo. She had the photograph framed and she hung it on the wall in our house in Rhode!

I got to know her then in Dubai that winter, the winter of 1997/98. She was working for the Emirates Racing Association, and she was riding out in the mornings for Dhruba Selvaratnam.

This was back in the early days of Dubai, in the early days of racing at Nad Al Sheba. The Jumeirah Beach Hotel had just been built and the Burj Al Arab was under construction.

I liked Frances from the start – she was straight up, she was lovely and she was easy to talk to. We started going out together in Dubai, and I think that we both knew quite quickly that it was fairly serious. So much so that Frances rang her parents to tell them about me, just in case they'd hear about it from someone else. There was no social media in those days, of course, but, you know, Ireland being Ireland, and given the strength of the Irish community in Dubai, news could travel quite quickly.

The only piece of advice that Joe gave Frances was to remember that, when she turned 40, I'd still be 35 and I'd have 25-year-olds chasing after me! That was one of the few things that Joe Crowley got wrong in his life: the 25-year-olds never came chasing after me, but Frances always slagged me about that. She always said that I was only staying with her to prove her dad wrong!

Aidan O'Brien was moving full-time to Ballydoyle in 1998, so Joe asked Frances if she would take out her trainer's licence and train out of Owning. Frances loved training on the hill. She and her dad were a great team.

Joe Crowley was a brilliant horseman: he had so much knowledge, so much experience, and he had a special affinity with horses. They had their moments, of course, they had their difficulties, but they worked great together as a team.

So Frances had her first runners in the autumn of 1998, and she hit the ground running. Golden Rule won the Listed Trigo Stakes at Leopardstown that October, and Promalee won the Drinmore Chase at Fairyhouse in November, a Grade 1 race. Some trainers go years before they train their first Grade 1 winner.

Ruby Walsh rode Promalee for Frances to win that Drinmore Chase in November 1998, and he rode Moscow Express to win the Galway Plate the following July. That was a great day. It was great for Frances, to train the winner of such a big race, such a high-profile race, so early in her training career.

Frances loved Moscow Express. He was quirky, but he had bucketloads of talent, and Frances got the best out of him. He won 26 races in his career, 19 of them for Frances, including the Morris Oil Chase at Clonmel and the Red Mills Chase at Gowran Park and the Newlands Chase at Naas, as well as the Galway Plate.

The Galway Plate was a massive win, a huge achievement by Frances and Joe; but actually Moscow Express's best performance was probably the one that he put up in winning the Powers Gold Label Tote Gold Cup at Fairyhouse in April 2001. He beat Florida Pearl and Dorans Pride and Native Upmanship and Commanche Court in that race. That was some race, and it was some performance by Moscow Express to beat those horses.

Frances kept Moscow Express on the farm after he retired from racing. Strange for a horse who won 17 times over fences, but he wasn't a great jumper of fences, and Frances was afraid that someone would get him and go point-to-pointing with him. So she had him in a field at the house, where he enjoyed a long and happy retirement.

She had lots of success with her National Hunt horses. Sackville won 18 races for her, including the Sefton Hurdle at Aintree and the Drinmore Chase at Fairyhouse. She also won the Drinmore Chase with Nil Desperandum.

Frances and I got married in 2001, and we had decisions to make. We were living in Carlow because it was the mid-point between the Curragh and the hill, but it was actually too far from both places. It wasn't working. Frances wanted to be closer to her horses, and Dermot was putting pressure on me to be closer to the Curragh. Something had to give.

Frances had always had it in her head that we would settle and live in Owning – she had her plot picked out and everything – but that wasn't really going to work for me, not if I was going to continue to ride for Dermot and give myself the best chance to be as successful a Flat jockey as I could be.

We discussed it for a while, we kicked all the pros and cons around and decided that we should live on the Curragh. I would be beside Dermot, and Frances could train on the Curragh. So in 2003, with Hannah on the way, we bought Clifton Lodge.

Frances built the yard up into quite a strong operation. The Curragh wasn't ideal for training National Hunt horses, but Frances always liked the idea of training Flat horses, and she would have had about 70 horses when her operation was at its peak. I used to ride work for her when I could, before I went to Dermot's in the morning or when I came home for breakfast. It was good to be able to help her out when I could, but it was all her operation.

There was a rule at the time that prevented me from riding a horse for Dermot in a race in which Frances had a runner. As Frances's husband, I wasn't allowed to ride against one of her horses. I had to either ride her horse, or not ride in the race. That didn't make sense, and it would have been a big obstacle for us. The Turf Club were very good on this, and once we brought it to their attention, they set about changing it. It was an old rule that maybe made sense at some stage, but I had a job to do as first rider for Dermot Weld, and Frances had a job to do as a trainer. When I could, I would ride her horses, but only when my commitments to Dermot allowed. The Turf Club recognised that, and they got the rule changed quite quickly.

That said, I probably tried extra hard when I was riding a horse for Dermot against one of Frances's horses. I always felt that I couldn't leave anyone in any doubt that I was riding to win, 100 per cent.

Frances had some nice horses, too, and she got the best out of them. I really enjoyed the training side of it in the beginning, being part of it with Frances. I loved riding work for her, and I think that we did very well for the period of time we were training on the Curragh.

We had some great days.

Saoire was a nice filly. I rode her in all her work, but because of my commitments to Dermot, I didn't get to ride her in many of her races. I rode her in the Moyglare Stud Stakes at the Curragh in 2004, and I got her beaten in that. I was kind of riding her to finish off her race, but I left it late enough before I asked her for maximum effort, and she ended up running on well to finish third. That was the one race for Frances that I regretted that I didn't win. I was thinking about the filly, getting her to finish off her race when, actually, if I had been more positive on her, she could have won it.

Then again, Frances always said that, if she had had a hard race then, as a two-year-old, she might not have made the progression that she made from two to three. We'll never know for sure. I was always happy to go with Frances's theory on that one!

Saoire was working well in the lead-up to the Irish Guineas. She had run well in the 1000 Guineas at Newmarket on her seasonal debut. The ground was just too fast for her at Newmarket, and she didn't really handle the dip. But she had turned inside out after that. I was thinking that she would have a real chance at the Curragh.

I was riding a Moyglare Stud filly for Dermot in the Irish 1000 Guineas that year, Utterly Heaven, so I wasn't going to be able to ride Saoire. I told Frances to try to get Mick Kinane for Saoire. If Mick Kinane was available, why wouldn't you get him?

The rest is history. It rained on Irish 1000 Guineas day that year. It rained all morning, which was liquid gold for Saoire. She was a filly who liked to get her toe into the ground.

That was a close-run race. There wasn't much between six or seven of us on the run to the line, and Utterly Heaven ran well to finish fourth, a neck in front of Maids Causeway, who had finished second in the 1000 Guineas at Newmarket. I drove her all the way to the line.

I knew that it was close between Saoire and Ralph Beckett's filly Penkenna Princess at the line, and I wasn't sure that Saoire was up. Saoire was tough, and she needed every assistance that Mick gave her. Every inch. Another jockey might not have won on her. Frances was watching from the stands, and she thought she was beaten. She thought, Second in an Irish 1000 Guineas, not too bad. But so close! Then she met her sister Annemarie on the way down from the stands, before the result was announced, and Annemarie told her that she had won. Then the announcement: first number 12, Saoire.

It was a great achievement by Frances, to prepare a filly to win the Irish 1000 Guineas. In so doing, Frances became the first woman to train the winner of an Irish Classic. Earlier in the day, I had won the Tattersalls Gold Cup on Grey Swallow. Two Group 1 races at the Curragh that day – I had ridden the winner of one and Frances had trained the winner of the other.

After a big win, we usually went to the Hanged Man's restaurant in Milltown. Frances and me; Kevin and Úna Manning; Declan McDonogh and his wife, Eimear; and Fran Berry and his wife, Laura. Kevin and Declan and Fran and I used to travel to the races together, we'd share the journey and share the driving, and we'd usually celebrate together as well, if any of us had a big winner. Then there were Ruby and Gillian Walsh, and Kevin O'Ryan and his wife, Angela, Frances's sister. That was pretty much our crew. There were others, of course, but that was the core crew.

That evening we went to our usual haunt to celebrate the two big wins. And it was my 28th birthday. That was a good birthday.

CHAPTER 21

I loved Cheyenne Star. She wasn't the best filly I ever rode or anything, but she was talented and, more importantly, she had a lovely personality. She'd do anything for you. And the fact that she was trained by Frances, and living just outside our kitchen door, meant that I got to know her well.

It is easy to get to like horses – gorgeous animals, majestic, willing to please. All we ask them to do, and the way they keep giving, it's quite remarkable. From something simple, loaded up into starting stalls with 10 or 15 other horses, into a confined space, primed athletes ready to run, to give their best, and to stand there until the stalls open. It's quite remarkable that a herd animal will do that.

And their bravery in a race. To give everything, run as fast as they can. We ask them to stick their heads into gaps, where it might be uncomfortable for them. I was always a huge admirer of horses.

When you were busy, sometimes you'd lose sight of that, of why you got into horses in the first place. Because you loved them as animals. On a busy day, in a busy week, you'd get off one horse and get up on another, get beaten on one, win on another, and then onto the next one. But when you step back, when it's all over, you realise what you're after asking all those horses to do for you, the pain barriers that you asked them to go through in races. And they did it, willingly, because you asked them to.

Cheyenne Star won her maiden at Thurles as a two-year-old, and I rode her to win a couple of times as a three-year-old, but it was really only as an older filly that she came into her own.

I rode her to win the Group 3 Ridgewood Pearl Stakes at the Curragh on Irish Guineas weekend in 2007. Actually, that was just two days after our son, Paddy, was born. We beat Mick Kinane on a Cheveley Park filly of Sir Michael Stoute's, Heaven Sent, and Kevin Manning on a filly of Jim Bolger's, Modeeroch, in a good finish. Cheyenne Star went on to win two listed races later that year with Seamie Heffernan on board, and Seamie also rode her to win the Group 3 Brownstown Stakes at Leopardstown the following year as a five-year-old.

It wasn't easy, though, Frances training and me riding. Not at the level at which we both wanted to be. It was difficult for us to do both and, in the end, something had to give.

There were lots of things that didn't work for me about Frances's training. There was the invasion of privacy, for starters. I felt like we didn't have our own space. You never knew when someone from the yard was going to walk into the house, looking for Frances, with a question or an issue with a horse.

I could be walking from the sauna into the house, just in a towel, and I'd meet one of the staff. Or owners – you never knew when an owner would call to the door. You have to do these things when you are training, of course, you have to be available to staff and to owners, but I just felt that our space wasn't completely our own.

And I know that I didn't support Frances's training. Not properly. I had my own issues to deal with. I was busy trying to be the best rider that I could be, shouldering all the pressures that I was shouldering, trying to justify my position as Dermot Weld's number one rider, trying to get my head around horses, trying to deal with defeats, with mistakes. I wasn't able to give Frances the support that she needed.

For a training operation to work well, you need a team of people and you need to be all-in. Frances was a very good trainer, she was brilliant with horses and with people, and I have no doubt that, if things had been a little bit different, we could have given the training operation a real go. We had different strengths and weaknesses, which complemented each other. If I hadn't been riding at the level at which I was riding, there is every chance that I would have chucked it and rowed in with Frances. There were lots of elements to the training of racehorses that I enjoyed.

But there were lots of elements that I didn't enjoy. Like, when a horse went wrong. Frances was always better at dealing with setbacks than I was. Or when a horse was just no good. When a horse simply couldn't run as fast as you wanted him to run, or as fast as you expected him to run.

In the end, Frances was trying to do everything on her own. She kept things from me. She wouldn't tell me if a horse had an injury or had a setback; she knew that I wouldn't have been able to deal with it, so she carried everything on her own. And she was trying to buy horses as well as train them; she was going through catalogues and going to the sales. These days, trainers have teams of people that go around the sales with them or for them, looking at horses, going through the catalogues, narrowing down the selection process. Frances was trying to do all of that on her own, as well as train the horses.

As well as that, she was trying to support me, trying to help me to deal with all the issues that I was trying to deal with myself. And she was trying to run a house, look after a family, with two young kids.

Frances's horses probably weren't right during her final year training, 2008, and everything suffered. Her mood, my mood, our marriage. I'd come home to her and, if a horse hadn't worked well there, or if something had gone wrong, or if I'd come home from the races having been beaten on a horse on whom I should have won, or if the horses had just run badly, I'd end up venting my frustration at home, and that just wasn't good. I was just letting off pressure, but unfortunately Frances was the one on the receiving end and that wasn't fair.

I think a lesser woman would have packed her bags and left. Seriously. Whatever perception people had of me on the outside, I don't know, that I was a nice happy-go-lucky type of fellow, that I was quiet, that I didn't say much, whatever. That wasn't true. I wasn't a nice person to live with at that time.

It's difficult enough, two small kids, sleepless nights. Every parent knows that. But for me, it was all about me and my job, riding winners, being successful. That was all that mattered to me at the time. When I looked back, and I had lots of time to look back when I got ill, I realised what a dreadful time that must have been for Frances.

I regretted, too, that I didn't take the time to help her, not only at home and with the kids, but in her work – play more of a role in the training, enjoy it more – but I just felt that I couldn't at the time. When you are riding at the level at which I was riding, you think that it's all about you; you think that everybody has to be helping you, pulling for you, not that you should be helping somebody else.

I stopped riding work for Frances. I just couldn't deal with the horses not going well. There was one morning I said that I would ride work. I rode the first horse and it worked poorly, so I just left. It wasn't a good thing to do, but I couldn't deal with horses working so disappointingly.

Financially, too, it wasn't making sense. My riding was making money, and Frances's training was losing money. It wasn't a difficult decision in the end.

That said, it wasn't easy, winding up the training operation, telling staff, telling owners. On the face of it, it was a successful operation. Frances was doing well. And make no mistake, Frances could train racehorses. She was a very good trainer. But behind the scenes, it wasn't working on any level. It wasn't working for us personally and it wasn't working for us financially. We were always perfectionists, both of us – if you were going to do something, you had to do it right. We could have kept going – it would have been easy to keep going, keep trundling away – but it would have been the wrong thing to do. Frances was sad in lots of ways when she called time on her training career, but in the end it was a relief to both of us when she decided to wind it up.

We had started to build our house in the Brick Field in Rhode, so we rented our yard on the Curragh out to Paul Deegan, and we rented a house in Gilltown for a year. That was nice. It was lovely living in Gilltown; it was like living in a holiday home for a year. And Frances was able to come to Dubai with me that year.

In the winters in those days, I would head off in November, off to Hong Kong and Dubai, and I wouldn't be back until February, which was tough on everyone. It was especially tough on Frances, with one and later two young kids – and that was before Sarah came along. So it was nice that, that year, Frances was able to come with me to Dubai, with Hannah and Paddy.

Grey Swallow was one of my favourite horses. The Tattersalls Gold Cup that he won that day, the day that Frances won the Guineas with Saoire, that was a top-class renewal of the Tattersalls Gold Cup.

He beat Bago, who had won the Arc de Triomphe the previous year, and who had already won a Group 1 race in France earlier that season, and Azamour, who won the Irish Champion Stakes the previous season, and who went on to win the Prince of Wales's Stakes and the King George in his next two runs.

Grey Swallow was an exceptionally good horse. I don't think that he really got the recognition that he should have got. He had this turn of foot over middle distances, 10 furlongs or 12 furlongs, that made him difficult to beat.

We were beaten in the Canadian International later that year: my old buddy Relaxed Gesture won that race. Relaxed Gesture was a Moyglare horse who had finished second behind Azamour in the Beresford Stakes as a juvenile, and who had finished second behind Yeats in the Derrinstown Stud Derby Trial as a three-year-old, before going to America to be trained by Christophe Clement. Anyway, he beat us that day. It was strange to see him racing in the Moyglare colours and Corey Nakatani riding him, not me. To make matters worse, we were demoted from third place to fourth place because I had accidentally smacked Mick Kinane's horse Electrocutionist over the head with my whip. It was just one of those things, driving finish, I didn't know that his head was there, and I caught him. Under the rules of racing in North America, I had to be demoted and placed behind him.

One of the great things about riding for Dermot Weld was that you got to travel. Dermot knew the international programme book like nobody else. He has had winners on every continent except Africa. He knew the international races, he knew the tracks, he knew the conditions and, most importantly, he knew the types of horses that would be suited to the races, or that would be good enough to be competitive in the races.

He took two fillies to Cologne on one day in September in 2005, Burren Rose and Society Hostess, both for listed races. He took me over to ride them, and they both won. There were not many trainers around at the time who would have known that there were two listed races for fillies on that day in Cologne, not to mind send two fillies over. Dermot knew, though – one race over a mile, the other over a mile and a half – and they both won easily. All I had to do was point and steer.

Our flight was delayed that day on the way home, and I sat with Dermot in the airport and talked about life. Away in a foreign country, on our way home, nobody else around, we had no option really but to hang out with each other. It was the first time that we actually sat and chatted together about life, not just horses. I enjoyed that lots. I thought that our relationship moved onto another level after that.

I loved being a stable jockey, I loved being part of a team, and it was made very easy for me at Dermot's. I wouldn't have to tack horses up or muck horses out, I just hopped on, rode them work, and hopped off, and when I was done I was into the Jeep and gone. I loved the routine. Up early in the morning, ride work, back home, go racing, home. Do it all again the following day.

In one sense, you can say that it's unusual for an elite athlete to have to ride work every morning and then go and perform to the best of his or her ability on the field of play in the afternoon. Like, you wouldn't see a Premier League football player working in the morning before going out to play a match at three o'clock. But I loved the routine. I loved being part of the team with the lads and getting to know the horses. That was massive for me. And anyway, there are lots of things about the life of an elite jockey that differ from the lives of other elite sportspeople. You're competing every day, for starters, often six or seven times a day. Usually you're riding at a weight that is way below your natural weight. Your friends are your rivals; you share a dressing room with all the people against whom you are competing. You travel to the games with the people you have to beat. It's bizarre, really, on lots of levels.

You form alliances; you are obviously closer to some riders than you are to others. It's the same in all walks of life. You form friendships. I always admired Kevin Manning, how he conducted himself, how professional he was, always. He was a very, very competitive person on the track, and I would have had my fallings-out with him, and we had our arguments, but the one thing we always agreed on was that what happened on the track stayed on the track. We'd have a falling-out during the day, and we'd end up having dinner that night.

Declarations would be in in the morning for the following day, and you'd check them on the system, and in later years on your phone, see what you were riding, see who the opposition was, see where you were drawn. The draw was always massive for me, as it is for most jockeys. Unlike in athletics, there are no staggered starts in horse racing: the stalls go straight across the track. It's more nuanced on a straight track, but on a round course, the closer you are to the inside, the shorter the distance you have to cover. If you were drawn wide at one of the tight country tracks, at Sligo or Ballinrobe, it made your task all the harder and you had to think about how you were going to mitigate that.

I studied form a lot. I always knew my own horses, even two-year-olds, even debutants – I knew them from riding them work and riding them in races. I knew their characteristics, if they had speed or stamina, if they liked being in front or behind, if they hung to the left or to the right, if they were keen or if they needed stoking up. As I have said before, Dermot's horses were almost always straightforward; they didn't have kinks or quirks in general. That was down to the way that Dermot trained them, the education that they got. So, nine times out of ten, I could ride them whatever way I wanted to ride them, whatever way would maximise their chances of winning. And nine times out of ten, that meant being handy, close to the pace. Usually, there is no point in being back behind other horses if your horse doesn't need to be covered up.

The more often you rode a horse, the better you got to know their characteristics. But I always studied the opposition too. Who my main dangers were, who the likely leaders were, where the pace was going to come from. That was always one of the most important aspects for me: where was the pace in the race?

Knowing the tracks was crucial too, and the more often you ride at a racetrack, the better you get to know it. In Ireland and in Britain, there are tight tracks and galloping tracks, flat tracks and undulating tracks, left-handed and right-handed, and soft ground at one of them might be different from soft ground on another. Galway is right-handed and tight and stiff and undulating, Leopardstown is left-handed and relatively flat with an uphill finish and galloping. Cork, up to seven furlongs, is flat and straight. Ballinrobe is tight and right-handed with a downhill finish. A horse that will be effective at Ballinrobe might not be able to operate at Leopardstown, and vice versa.

I think that's why Irish jockeys are so good: they have to adapt, they have to think about how they are going to ride at different tracks, and they have to change riding styles or tactics accordingly, often mid-race. Your intelligence as a rider comes into play, your ability to figure things out. The subtleties of racetracks: where you can make ground at Sligo, where you want to be at the end of the back straight at Limerick, where the best ground is at Gowran Park when it rains. Like, the Curragh is seen as a galloping track, and it is, but you usually don't want to be too far behind at the Curragh. You don't want to be too far off the pace because it's difficult to make ground from the back, unless, of course, they have gone too fast in front. Then it is a disadvantage to be close to the pace.

When I went to the races after I retired, I was lost. I didn't know where to go, where to get something to eat, where I could go to the toilet. I wandered through the Curragh, lost. Leopardstown was a track at which I always felt completely at home, but when I went there after I had retired, I didn't know what to do with myself. It was all new to me, the whole place.

I won the championship again in 2005, my third championship and my first since 2001. It was close enough: Fran Berry ran me close, and I only won by nine in the end, 67 to 58, with Kieren Fallon on 57 and Declan McDonogh on 52.

It was great to be champion again. It was my goal every year. You are riding for Dermot Weld, you should set out to be champion. Every jockey wants to be champion, and any jockey who tells you anything different is not being straight either with themself or with you. It would be like the Dublin captain, at the start of the season, saying that he didn't really mind whether they won the championship or not. Or Shane Lowry saying that it didn't really make any difference to him whether he won the Open or not. That he was just going to go out there and play as well as he could play and that, if that was good enough to win it, so be it.

Bananas.

Champions

I announced my retirement in May 2019. I had known for a while that I would never race-ride again, but it was still a sad day for me when I actually stated publicly that I would never ride professionally again.

I had just finished another round of post-operative chemotherapy, and I knew that I wasn't going to be able to put my body through what I needed to put my body through if I was going to ride at the highest level again. I couldn't compromise my immune system like that. And if I wasn't going to be able to ride at the highest level, I didn't want to ride.

My oncologist was very happy with me, and he put me on this new medication, a PARP inhibitor, which was basically designed to stop the PARP enzyme from carrying out repair work on the cancer cells, so that they would die off. It was just one tablet a day, so no extensive treatment, no hospital visits. The whole premise was that you could live with cancer, but it wasn't going to kill you. The way we looked at it, it was like living with high blood pressure, or living with diabetes. One tablet a day, I could manage that.

So this was it, Frances and I thought, the start of the rest of our lives. Normal life. I got to go to Royal Ascot in 2019 with Frances, and I was feeling good. It was strange, though. I would have loved to have been out there competing, but it was nice to be there with Frances too and a few friends, and experience Royal Ascot as a racegoer.

It was at Royal Ascot that I mentioned the idea of a charity race to Margaret Heffernan. Margaret, formerly CEO of Dunnes Stores and an honorary member of the Turf Club, has done amazing work for a number of charities, raising millions through her work with the People in Need Trust and other charities. She invited us up to her box for lunch, and it was there that I put it to her that we were organising a charity race on Irish Champions' Weekend. She asked me how much I hoped to raise. I said a million. A million euro. Crazy figure. I was almost embarrassed saying it. She said good. No point in doing it if you're not going to do it properly.

The idea had started a while ago and it had grown legs. I was lying on my bed in St Vincent's Hospital one day when my nurse Dee said to me, 'You know, you should do something. You have a bit of a profile and you could use that to raise awareness, to raise funds. Pancreatic cancer research is not getting the funding that it needs.'

I wanted to do something, and Frances and I chatted away about it for a while, without ever really making any progress. We were thinking about a race, all right, but we hadn't decided on anything when, out of the blue, in June 2019, Joe Foley rang me and asked me if I would be an ambassador for Irish Champions' Weekend. I said of course. I was honoured.

Joe owns and runs Ballyhane Stud, a very successful operation. He was also one of the primary instigators of the whole concept of Irish Champions' Weekend, that weekend in September on which some of the best races from Leopardstown and some of the best races from the Curragh were put together in order to form a fantastic weekend of racing.

Joe also said that we could do something for charity, for the hospital or for cancer research. That's when the idea of having a charity race on the weekend started to come into sharper focus.

But I was nervous about it all from the beginning. I was nervous first about getting the riders, and it was tight enough in terms of time if we were going to get everything organised. We were into June, and Irish Champions' Weekend was in mid-September. So we had three months to try to get everything in place, starting from scratch.

The priority was to get the jockeys in place. I said it to AP McCoy, 20-time champion jockey, and he was brilliant. He had only ridden once since he had retired, in a charity race at Doncaster four years earlier (which he won!), after which he said that he would never ride in another race. So it would have to be something special if he was to go back on his word. It was AP who suggested making it a champions' race, that every rider in the race had to be a champion jockey, and that made lots of sense to me.

I had to recruit the riders, the champion jockeys, and that was an anxious time for me. What if they said no? But they didn't. Not one of them. AP McCoy was joined by Ruby Walsh (who was champion jockey 12 times), Charlie Swan (nine times), Ted Durcan (seven times), Kieren Fallon (six times), Johnny Murtagh (five times), Richard Hughes (three times), Paul Carberry (twice) and Joseph O'Brien (twice). And me. Nine times. That was 75 championships between the 10 of us.

I was lucky that I could pick up the phone to all of the jockeys and ask them. That I didn't have to go through an intermediary.

Ruby Walsh had been a great friend of mine for years, Ted Durcan was always one of my best friends from our years in Dubai and Joseph O'Brien was my nephew, Frances's sister's son. And I knew all the other lads very well. When I rang Paul Carberry and asked him, he said that he had heard about the race and that he was hoping I would ask him! I was pushing open doors all over the place.

It was some array of talent, and me in among them. And it was going to be an opportunity for me to ride in a race at the Curragh one final time.

The one person who couldn't do it was Mick Kinane, 13-time champion jockey Mick Kinane. I would have loved if he had been able to ride in the race, and he would have loved it too, but, after considering it for a while, he just decided that he couldn't do it. It was 10 years since his retirement from the saddle at that stage, and he just thought that he wouldn't be fit enough to compete, and if he wasn't going to be able to compete, he wasn't going to be able to do it.

Horse Racing Ireland (HRI) and the Irish Horseracing Regulatory Board (IHRB) were brilliant in arranging everything so that the race could take place. They had to frame the conditions of the race so that we would get the horses – horses of similar levels of ability – and they had to allow for a ninth race on the day. It was the first time that nine races were run on the same card in Ireland. The Curragh were great, too, in helping us arrange the race. And I was glad that the race was scheduled for the middle of the day, after the St Leger, not as the last race on a nine-race card, when people might have been drained from the day.

Frances and I met with my oncologist, Ray McDermott, and his wife, Grace, in June to discuss how whatever funds we raised might best be deployed, and they suggested Cancer Trials Ireland. I was very specific that I wanted whatever money we raised to go to pancreatic cancer. When I said to Eibhlín Mulroe, CEO of Cancer Trials Ireland, that I wanted to raise a million euro, she nearly fell off her chair. I'm sure she thought that I was mad.

There were times during the preamble that I thought I was mad too, that I thought, what am I at here? What was I thinking? A million euro is such a massive amount of money; how are we going to raise a million euro?

But that was without recognising the generosity of racing people. I was very lucky in my life in that I came in contact with, and rode for, some very generous people. There were estimates in the lead-up to the weekend that we could raise as much as €500,000, but in the end we went way past that.

People's generosity astonished me. JP McManus donated a hundred thousand euro as soon as the race was announced. He was the first person in. That was incredibly generous, and it was important in order to get the ball rolling.

The late Sheikh Hamdan Al Maktoum donated €500,000 at the Irish Champions' Weekend dinner on the night before the race. Eva Haefner donated a million euro. Just like that. She didn't want any recognition, she didn't want it known, and not many people knew about it at the time, but she donated a million euro.

There were so many other fundraising activities that people organised as well. So many people who were so generous with their time as well as with their donations. The stable staff, for example, donated their best-turned-out prizes and their expenses for that day at the Curragh to the fund. That was so generous of them.

The stable staff do a fantastic job, often an underappreciated job. They are among the most important people in racing, and I like to think that I always respected them. I always appreciated the work that they did.

I always tried to conduct myself well with them. I would always respect the groom who was leading up a horse that I was riding, ask them what they thought. Apart from the importance of being courteous, they would often give you a piece of information that would be valuable in a race. Nobody spends more time with a racehorse than the groom, few people know the horse better, so it is always worthwhile listening to their opinion.

And the general public, donating one euro or two euro. People coming up to Dermot Weld or Ruby Walsh at the races and giving them cash and cheques to put towards the fund. Jennifer Walsh came up with the idea of designing and producing coffee mugs and selling them in order to raise more funds. It was unbelievable. We were over 2.5 million euro by the day of the race. I was blown away.

And the owners and trainers who made the horses available for a charity race worth just €100. Any of them could have run in the 10-furlong handicap later on the day at the Curragh, or in the 7-furlong handicap at Leopardstown the day before, and both of those races were worth €90,000 to the winner.

In total we got to €2.6 million, and that was just unbelievable, a testament to the generosity of the racing community, with every penny going to Cancer Trials Ireland for pancreatic cancer research. And that day, the day of the race at the Curragh, 15 September 2019 – that was a memorable day.

CHAPTER 22

I won the Irish 1000 Guineas on Nightime in 2006. She was a tough filly, bred by Dermot's mother out of her mare Caumshinaun, on whom I had won a listed race at Cork five years earlier. Mrs Weld didn't have many mares, so for her to breed an Irish 1000 Guineas winner was a fantastic achievement.

Nightime was a backward filly; she only raced once as a juvenile, in a seven-furlong maiden at Cork, and she was well beaten in that. She did win her maiden back at Cork, though, early in 2006. It's obviously a big step up, from a maiden win into a Classic, but that's Dermot Weld for you. She was working so well at home that he thought that she could be good enough to be competitive in the Guineas.

I never envisaged that she could put up a performance like the one that she put up in winning the Guineas. I thought that she would run well, but to win the Guineas like she did, to win by six lengths, as easily as she did, against some of the top three-year-old fillies in Ireland and Britain, you couldn't have seen that coming.

The rain that fell on the day helped, of course. She loved that heavy ground. Sir Mark Prescott had a good filly in the race, Confidential Lady, who had finished second to Speciosa in the 1000 Guineas at Newmarket, and she went off in front. I was happy to take my time on Nightime, let her make her ground gradually. I took her towards the stands side – you usually want to be on the stands side when the ground gets heavy at the Curragh – and asked her to pick up, and she was great. We hit the front between the two-furlong pole and the one-furlong pole, and she just carried me further and further clear.

That was some feeling, an Irish 1000 Guineas, another Classic. It was a special day for Dermot, too, and for Mrs Weld. She was there on the day, in the winner's enclosure. She bred Grey Swallow too, of course, and part-owned him, but this was a filly that she had bred who was racing in her colours.

I always had a very good relationship with Mrs Weld, but she was a strong woman, a tough lady. Any time I was riding one of her horses, she'd call me on my way to the races, and she'd call me on my way home from the races. She'd speak her mind, she'd let you know how she wanted her horses ridden, she'd never leave you in any doubt. 'Here's what I want you to do, don't mind what Dermot tells you!' I don't think I ever told Dermot that. 'Don't listen to Dermot; this is how I want you to ride this horse!'

But I enjoyed my time with Mrs Weld; I enjoyed my conversations with her. She was a very intelligent and hugely successful lady, who had a depth of knowledge about racehorses, training and breeding. She and her husband, Charlie, had been very successful before Dermot came along and took over the training of the horses. I suppose Dermot didn't lick it off the stones.

Mrs Weld was a really successful breeder, and that doesn't happen by accident. Nightime is by Galileo. The Galileo of 2006 was not the Galileo of today. He was a Derby winner then, of course, and a King George winner, but he was only starting out as a stallion in 2005, and nobody could have known then that he would develop into the stallion that he became. Nightime was in his first crop of foals, as was Sixties Icon, who won the St Leger later that year. Galileo went on from there to become the most successful thoroughbred stallion in the world, eclipsing his own sire, Sadler's Wells.

And Nightime went on to be a brilliant broodmare. She bred Ghaiyyath, who was bought by Godolphin for €1.1 million as a foal at Goffs, and who went on to win the Coronation Cup and the Eclipse and the Juddmonte International. Nightime is also the dam of Zhukova, whom I rode to victory five times, including in two Group 3 races, and who won the Grade 1 Man o' War Stakes at Belmont Park in America.

I was getting noticed a little by British trainers by then. My win on Refuse To Bend in the 2000 Guineas was obviously a big help, plus, I suppose, the fact that I was champion jockey in Ireland. It just meant that, for a few of the British trainers, if they were sending horses over to race in Ireland, they'd book me for the ride if I was available, instead of sending their own riders over.

My agent Kevin O'Ryan was really good with the British trainers. As soon as the entries were out, as soon as Kevin saw that there was a British horse entered, as long as Dermot didn't have a runner in the race, he would be straight on to the British trainers, telling them that I was available if they wanted me.

Rae Guest, Kevin Ryan, Mark Wallace, Michael Bell, Ralph Beckett were good to me, trainers like that who would have been looking beyond the very big days in Ireland, looking for races that might suit their horses. I won the Ballyogan Stakes on Yomalo for Rae Guest, and I won the Mooresbridge Stakes on Regime for Michael Bell, and I won three Group 3 races in the summer of 2007 on Benbaun for Mark Wallace.

Mark was a good friend; we had a great day at his wedding some years later, and Benbaun was some horse. He was so fast. In his day, there wasn't a sprinter who could go with him. Back then, British sprinters were generally better than the Irish sprinters. Back then we didn't seem to have a lot of high-class sprinters in Ireland. Things have changed recently, but there was a long while there when there wasn't a good programme in Ireland for sprinters. We didn't have a Group 1 sprint, for starters. If you wanted to win a Group 1 sprint, you had to go to Britain or France. Dermot didn't have any sprinters at that time, so any time Benbaun was coming over to Ireland, I was available and bursting to ride him.

I was good friends with one of Benbaun's part-owners, Steve Hillen, as well as with Mark, and they were great in wanting to put me up.

Benbaun was obviously talented, but he wasn't flawless. He was a chronic bleeder, for starters, and Mark did a phenomenal job with him, to get him to achieve all that he achieved. And when he would come under pressure late in his races, he used to lean, which may have been down to his bleeding. He was better over five furlongs than over six, I always thought, because he could do five furlongs in one breath. It was when he needed to take a breath during the final furlong, that was when he used to get into difficulty.

Benbaun came over to Ireland quite a lot in 2007. Kieren Fallon or Jamie Spencer would generally ride him when he raced in Britain, but I rode him to win his three Group 3 races in Ireland that year, and I also got the call up to ride him in the King's Stand Stakes at Royal Ascot. And when it came to the Prix de l'Abbaye in October, towards the end of the 2007 season, I was delighted to be asked to ride him again.

The Prix de l'Abbaye is on Prix de l'Arc de Triomphe day at

Longchamp, which has always been, for me, one of the best race days of the year. The racing on that day is always top-class. Six Group 1 races. And everyone comes together there on one day. The best jockeys, the best horses, trained to the minute by the best trainers. I always wanted to win the Arc, which, regrettably, I never got to do, but, failing that, I always wanted to ride a winner on Arc day. Thankfully I got to do that twice, on Covert Love in the Prix de l'Opéra in 2015 and on Benbaun in the Abbaye in 2007.

I walked the track on the morning of Arc day 2007. As I was on my way to the sprint track, I met Sir Mark Prescott, so we walked the sprint track together. When we were at the stalls, he asked me to look down the track towards the winning line, and he asked me what the track looked like. I told him that it looked to me as if it was downhill the whole way, which it did, from the starting stalls to the winning line.

So we walked down the track, the five furlongs from the stalls to the winning line, and when we got there, Sir Mark asked me to turn around and look back at the stalls. It was mad. 'You're going to think that I'm a complete idiot now,' I said to Sir Mark, 'but it looks like it's downhill, too, from the winning line to the starting stalls.'

'Exactly,' said Sir Mark, as I breathed a small sigh of relief. 'You know what that tells you?'

I didn't say anything. I thought of saying, it's dead flat, but decided against it. I didn't want to appear like a complete idiot again, twice in the space of 15 seconds.

Sir Mark didn't leave me in suspense for too long.

'It tells you that it's dead flat.'

That always stuck in my mind. The five-furlong track at Longchamp: dead straight, dead flat. It's about going as fast as you can for as long as you can.

I loved the buzz of Arc day. And when I was younger, for some reason, they put me sitting close to Cash Asmussen in the weigh room at Longchamp on Arc day. I loved Cash. He was a brilliant jockey, and he was one of my childhood heroes. I loved watching him ride. He was only in Ireland for one year, during the 1980s, with Vincent O'Brien, but I loved watching him ride on telly, too, when I could see him in Britain or in France, and then when he would come back and ride in Ireland again on the big days, Dream Well and Montjeu in the Irish Derby, Suave Dancer in the Irish Champion Stakes, Spinning World in the Irish 2000 Guineas. Cash was behind Mick Kinane as a jockey in my book – everybody was behind Mick Kinane as a jockey in my book – but he was only a short head behind him.

And, just like with Mick in the early days, I wasn't shy about asking Cash questions. I was generally a shy young fellow, but, strange thing, when it came to going up to these iconic jockeys, childhood heroes of mine, and asking them questions, I was quite forward. I don't know why that was. When Cash was sitting there beside me in the weigh room, it just seemed like the most natural thing to me, to ask him for advice.

Cash was great. He told me lots of things, but the thing that stuck with me most was when he told me not to make a move in the false straight. It was brilliant advice. There is a part of the round course at Longchamp, after you leave the back straight and before you get into the home straight. They call it the false straight. Jockeys who don't know any better make the mistake of asking their horses for their effort in the false straight. It does feel like you are closer to home than you actually are at that point, and if you make your move there, you have made your move too early. You won't get home. It was sage advice. Cash's words rang in my ear every time I got to the false straight.

I marvelled at Cash. To see him there, so close to me in the weigh room, to see how he operated. It was the first time that I started to think that there was more to being a jockey than being a jockey. He had a sales catalogue for the Deauville Sales in the weigh room with him, and he was going through it between races. Other lads would be reading the *Racing Post* or studying form or just sitting there, trying to get their thoughts together, trying to figure out tactics, whereas Cash was buying and selling horses at Deauville!

I just thought to myself, he's an operator. I was in awe. He was a brilliant rider, but he was more deeply involved than that. It made me think about the possibilities for me in racing beyond race riding.

Benbaun was great in the Abbaye that day. He was sharp early on, he got me into a lovely position just behind the leaders, and when I asked him to pick up, he was very good. We hit the front on the run to the furlong marker, and he kept on strongly all the way to the line to win well.

That was brilliant for me, another Group 1 race in France to add to Vinnie Roe's Prix Royal-Oak in 2001. But a winner on Arc de Triomphe day, that was pretty special.

Declan McDonogh beat me in the jockeys' championship in 2006. I was gutted about that. I was very happy for Declan – Declan had always been one of my very close friends, and he is Paddy's godfather. Even so, mainly, I was gutted for me!

Declan had one of those years. He rode good winners for Kevin Prendergast, Mustameet and Decado and Brazilian Bride, and he struck up a really good relationship with Ado McGuinness, who just had winner after winner that season. He won four handicaps in a row on Breaker Morant that season, and he won five times on Miracle Ridge. I just couldn't catch him.

I knew in September that I would struggle to catch him. That year, the declarations would come in, and I'd look at my own rides, then I'd look to see what Declan was riding, and he always seemed to have lots of chances. If I wasn't riding in a race, I'd be hoping that Declan wouldn't win it. And if I was, if my chance had gone, I'd be hoping that Declan wouldn't win it. ABD, Anyone But Declan!

It's mad, really. Declan was one of my closest friends. When we were going racing, sharing lifts, it was always me, Fran Berry, Kevin Manning, and Declan. I was always delighted when Declan was successful, but that year, 2006, when I was trying to beat him in the jockeys' championship, I wanted him to get beaten on everything that he rode. It's human nature. It's the competitive spirit, the will to win that is in all of us. I'm sure that Declan was the same with me that year.

When Declan won the championship, though, when I knew that I couldn't catch him, I was delighted for him. He deserved to be champion; he rode like a champion. And it wasn't really that close in the end: he beat me by 13, 89 winners to 76.

I got the championship back in 2007. I rode 94 winners, I beat Declan by 12, and I thought to myself, a hundred winners is achievable. I didn't say too much about it at the time, but I knew that if the ball had hopped a little better for me in 2007, I could have got to a hundred. I could have ridden six more winners that year with a little bit more luck.

So riding a hundred winners in a season became a big goal for me then.

CHAPTER 23

Johnny Murtagh was a top-class jockey. He always was. From the time that he was apprenticed to John Oxx, he was destined for the top. He was champion jockey for the first time in 1995, and he was champion again in 1996, the year that I went in to John Oxx's as second jockey behind him.

In one sense, I probably wasn't the ideal second jockey. It wasn't that I wanted Johnny's job, it wasn't that I wanted to prove that I was better than him, that I was more deserving of the top job at John Oxx's than he was. No way. But I did want to be first jockey at John Oxx's at some stage. I had it in my head from early at John's that, if and when Johnny moved on – if he went abroad or if he moved to another trainer in Ireland – I would be the automatic first choice, that John wouldn't be in any doubt that I was the right person to take over from Johnny.

I'd like to think that I was a team player at John's, as I was at Dermot's and wherever I was, but I rode to win. Always. That was what John wanted. And if that meant riding to beat Johnny, even if he was on another horse of John's, that was what I did.

I know that John wanted me to always ride to win, even if it was to beat a better-fancied stable companion of the horse that I was riding. And I know how it feels when you get beaten by a stable companion, by a horse that you could have ridden. Even though you are happy for the trainer, your boss, and even though you know that you will probably be riding that horse next time, it's not a nice feeling, knowing that you could have ridden the winner.

And I think that John quite liked that I was in there, snapping at Johnny's heels, keeping Johnny on his toes. It wasn't great for my relationship with Johnny, though.

I understood Johnny's position. This young whippersnapper coming here from Tom Lacy's. Who does he think he is?

Johnny probably saw me as a bit of a threat, which was no bad thing, really, for me. The fact that he thought enough of me to see me as a threat was a positive. If he hadn't regarded me at all, if he hadn't seen me as a challenger to him, well, that wouldn't have said much for my ability as a rider.

There was a rivalry there between us from the very beginning, and it lasted years. When I left John's and started riding for Dermot, we inevitably ended up fighting out a lot of finishes. On occasion, Johnny would tighten me up in a race, and on other occasions, I would tighten him up. That was just the way it was. If either of us had an opportunity to tighten the other up in a race, we usually took it. Usually the rivalry was restricted to racing and to race riding and to the racecourse, but sometimes it spilled over.

Like one Sunday afternoon at Leopardstown in August 2005, I was riding a Moyglare filly, Polished Gem, for the boss in the first race, a two-year-olds' maiden. She was a lovely filly, a well-bred debutante whom we liked a lot. Johnny was riding a colt for Thomond O'Mara, Famous Seamus, who had run three times and who had been beaten three times. There was a bit of crowding just around three furlongs out, involving me and Johnny and Valdir de Souza on a filly of Liam McAteer's called Nans Lady.

I was in the wrong. I ran Johnny up the back of the other horse on the run around the home turn. I saw him on the inside, and he was trying to edge out off the rail, but I didn't let him out. Usually, in an instance like that, you'd let a jockey out. You'd let him out because you'd hope that, if and when the next race comes along and positions are reversed, he'll let you out.

There's race riding and there's race riding, and there are fine lines. On the face of it, I didn't do anything wrong. The stewards had a look at the incident and decided that I didn't do anything wrong. I held my racing line. But actually, in terms of what you should do in instances like that, in terms of what is accepted and understood and expected among jockeys, I was in the wrong. I left him in there, and he clipped heels and could have come down, which was bordering on dangerous, and that was the last thing that I ever wanted to do.

Johnny started shouting then and he didn't stop shouting until we had crossed the winning line about 40 seconds later. You couldn't print what he was shouting. You probably couldn't spell it.

He finished just behind me. I finished fifth on Polished Gem and he finished just beside me on Famous Seamus, a neck behind me. Then, all of a sudden, before we had pulled up, just after we had passed the winning post, I heard the crack and I felt this searing pain in my face. Johnny had boxed me on the jaw!

I was shocked and sore all at the same time. I was rocked, but thankfully I managed to stay on my filly. If I had come off, it would have been much worse for me and for Johnny.

It was a heat-of-the-moment thing, and Johnny said afterwards that he missed me. But he didn't. Or, if he did, I wouldn't have liked to have been there if he had actually hit me. Johnny was a boxer as a young fellow, he knew how to hit me, and the video evidence showed that he hadn't missed me, not even a little bit.

Johnny was suspended for 21 days for that. And he got two more days for his ride on Back To Paris later on the day, in the second-last race, when he cut me and Absolute Image up as he was coming through to win his race. He didn't need to do that, as he was going to win the race anyway, but he obviously had the opportunity to do it, to get me back for the earlier race, so he took it. I'm sure he thought that it was worth the two days.

We had our moments, Johnny and me. There were other incidents on the racecourse, in the weigh room. It never came to blows before or since – I wouldn't have wanted it to come to blows, because Johnny would have boxed the hell out of me!

As we got older, we got a little bit more mature, and I remember having a chat with him one day and saying, 'This has to stop.' The thing was, we were very similar. We both had this competitive streak, this will to win that rose above most other motivators or sentiments. Johnny obviously retired before I did, but even towards the end of his riding days, we had become less intense with each other; we had moved towards a truce.

I always had the greatest respect for Johnny Murtagh as a jockey. He was a world-class rider. He was champion jockey in Ireland five times, and he rode as first jockey for Ballydoyle for three years, and he rode all those big winners. He won every Irish Classic and he won most big races in Britain, he won the Arc de Triomphe on Sinndar and he won the Epsom Derby three times in five years. And he proved quite quickly after he started training that he was going to be a top-class trainer, too, which wasn't at all surprising.

I probably wanted to emulate him; I probably thought that I wanted to be as good as him as a rider. And maybe I wanted to show him that I was good. Maybe that's where it came from, the rivalry. Coupled with the fact that maybe he saw me as a threat, that he was wanting to put me back in my box. It was probably a combination of all those things.

And when I got ill, Johnny Murtagh was one of the first people on the phone to me, he and his wife, Orla, asking if there was anything that they could do. On reflection, when a little bit of maturity set in, a little bit of perspective, we realised how ridiculous our rivalry was and that, actually, we quite liked each other.

I was very lucky in that, during my career, I didn't suffer any serious injuries, and I didn't really have many lengthy bans.

And the only real injuries that I ever got were off horses that were trained by Frances! I won the Madrid Handicap at the Curragh in 1998 on Goldman. I got up to beat Johnny Murtagh on a filly of Eddie Lynam's, Hartstown Girl, in a tight finish, which was great. Then Goldman shied after the line, probably at the shadow that the stewards' tower cast on the ground, and dumped me on the ground. I broke my collarbone in that one.

And on the Thursday before Guineas weekend in 2001, I was riding a horse for Frances in a maiden at Clonmel, Nonchalant, and he slipped up on the bend on the run into the straight, bringing down Warren O'Connor on a horse of Noel Meade's. I was fine, a little sore but fine, except for the little finger on my right hand, which felt sore and looked deformed!

This was about 10 days before Irish Guineas weekend, and we had a good Moyglare filly, Cool Clarity, for the Guineas. We thought that she had a big chance in the Guineas; she had just won the Athasi Stakes and she was a progressive filly, or one who had the potential to be better than she had shown on the track up to that point. So my first thought was, if the doc sees my finger, he'll stand me down and he won't let me ride in the Guineas. So I put my little finger into my mouth and I tugged it and put it back into place. It was painful, all right, but not nearly as painful as missing out on Guineas weekend would have been.

Cool Clarity didn't win the Guineas, and my little finger remained deformed-looking.

I had a few more falls. I had a fall in Hong Kong, when a horse flipped over on me in the stalls and I got a small hairline fracture in my wrist, but it never stopped me riding. And I had quite a bad-looking fall at Ballinrobe – I was caught in a sandwich as two horses converged on me, and I clipped heels and came down. But I got up and walked away from that, pretty much unscathed. Like I say, I was very fortunate with injuries throughout my career. The longest I was ever on the sidelines through injury was that three-week spell that I missed with a broken collarbone. Frances and I took the opportunity during that time to go to Paris together.

There was one evening, we were all out in Carlow, a gang of us, Frances and me and Ruby and Gillian, and Ian Amond, Busty, who was riding over jumps at the time, and a few others. The jumps boys were talking about their injuries. Most of them had broken most of the bones in their bodies at that stage, and had had pins and plates inserted all over the place. The best that I could muster was that I had just returned from America, I had slept in an awkward position on the plane, and I had a crick in my neck!

I didn't lose much time through suspensions throughout my career, either. I was never a whip-happy jockey. I always tried to get horses to run for me, without relying on the whip too much. I got a couple of days for giving a filly two cracks of the whip at Galway when we were clear, in an unassailable lead. That infuriated me at the time. I was annoyed with the stewards but, actually, the stewards were right. If I was being honest, I should have been annoyed with myself. There was no need to give the filly a smack: the race was in the bag. I put it down to the occasion, Galway, the pressure, the atmosphere and the crowds and the importance of it all, of winning.

I got seven days from the Ascot stewards for my ride on Pale Mimosa in the Long Distance Cup on British Champions Day in 2013, but that was my own fault. I left her with too much to do and, when I realised that, I got a bit frustrated. That was just stupidity on my part.

The stewards were busy after that race. Johnny Murtagh got seven days for his ride on Royal Diamond in winning the race, and Billy Lee got nine days for his ride on Eye Of The Storm in finishing third. All Irish-based jockeys.

And I deserved the 10 days I got from the stewards at Listowel in 2005. I deserved at least 10 days! It was the second day of the Listowel Festival in September, the first race, a six-furlong handicap, and I was riding a filly for Frances called Miss Isabela.

There was a thing going on with Colm O'Donoghue at the time. It was probably all in my imagination, but Kieren Fallon was my main rival for the jockeys' championship that year; he was first jockey for Ballydoyle, and Colm was riding for Ballydoyle too, and I just got it into my head that Colm was out to get me.

Maybe it was paranoia on my part, but it seemed to me that Colm used to come out of nowhere in races and hinder my prospects of winning. There was no evidence of it whatsoever, but on several occasions he just seemed to arrive there and hold me in pockets or force me wide, and I just thought, Ah here, this is getting out of hand.

So in this race at Listowel in September 2005, Colm was riding a horse for Peter Casey called Tubbertown Rose. I was delivering my challenge on Miss Isabela and, lo and behold, there's Colm again up on my outside, pushing me back in. I just lost the plot. It was the culmination of everything, the pressure that I was putting myself under, the jockeys' championship, the wasting. My dad wasn't well at the time either, so that was probably having an effect on me. Add all of that to this feeling that Colm was out to get me. (Just because you're not paranoid, it doesn't mean that they're not all out to get you.)

I just saw red. I struck out with my elbow and I caught him in the face. There were words and there were expletives, lots of expletives. I didn't calm down, either. I finished fifth, Colm finished fourth, but that was almost secondary, and the argument raged.

I still hadn't calmed down by the time we got to the stewards' room. (It was inevitable that we were going to be called there.) I always thought that I was quite good in the stewards' room. I always thought that I could present my case, argue my corner, whether I should get the race or not, whether I should keep the race or not, that the interference was not significant enough to warrant changing the result if I had passed the post in front, or that it was if I hadn't. But on that day at Listowel, I wasn't good.

I hadn't calmed down at all; I was out of control in the stewards' room. I told the stewards what I thought was going on, that Colm was out to get me. I told them about other incidents. I couldn't believe that they couldn't see it. I couldn't believe that they didn't agree with me and ban Colm. They were right, though; I was wrong. It was the one time that I lost it in the stewards' room, and it wasn't pretty.

I got a 10-day ban for that, which wasn't pretty either. It put me under more pressure in the jockeys' championship. I went out and won on my next ride, Kempes in the two-year-olds' maiden, also for Frances. He was a nice horse, and Frances did well with him – she won four races with him, including the Ulster Derby at Down Royal. He was later bought by JP McManus, and he won the Hennessy Gold Cup for him and Willie Mullins in 2011 under David Casey after Frances had stopped training.

My win on Kempes put me on 65 winners for the season, 13 clear of Kieren Fallon. I hoped that it would be enough of a buffer to see me home in the championship, and it was. Kieren was riding abroad a lot that autumn for Aidan, and he won the

Arc de Triomphe that year on Hurricane Run. He actually only rode three more winners in Ireland between then and the end of the season and, in fact, it was Fran Berry who finished second to me in the championship, nine winners behind.

And there was a serious silver lining to my 10-day ban. As I mentioned, my dad wasn't well at the time, and it meant that I got to spend that time with him. If I hadn't been banned, I would have been riding. I wouldn't have taken the time off. I was blinkered like that. It was like I was forced to take the time off so that I could spend it with my dad. I cherished that time, and I was always grateful that I got to spend it with him. The following month, in October 2005, my father, Paddy Smullen, died.

CHAPTER 24

The lads used to say that Famous Name was my ATM. It was like, every two or three weeks you'd just pull him out and run him, and you'd get your payment from him, guaranteed!

It was a huge deal when Prince Khalid Abdullah sent horses to Dermot for the first time in 2007. It was a real coup for Dermot, the first Irish trainer to have horses for Prince Khalid. To have an owner like that in the yard, the strength that he had, the power that he and his Juddmonte operation had in racing and bloodstock on a global scale. And the horses that raced in Prince Khalid's famous green and pink and white colours, from Warning and Danehill and Zafonic through to Oasis Dream and Workforce and Enable. And Frankel, of course. It was always a privilege to put on those colours.

Famous Name was in the first group of horses that Prince Khalid sent to Dermot, and we loved him from the start. He won his maiden on his racecourse debut by seven lengths, and he kicked on from there. He won the Guineas Trial at Leopardstown on his first run as a three-year-old, and Dermot decided that the Prix du Jockey Club, the French Derby, was the ideal target for him. The race had been shortened a couple of years earlier, from a mile and a half to a mile and two and a half furlongs, and Dermot thought that that would be an ideal distance for Famous Name.

We were very unlucky with the draw, we got stall 17 of 20, and you don't want to be wide at Chantilly over 10 and a half furlongs. You are turning all the time until you get to the home straight, so you have to get in as far as you can so that you're as close to the inside rail as you can be – but ideally you don't want to be too far back in the field.

I took Famous Name back in the field early on so that I could tuck in a bit, but we were still wider than ideal. We were about fourth last turning for home, we were about 10 lengths off the leaders, but when I took him towards the outside and into clear sailing, he picked up really well for me. We got to within about half a length of Vision D'Etat at the 200-metre mark, but Vision D'Etat had enjoyed a dream run around towards the inside from stall four, and he got a lovely split about three hundred metres out. We closed on him all the way to the line, but we just couldn't get to him. In the end, he beat us by a neck.

Looking back on it afterwards, there was nothing that I would have done differently. And any time you can look back on a ride and say, hand on heart, that there was nothing really that you would have done differently, then you know that you have given that horse a good ride, that you have maximised his chance of winning. It was the draw that beat us at Chantilly that day.

Dermot seemed to share my view. It was just one of those things.

On the plus side, if Famous Name had won the French Derby as a three-year-old, there is a good chance that he would have been whisked off to stud before he got to race as a four-year-old, and that would have deprived me of many, many good days and, of course, my ATM.

He ran in 38 races in his career; he won 21 times and finished second or third 13 times. He was only out of the first four three times in his life, all in Group 1 races. He never did get to win his Group 1, but he won his Group 2 and he won bundles of Group 3 races and listed races. He was brilliant at Leopardstown in particular: he knew when to relax at Leopardstown, he knew when to pick up, just on the run into the little dip between the three-furlong pole and the two-furlong pole – that was when he got rolling; he would have got rolling there even if I hadn't asked him to – and he won at Leopardstown 13 times.

I rode Famous Name in 37 of his 38 races. The only race in which I didn't ride him was in the Tattersalls Gold Cup at the Curragh in May 2009, because I rode Casual Conquest instead.

They were both top-class horses, and they both deserved to take their chances in that race, a Group 1 race, which wasn't ideal for me. I could obviously only ride one of them. I just thought that Casual Conquest had a better chance. Also, he was owned by Moyglare Stud, and I was always going to ride a Moyglare horse in a Group 1 race over any other horse.

I tried to convince Dermot not to run both Famous Name and Casual Conquest in the Tattersalls Gold Cup. Run one of them; whichever one we ran I thought would win. Keep the other for another race, a race in which I would be able to ride him. But Dermot was right to run the two of them – Dermot was usually right. It was the right race for both horses, a Group 1 race over 10 furlongs at the Curragh in May, early in their four-year-old seasons.

Mick Kinane rode Famous Name, which was strange for me. I didn't want to see anyone else riding him. The bookmakers sent Famous Name off as favourite. I knew that both horses were well, both horses had been working well, but I also knew that Casual Conquest stayed well; he was a 12-furlong horse running over 10½. Famous Name, by contrast, stayed 10 furlongs all right, but he was probably at his absolute best over nine. So I figured that the way to maximise Casual Conquest's chance of winning the race, and to expose Famous Name's potential vulnerability, was to make it a test of stamina.

I had never made the running on Casual Conquest before – he wasn't a front-runner – but I made the running that day. I set a good pace, which ensured that we had to stay if we were going to win, and he stayed on better than Famous Name. We won by over five lengths in the end from Famous Name, who was a good second. So it turned out that I was right: either one of them would have won it!

Both Famous Name and Casual Conquest were lovely horses. Talented, genuine, willing. Muhannak was talented, but sometimes he wasn't that willing. Actually, he wasn't a nice horse at all.

Kevin O'Ryan saw that Muhannak was entered in a listed race at Dundalk in September 2008, the Diamond Stakes, and Dermot didn't have a runner in the race, so Kevin was straight onto Muhannak's trainer, Ralph Beckett, to tell him that I was available.

The ten-and-a-half-furlong start at Dundalk is just in front of the grandstand, so you have to canter down the track and turn around and come back to the start. Muhannak cantered down the track all right, but when I turned around to come back, he wouldn't come back. He wouldn't budge. So I had to get down off him and lead him back, me running along in front of him, dragging him back to the start. Thankfully, he was a different proposition when the race started – he ran on well and we won by a neck.

After that, Ralph and his owner, Richard Pegum, decided that the Breeders' Cup Marathon in America would be a good race for him and – right place right time – because I had ridden him to victory at Dundalk, they asked me if I would ride him again.

I had always loved watching the Breeders' Cup on television when I was younger, on a Saturday night in the darkness of late October or early November, watching live racing from America, on the other side of the world, where daylight was. I always thought that I would love to ride at the Breeders' Cup, and wouldn't it be amazing if you could ride a winner of a Breeders' Cup race?

The Breeders' Cup Marathon was a new addition to the Breeders' Cup schedule in 2008. It was run over a mile and a half in 2008, which just shows you. In Ireland and Britain and Europe, a mile-and-a-half race is a middle-distance race. Races that we consider to be marathons are run over two miles or two and a half miles. In America, because there is such an emphasis on speed, they thought it would be appropriate to call a mile-and-a-half race a marathon, even though the Breeders' Cup Turf is also run over a mile and a half. The following year, they increased the distance of the Marathon to a mile and six furlongs, which made more sense, before they removed it from the Breeders' Cup schedule in 2014, which I thought was a shame.

The Breeders' Cup moves around: it is run at different tracks around America in different years. In 2008, it was run at Santa Anita in California, one of the most picturesque racecourses in the world. The Europeans usually do well when the Breeders' Cup is run at Santa Anita and, in 2008, the races that were historically run on American dirt were run on a surface called Pro-Ride, a surface that is more like the Polytrack that we have on the all-weather tracks in Britain and Ireland than it is like American dirt.

All of that played into our hands, and Muhannak was great on the day. I was always happy with our position. I moved him up as we ran around the home turn, wide but making ground and travelling well. The favourite, Sixties Icon, and Frankie Dettori were on our inside; we got first run on them, and we hit the front at the top of the home straight. We were closed down late on by

Edgar Prado on an American horse named Church Service, but Muhannak ran on well for me.

I wasn't sure whether or not we had won – I wasn't sure where the winning line was. In the end, we won by a head; there never really was any doubt if you had been watching the race from the stands or on television. But there was a doubt in my mind until the result was called.

It was a big deal for me, to win a Breeders' Cup race. I really did treasure that trophy.

CHAPTER 25

You miss things when you are a jockey. You miss going to things. Events. Sporting events. Family events. Life. Literally.

Frances went into labour on the morning of the Pretty Polly Stakes in 2010. I was due to ride Chinese White in the Pretty Polly Stakes, a Group 1 race at the Curragh on Irish Derby weekend, so you'd think that I would have had a difficult decision to make, but it wasn't a difficult decision at all. Indeed, there wasn't a decision to be made. I was down to ride, I had a great chance of winning a Group 1 race, so I was going racing.

We had only just moved into our new house in Rhode, and there I was, in my suit, all set, all decked out, Pretty Polly day at the Curragh with a good book of rides.

'Right, I'm off now,' I said to Frances.

'I'm off too,' said Frances. 'I'm off to the hospital.'

There was never any question of me going to the hospital with Frances, of not going racing. Frances didn't ask me to. She never would have. It just shows you how lucky I was to have met and married somebody as generous and as understanding as Frances, who came from a racing background, who understood everything that went with it. So my brother took Frances up to Mount Carmel Hospital while I headed off to the Curragh.

I finished fourth in the first race, a two-year-old fillies' maiden, on a filly of Eoin Griffin's called Light Footsteps, and I won the second race, the Group 3 International Stakes, on a filly of Dermot's, Precious Gem, a progressive filly who had won her previous two, and I went out to ride Chinese White in the Pretty Polly.

Chinese White was a high-class filly, a grey filly owned by Lady O'Reilly (who was always a great supporter of mine and of Dermot's). I had won three races on Chinese White the previous season, including the Group 2 Blandford Stakes at the Curragh, and we had won the Listed Victor McCalmont Stakes at Gowran Park on her debut in 2010 before finishing third in the Tattersalls Gold Cup.

We fancied her for the Pretty Polly, though; we knew that she was well and we thought that she was good enough to win the race. Also, she was in-foal to Cape Cross, and fillies and mares can often improve in terms of performance on the racecourse when they are in-foal.

She was nicely out of the stalls and I allowed her to move up to take second place behind Kevin Manning on a filly of Jim Bolger's, Akdarena. Kevin set a good pace, but I was happy to let him go on about five or six lengths in front of us as we raced across the top of the track. I was happy that we were going as fast as I wanted to go on Chinese White. I asked her to pick up when we straightened up for home, and she did. We joined Kevin just inside the two-furlong marker and went on. I knew that we had gone fast, I knew that there was a chance that something would come from behind to challenge us, so I just kept my filly up to her work. Frankie Dettori closed on us a little on Flying Cloud but, while I could hear him, I never saw him, and my filly kept on well. I gave a little punch of the air when we crossed the winning line.

That was great, another Group 1 race in the bag, and it was a Group 1 win for Chinese White on her final attempt. She was obviously always going to be retired from racing after that race, given that she was in-foal, so it was great for her, and for Lady O'Reilly to get a Group 1 win for her latest broodmare.

Incidentally, the foal that she was carrying at the time was named Best Effort, and he won a couple of races in Britain for Sir Mark Prescott and Lady O'Reilly before being sold to Hong Kong and winning a few more.

My last ride on the day was on Profound Beauty in the second-last race, the Curragh Cup. We finished second behind a horse of John Dunlop's, Tactic, and I high-tailed it out of there and headed for Mount Carmel Hospital. All was well; I made it to the hospital on time. Sarah waited for me to arrive before she was born.

I made it on time for that event, but I did miss lots of family events because of racing. That was the job, that was the path that I had chosen. I never missed a day's work. Even if I was feeling bad or sick or if I had a bit of a flu, I never missed a day of riding work or riding out, and I only missed a day's racing if I was suspended or if I had a broken collarbone.

That's just the way it was. That was my mindset. Communions, weddings, confirmations, christenings, they were all second to racing. Call it dedication or determination, call it selfishness, it was probably a combination of all of that, but that was the way I looked at things. I never felt that I was being selfish about it, though – I just thought that that was the way it was, that that was the way it had to be.

When I looked back on it at the end of my career, maybe there was some kind of a happy medium that I could have found, but I don't think that I would have had the career that I was lucky enough to have if I had gone with a happy medium. It was a mindset as much as anything else.

I could never understand the mentality of any rider who could give up a day's racing, and the chance of riding a winner or two, because they had a wedding or some other personal event on. Or a rider taking holidays or days off when racing was on. That wasn't me. If you have an attitude that says that you are going to take a day off so that you can go to a wedding or a christening, you are not completely focused on the job. If you're going to be a jockey, and if you're going to try to be a successful jockey, you take every opportunity. You don't leave the door open for anybody else. That was my attitude. I even missed my brother Ger's wedding because I was riding.

As well as that, I would never have been able to enjoy a day, an event, if I had given up a day's racing for it. I would have been all the time checking my phone, checking results, watching racing, checking to see if the horses I would have ridden or could have ridden would win. And if one or two of them happened to win, that would have ruined any day for me. I would have been no company for anybody on a day like that, so it would have been a waste of time me being there.

I know that because, when it was forced on me, when I missed a day's racing because of suspension, I used to try to make the best of it, to go off and do something with Frances or with the kids. I'd say that I'd stay away from phones, just try to enjoy the day, but I couldn't help myself. I'd be checking results all the time and, if I missed a winner, which I usually did, or convinced myself that I could have ridden the winner, the day would be ruined. I'd be a horrible git for the rest of the day.

And I didn't try to catch the ends of events after racing, either. I didn't try to go to the afters of a wedding. If I was doing light the next day, there was no point: I wouldn't have been able to eat or drink anything. And if I had had a poor day at the races, there would have been no point either. If I missed it, I missed it.

❖

I always tried to ride for outside yards whenever I could, when my commitments to Dermot allowed. The way I looked at it, they were very good to me when I was trying to get established, so I was always going to ride for them when I was able to ride for them. Even though I'd be riding for Dermot Weld and for all those big owners, I still thought that it was very important to keep those relationships that I had formed in the early days.

As well as that, the smaller trainers were a massive help to me in winning my nine championships. There'd be a seven-race card, and I'd be riding for Dermot in three or four or five of the races, but it was great to be able to have a good ride in some of the other races too.

Harry Rogers was always very good to me. He was a very underrated trainer; he was a great target trainer, and if Harry rang Kevin and said, 'You know what, I think Pat should ride this,' I'd ride it, even if I thought that something else in the race had a better chance.

John Kiely was similar. When John rang Kevin looking for me, Kevin very rarely said no. John and Marian were always great supporters of mine. David Marnane, too, and obviously Joanna Morgan. Joanna continued to support me even when she had only a small team of horses.

Mick Halford put me up on Casamento for the Group 2 Beresford Stakes in September 2010, and we duly won that easily. Casamento was owned by Sheikh Mohammed, though, so when he ran in the Group 1 Racing Post Trophy at Doncaster the following month, he was ridden by Frankie Dettori, who was obviously riding for Sheikh Mohammed at the time.

I rode the Eddie Lynam-trained Sole Power when he was two and three but, when he was running in the Nunthorpe Stakes at York in August 2010, I was riding for Dermot at home, so Wayne Lordan rode him, and duly won on him, at 100/1! I didn't get to ride Sole Power again then until he was a nine-year-old, when he was well past his best, after he had won all those Group 1 races. And I rode Slade Power for Eddie once – I rode him to win his maiden at Dundalk as a two-year-old in December 2011. I never got to ride him again, so my 100 per cent record on him remained intact!

Other trainers were great – Tracey Collins and Reginald Roberts and Joe Murphy and Sabrina Harty, and Willie Mullins and Michael O'Callaghan in later years. And it was nice that, again in later years, some of the British trainers wanted to use me. Mark Wallace and Richard Fahey, obviously, but also Hugo Palmer and Mick Channon and Michael Bell and Robert Cowell and Ralph Beckett and William Muir.

And Kevin Ryan.

Kevin Ryan was always a great supporter of mine. I won the Greenlands Stakes in 2012 on Tiddliwinks for him, and he asked me if I would ride Captain Ramius for him in the Ayr Gold Cup the following September.

Kevin had four runners in the race, they were all priced up similarly, but it rained lots in Ayr that weekend, and Captain Ramius loved rain. He loved soft ground. I had breakfast with Kevin that morning, and he said, 'You know, I think your lad will win. The ground has come right for him and, of my four, he's the one I'd like to be on.'

He did win. He won doing handsprings.

CHAPTER 26

We thought that Rite Of Passage was a good horse from early on. He was a National Hunt horse, a horse for bumpers who might go on and be a good hurdler, but I still rode him in a lot of his work. I rode most of the young National Hunt horses in their work.

Did I think that he could win races? Yes, I did. Did I think then that he could win an Ascot Gold Cup? Never even considered it!

Even as a young horse, though, Rite Of Passage was plagued with leg trouble. He was an upright horse, a conformation flaw that meant there was always a lot of pressure on his tendons. If he hadn't been trained with the care and attention that Dermot Weld gave him, he wouldn't have achieved half of what he achieved on the racecourse. If I had to pick one horse that epitomised Dermot Weld's skills as a racehorse trainer during my time there, one horse with whom Dermot's training methodology made the greatest difference, it was Rite Of Passage.

He won his bumper at the 2008 Galway Festival on his racecourse debut under Robbie McNamara, and he followed up by winning another bumper at Naas the following February impressively, beating a hotpot of Willie Mullins's, Quadrillon, by six lengths. We had been thinking about the Cheltenham Bumper for a while and, after his win at Naas, there was only one obvious target for him.

I was desperate to win the Cheltenham Bumper. Bumpers are unusual in that they are restricted to amateur riders in Ireland, but open to professional jockeys in England. I couldn't ride in the Champion Bumper in Punchestown, or in any bumper in Ireland – hence my fixation with Cheltenham.

I loved riding at Cheltenham. I loved the occasion. I loved going into the weigh room, the slagging – here's this fellow coming in now, this Flat jockey – but it was all in good fun. The jump jockeys knew how serious I was about winning the race, that I wasn't just a day-tripper who was swanning in, taking somebody else's ride. I was invariably riding a horse for Dermot in the bumper, one of our own.

I was usually sitting beside AP McCoy in the Cheltenham weigh room, and that was great too, if a little intense, especially if AP wasn't having a good day or a good meeting! Because it was serious, it wasn't about banter or slagging or having fun. It was a massive day, it was a massive occasion, a massive race, and everybody there desperately wanted to win it.

I always thought that Cheltenham was a dreadful racetrack though! It was never a galloping track in my eyes. Jump jockeys will probably disagree with that; they'll say that it's a demanding track, and it is. The finish is stiff. But it's an undulating track on which you can never really get into a rhythm. I've had some terrible runs around there on good horses, and it doesn't help that the Champion Bumper can be a really rough race.

Rite Of Passage was well backed: he was sent off as favourite, and he deserved to be favourite. The race went well, too. Katie Walsh on a mare of Willie Mullins's, Morning Supreme, set the early pace, and I was able to get Rite Of Passage nicely settled in behind, towards the outside early on.

We travelled well the whole way, we travelled really well to the top of the hill, and I thought we would win as we started down it. But I had to ride him along as we approached the home turn, and Brian O'Connell on Dunguib loomed up, running all over us to my right. I couldn't believe how easily Dunguib travelled up alongside us, or how quickly he went away from us as we straightened up for home. In the end, we finished third. Some Present and Davy Russell stayed on past us up the hill, but we were all miles behind Dunguib.

It took Rite Of Passage a little while to get over that race. It left its mark. The Cheltenham Bumper is a tough race: it can be a brutal race and it can have a lasting effect on a young horse. I always said to Frances, if I had had a good young National Hunt horse, the last race I would have run him in would have been the Cheltenham Bumper.

Rite Of Passage ran in a bumper at the Curragh two months later. He got beaten, and Dermot put him away for the summer after that. He came back after a nice break, refreshed, to run in a maiden at Ballinrobe. That was just the second time I rode him in a race and, while he won all right, he wasn't overly impressive. He was a big horse, and it was a struggle just to get him around a tight track like Ballinrobe.

On the back of that run, the handicapper gave him a mark of just 88, which I thought was lenient. I thought that he was a certainty in the November Handicap at Leopardstown six weeks later, and he duly won like one.

He went hurdling then that National Hunt season – he won his maiden hurdle at Leopardstown the following January, and he won a novices' hurdle at Punchestown in February, and they sent him off as favourite for the Neptune Hurdle back at the Cheltenham Festival the following March. But he was a straight, angular horse with a long back, and jumping just wasn't his forte.

It didn't come naturally to him. Even so, he battled on well to finish third behind Peddlers Cross in that Neptune Hurdle.

He had the heart of a lion, though. He gave you everything in all his races, always. He was one of those horses who left it all out there on the track; he kept nothing for himself, and that was why he was so good. He never knew when to stop.

He was always going to run on the Flat when he came back, and Dermot started to think that Rite Of Passage could be a contender for the Ascot Gold Cup.

We were hopeful that he would run a big race, but you couldn't have thought that he would win the Gold Cup. We did think, though, that there were a lot of non-stayers in the race. There were horses in there who would stay two miles, maybe even two and a quarter miles, but the last two furlongs of the Gold Cup, that is the red zone of the race. We knew that Rite Of Passage would stay, and we knew that he had the mental toughness to keep going when most of his rivals would have had enough.

It was a messy enough race, that Ascot Gold Cup. I had a nice position early on, along the inside and just behind the leader, Akmal, but he had had enough as we raced to the home turn, and was starting to drop back on top of me, so I had to manoeuvre my way out around him. Ryan Moore was just to my outside on Ask, keeping me in, as was his right, but I had to try to engineer a bit of racing room for myself so that I could get past Akmal. I upset Ryan a little bit in moving to my left, and the stewards gave me a two-day suspension afterwards for the manoeuvre. I couldn't complain about that, but I was travelling well enough to make the move and, if I hadn't moved out when I did, I would have got shuffled back in the pack, and I would have lost all chance of winning the race.

Johnny Murtagh had hit the front on Age Of Aquarius at that point, and he kicked for home off the home turn. We went around the home turn behind him. From there, from the top of Ascot's home straight to the winning line, for two and a half furlongs, it was some tussle between the two of us.

We had two lengths to make up on Johnny from the top of the home straight, and we made them up before we got to the furlong pole. Rite Of Passage was about a neck in front of Age Of Aquarius at that point. I thought that I had him, I thought that we would go on and win by a length, but Age Of Aquarius battled back. He was brave and tough, we couldn't get away from him, but Rite Of Passage was brave and tough as well, and he just wouldn't let Johnny's horse past him again. At the winning line, we were still a neck ahead.

That was phenomenal, an Ascot Gold Cup. After going so close on Vinnie Roe in 2002, to go and win it then eight years later, it was just amazing. It was one of the most satisfying days of my professional career, too, because Johnny Murtagh was the one rider that you didn't want to come up against in a one-on-one fight to the line. It was desperately difficult to beat Johnny in a finish. So to come out on top like that, by a neck, in the Ascot Gold Cup, at the end of a two-and-a-half-furlong run to the line, that was very satisfying.

I appreciated everything about the win, even immediately afterwards. When I was pulling up, just after crossing the winning line, as Johnny was saying, 'Well done,' to me, I appreciated what was after happening – the race that had just taken place, the duel that we had just witnessed, that we had been a part of, what the horse had given me. And the fact that it was the Gold Cup, the Ascot Gold Cup.

There are more important races run during Royal Ascot, but there aren't any more prestigious races.

I took the time to soak up the atmosphere as we were making our way back in to the winner's enclosure. That was the best horse race I ever rode in. Maybe not in terms of the horses' abilities, but in terms of the competition. It was the best performance from a thoroughbred horse, to give you everything like that, to get the better of another thoroughbred who was giving everything, after such a protracted duel. I just thought that it was a brilliant horse race.

CHAPTER 27

I hated it when planes got delayed. The angst. I always gave
myself lots of time to get to race meetings in Britain or abroad
just so that I wouldn't be fretting, but when there was a delay
to a flight, that was only the start of it. You never knew how long
that delay was going to be for.

Like on 20 October 2012, when I was flying to Ascot for
British Champions' Day. It was just the second year of British
Champions' Day at Ascot, a race day that was newly created.
They took a few races from Newmarket, the Champion Stakes,
the Jockey Club Cup and the Pride Stakes, and put them together
with the Diadem Stakes and the Queen Elizabeth Stakes from
Ascot, added a handicap and put it all together to form one day,
British Champions' Day, at Ascot in mid-October.

It was a great idea, a great concept, similar to Irish Champions'
Weekend, or Arc de Triomphe day in France, or Breeders' Cup
day in America, and it made for a fantastic day of top-class Flat
racing. It was just a pity that sometimes the ground had gone by
the time mid-October rolled around.

The first race was early enough on British Champions' Day
2012, so we were getting an early flight on Saturday morning.
But it doesn't matter how much time you have given yourself
– if there is fog, the plane just can't take off. There was fog that

morning, really bad fog, which left us sitting on the plane on the tarmac for ages.

The only good thing was that Dermot was with me, so I didn't have to ring him to try to explain why I might not make it to Ascot on time!

Eventually we took off, but I was resigned to the fact that we probably weren't going to make it on time for me to ride Rite Of Passage in the first race, the Long Distance Cup, which was due off at 1.45 p.m. That was a pity, but it wasn't a disaster. Rite Of Passage had only run once since he had won the Ascot Gold Cup on that memorable day in 2010. He didn't run again in 2010, and he had only run once in 2011: he had finished third behind Fame And Glory in the Saval Beg Stakes at Leopardstown in the early part of the season.

His leg problems resurfaced – he was such a fragile horse – and it was only because he was trained by Dermot Weld that he had got to a point where he could even run in the Long Distance Cup at Ascot. It was big leap of faith to think that he had a real chance of winning it.

Sapphire was different, though. I was thinking that, as long as I made it in time for Sapphire in the Fillies and Mares Stakes at 2.55 p.m., I would settle for that. We thought that Sapphire had a big chance. She had won the Noblesse Stakes and the Give Thanks Stakes at Cork during the summer, both Group 3 races, and she had finished second to Izzi Top in the Group 1 Pretty Polly Stakes at the Curragh. She had been working well in the lead-up to Ascot, and Dermot had had the race in mind for her for a while.

Dermot had Richard Hughes lined up to ride Rite Of Passage if I didn't make it on time, but there was still a chance. Once the flight took off, it was all seamless. We landed, got in the car, and made good time. Then, about two miles from Ascot, disaster. The traffic was all backed up. So close and yet no chance.

I grabbed my bag and opened the back door.

'I'm going to make a run for it.'

So I jumped out and started running. It must have been a sight for any racegoers sitting in traffic, this strange guy, running down the road with this big bag over my shoulder, in a suit, not long before the first race. Especially if anyone recognised me.

'Was that Pat Smullen?'

I got into Ascot about 20 minutes before the first race, dripping with sweat, got changed, got my saddle, got on the weighing scales. You have to weigh out 15 minutes before race time at the latest, and I literally got onto the weighing scales with minutes to spare. And as I was there, sitting on the scales, Richard Hughes walked in through the door. He had been caught in traffic too, so he actually wouldn't have made it on time!

Turned out, it was all worth it. Rite Of Passage was brilliant. I rode him for luck that day. I thought that I had to ride him for luck, his first run in 17 months, conserve every little bit of energy in him that I could on the soft ground, and hope that the gaps opened up. I dropped him out at the back of the field and got him settled. We were still second last and along the inside as we started to turn for home, but I knew that I still had plenty of horse underneath me. I could have gone outside in the home straight, but we would have had to cover more ground, use up more energy than we would by staying on the inside. A gap opened up on the rail as Jim Crowley's horse Ile De Re rolled to his left, so we went for that gap. Jamie Spencer hit the front on Fame And Glory, but he didn't put the race to bed, and I knew that my horse would give me everything.

We closed on the leaders as we passed the furlong pole. It all got a little tight against the inside rail, and I had to engineer some racing room for myself as Adam Kirby on the grey horse

Electrolyser kept us in a bit but, luckily, Rite Of Passage had enough energy left to enable him to muscle his way out a bit. Once we got outside William Buick's horse Aiken, Rite Of Passage picked up again. He was so tough. He forged his way up alongside Aiken and went on to win by a neck.

Rite Of Passage was an unbelievable racehorse. He wasn't the fastest horse that I ever sat on, but you'd never find a tougher horse, a more willing horse. He gave you all that he could give you, every time. And for Dermot Weld to get him back to win the Long Distance Cup on British Champions' Day at Ascot, after being off the track for 510 days, to have him in that form, that fit – Dermot has accomplished so many remarkable feats as a trainer of racehorses but, to my mind, this was up there with his very highest achievements.

For me, I was just happy that I got there in time to take the ride!

It was a different situation with Sapphire. I thought that she was the best filly in the race, and she loved that soft ground, so I rode her like the best filly in the race, in mid-division, fifth or sixth of the 10 runners and one off the rail. She travelled really well for me to the home straight. I didn't ask her to pick up until we had straightened up for home and were on the run to the two-furlong marker. She picked up really well for me, as I hoped she would; we hit the front at the furlong pole and she came away from her rivals impressively.

Dermot was great with fillies. He was great with all horses, obviously, but fillies and mares generally needed just a little more empathy than colts and geldings did. There was more emphasis on keeping them happy than there was on getting them hard fit. You had to strike a balance, get them fit without asking them to do too much.

I always enjoyed riding fillies and mares. I always thought that you had to cajole them more than be aggressive on them.

You couldn't bully them. You had to encourage them. And I had the benefit of knowing all those breeders' families through the years: you got to know families' traits, their temperaments, what worked for them, what didn't work.

I had had a good tussle with Johnny Murtagh for the championship in 2011 (he beat me by four in the end, 83 to 79), and I had another good tussle with Joseph O'Brien for the 2012 championship. In one sense, it was strange, going toe-to-toe with your nephew for the championship, but, in another, it was the most natural thing in the world.

Joseph was a competitor for me from the very start. He was always a very competitive young fellow. He was joint champion apprentice in 2010, his first full year with a licence, and he kicked on from there. He rode his first Classic winner in May 2011, so he was up there among the top echelons of riders very quickly, at a very young age.

Of course, there was a family connection there, but he didn't need Uncle Pat to look after him in the weigh room! He was very much his own man, and he was a rival from the very beginning. He was riding for his father, Aidan O'Brien, so very quickly he was the person who was my biggest threat in the jockeys' championship.

Joseph was my main rival in lots of races as well. That was always going to be the case, given the horses we were riding, the trainers for whom we were riding. You'd be going through a race the night beforehand or on the morning of the race, going through your main dangers, and very often your main danger would be Joseph's horse.

You had to be respectful, you had to ride within the rules and you were never going to put anybody in danger, but when the gates open, everything goes out the window. Friendships, family connections, everything. It's every person for themselves. If you started to let your guard down, if you started to think, Oh I'll give him a little bit of room, because he's my friend or because he's family or because he's not going well, you weren't doing your job. If you didn't commit to a gap, people would see it, connections would wonder why, and then they'd be saying that you were helping the other guy or that you'd lost your competitive edge or, worse, that you'd lost your bottle.

I never lost my bottle and I never lost my competitive edge. I tried to never leave the door open, not even a little. If you left it open a little, even slightly ajar, it could open a lot. People could use that slight gap to prise it open further. Best to keep the door firmly closed and leave no room for manoeuvre or for doubt.

That all led to a little animosity between Joseph and me while we were riding.

That wasn't surprising. If you put two highly competitive souls into a cauldron, both seeking the same outcome, and make it so that only one can achieve that outcome – victory – then you are going to have a certain level of animosity.

It was a bit like Johnny Murtagh and me, the competition between Joseph and me. I could have concluded that there was one common denominator at the heart of all of it: me! I always preferred to think, though, that it was the competition and the competitiveness. And, as with Johnny, it was only there when we were both riding. After Joseph retired from race riding, once the competition aspect of it had gone, we were good. And when I got ill, Joseph and Aidan were brilliant with me. They couldn't do enough for me.

Joseph was a top-class jockey, one of the best riders I ever rode against, and he deserved to be champion in 2012. The last Flat meeting of the year was the November Handicap meeting at

Leopardstown on 4 November, but it didn't get that far, as we were both at Santa Anita riding at the Breeders' Cup that weekend. So our battle for the championship ended the week before, at Leopardstown on 27 October, where I rode a treble, all three for Dermot, including the steering job that was Famous Name in the Listed Trigo Stakes (again!). Even so, I came up three short, 87 to 84.

It had been a gruelling contest, though, and I think that it took its toll on both of us. I didn't want to get beaten, and neither did he. We both went to the buckle end in every way, and it wasn't pretty on occasion. We had our moments; we had our arguments both on the track and in the weigh room afterwards. He was as competitive as I was: he wanted to win his first championship as desperately as I wanted to win my seventh, and I wouldn't have expected anything else from Joseph.

The fact that Kevin O'Ryan was agent for both of us added an extra dimension! But Kevin made it very clear that he offered both of us to everyone. If any trainer rang him looking for a rider, and if we were both available, he'd tell that trainer that we were both available, and it would be up to the trainer to choose one of us. Kevin handled it extremely well – he was straight up with both of us and with all the trainers, and everybody knew where they stood.

There was a lot of talk at the time that Joseph was lucky, that he was only getting to ride all those good horses because he was Aidan O'Brien's son. But all those horses had to be ridden. Joseph was riding at the highest level, for the biggest operation in the world, and under all the pressure that those high-level rides bring. And he was absolutely crucifying himself to keep the weight off. Fundamentally, he was a top-class rider. He wouldn't have got or kept the rides on all those top-class horses in all those Group 1 races if he hadn't been a top-class rider. I don't think that he really got the credit that he should have got during his riding career. I don't think his talent as a jockey got the recognition that it deserved.

CHAPTER 28

Voleuse De Coeurs was always a talented mare, owned by Lady O'Reilly. I rode her to win at Wexford early in the summer of 2012 over a mile and a half, and Dermot stepped her up to two miles for the Topaz Handicap at the Galway Festival that year.

I wasn't sure about her stamina for two miles, and the ground on the day was softer than any ground she had encountered before, but Dermot had lots of confidence in her. We had a poor draw, 18 of 20, right on the outside.

I dropped her in at the back of the field early on, and we were still about fourth last with six furlongs to go, but once I got her out and got her rolling, she made up the ground very quickly. I was able to sit up on her as we raced down the hill. We hit the front on the run around the home turn, and we cleared away in the home straight to win by eight lengths. It was a fair performance by a three-year-old filly, taking on her elders in a competitive handicap like that, on soft ground and stepping up to two miles for the first time.

Voleuse De Coeurs's big target in 2013 was the Irish St Leger. I rode her in all four of her races in 2013 before the Leger; we won the Listed Vintage Crop Stakes at Navan, and we were just beaten by Royal Diamond in the Group 3 Irish St Leger Trial at the Curragh in August.

The problem for me was that Pale Mimosa was also on track for the Irish St Leger. Pale Mimosa was another high-class staying mare, owned by Dr Ronan Lambe. I had won the Galtres Stakes at York on her the previous year and, in her only run in 2012 before the Irish Leger, she had won the Saval Beg Stakes at Leopardstown.

It was a quandary for me. You can only ride one horse in every race, and I had to choose. Dermot left it up to me, but I felt that he was kind of leaning towards Pale Mimosa. There wasn't much in it, but I was leaning towards Pale Mimosa too. Her final piece of work before the Leger was very, very good, whereas Voleuse De Coeurs's was only ordinary, and that swung it for me. I rode Pale Mimosa.

It just shows you: sometimes when a horse's final piece of work before a big race is very good, they can underperform in the big race. Pale Mimosa underperformed in the Irish Leger.

That was Voleuse De Coeurs for you, too. While she wouldn't always impress you with her work in the mornings, she was always at her best on the racecourse, and she was very good in the Irish St Leger. Chris Hayes rode her, and she was the best horse in the race on the day by far. I saw her moving up on my outside as we rounded the home turn while I was flat to the boards on Pale Mimosa on the inside, and I thought, Ah, here we go. She hit the front on the run to the two-furlong pole, and she just went clear. It was great for the mare, great for Lady O'Reilly, great for Chris Hayes, and great for Dermot, of course, and all the team, but it was a tough one for me. It was a Classic winner that got away.

And just to compound matters, she was sold after the race to Australia, so I never got to ride her again.

I did get to ride Pale Mimosa again, though. I won a listed race at Leopardstown on her in July 2014, on her seasonal debut, and then we went to York and won the Group 2 Lonsdale Cup, where we beat the Queen's mare Estimate, who had won the Ascot Gold

Cup the previous season and who won the Doncaster Cup on her next run.

Pale Mimosa was very good that day; she was very strong all the way to the line. That was the real Pale Mimosa.

The 2013 championship was well out of reach by the time the Irish St Leger was run. Joseph was having an unbelievable season. He had ridden lots of big winners, including Magician in the Irish 2000 Guineas and Declaration Of War in the Queen Anne and in the Juddmonte International, and he was well clear of me in the championship by the time mid-September rolled around. He rode 126 winners in Ireland that season, which was a record in an Irish Flat racing season, beating Mick Kinane's record by 11. There was no arguing with that total. I finished second again, 43 behind Joseph, but 29 ahead of Chris Hayes in third.

My appetite for rides and for winners remained as strong as ever, though. I wanted to ride in every race. If there was a race in which I didn't have a ride for Dermot, I wanted Kevin to be on to other trainers, getting me as good a ride in that race as he could get me. I wanted to have a full book of rides every day, and if I didn't have a full book, I was disappointed.

Maybe I should have done it differently, maybe I should have been concentrating on quality over quantity, conserving myself, but my attitude was that if I was there anyway, if I was at the races, I might as well ride in a race. Better that than sitting in the weigh room watching it. If you had a ride in a race, you had a chance of winning it. One thing was certain: if you were sitting watching the race in the weigh room, you had no chance of winning it.

In early spring of 2014, I got myself ready to try to win the championship back.

CROSSING MOORE'S BRIDGE

We drove over Moore's Bridge and it hit me. The cars, the traffic, the crowds.

It's a landmark, Moore's Bridge. The bridge that goes over the railway line on your way to the Curragh. You get your first glimpse of the racecourse when you cross Moore's Bridge. It had been a long time since we had seen people in the stands at the Curragh from Moore's Bridge. Years ago, on Irish Derby day, when you had 30,000 or 40,000 people there on the day, you would have seen people in the stands when you were going racing. And we saw them again that morning, people gathering more than an hour before the first race.

'My God.'

The kids were unusually quiet in the back of the car. It was just like a normal race day for them in many ways. They were always used to going to the Curragh, they were used to the panic in the morning, getting dressed, getting ready, all the hullabaloo, getting out the door on time. Up to that point, that day had been no different from any other in that respect.

But it was different in a thousand ways. For starters, I was with them. Usually, even when the kids were going racing, I would have been gone long before them, up the road early, to get there in good time, and Frances would follow later with the kids. So it was different before we ever got to the racecourse. Then we saw the people on the stands, and that was different too.

I could feel Frances watching me from the passenger seat. I just looked ahead, hands on the steering wheel, eyes on the road. I was nervous. It wasn't nervous like before-a-big-race nervous. I had driven that road many times before, often with big rides ahead of me, pressure rides. It was different that day, though. It was daunting. Scary.

It was Irish St Leger day at the Curragh, one of the most important days on the Irish racing calendar, with three Group 1 races. Yet some people were calling it the Pat Smullen Race day, and that was just bizarre.

❖

Hannah, our eldest, was 16 at the time, so she had a bit of an inkling that this was different, that this was a big day, but she probably hadn't fully grasped the magnitude of it. None of us really had.

The idea had grown and run away with itself. A million euro, I'd said to Margaret Heffernan. Raise a million euro. What was I thinking? A million euro was a massive amount of money.

What had started out as an idea for a charity race – another charity race – had morphed into something special, something unique. A race for champion jockeys.

There are lots of charity races, and they raise lots of money for really worthy causes, but this was a one-off and, if it was going to be a one-off, it needed to be special.

It was a big ask, asking so many riders to come out of retirement for the Pat Smullen Champions Race for Cancer Trials Ireland. But they were all brilliant. Every one of them. Nobody hesitated. Ruby Walsh said afterwards that there are some people in the world who, when they ask you to do something, you just do it. It was all very humbling, really.

That feeling of humility continued to the day and through it. From the time that we walked into the racecourse through the turnstiles. People coming up to me and shaking my hand, wishing me well. I couldn't go 10 steps without the next person coming up to me and saying, 'Good luck with everything.' I was a little bit overcome by the whole thing.

Eva Haefner very kindly gave us the Moyglare Stud box for the day, for the jockeys who were riding in the race and their families, so it was great to have a base there, to be able to relax there for a little while.

The racing started and the day flew, helter-skelter from start to finish, and some of the stories, you couldn't have written them. Tarnawa winning the Blandford Stakes was fantastic, for the boss,

Dermot Weld, with Chris Hayes wearing the famous green-and-red Aga Khan colours that I had worn so often in the past. Pinatubo, the champion juvenile colt, putting up the performance that he put up in winning the National Stakes by nine lengths.

And then Search For A Song winning the Irish St Leger.

It was a pity that Eva couldn't have been there to see her filly win the Irish St Leger. She and Moyglare Stud were always massive supporters of mine, during my riding career for sure, and probably even more so after I retired. Search For A Song was Moyglare's first Irish St Leger winner, and she was the first three-year-old filly to win the race in 30 years.

It was the way she won it, too. I watched the race with Eva's children, Chiara and Mischa. I didn't say it to them at the time, but their filly was so keen and free in the early stages of the race that I was certain she had no chance of lasting all the way home. I was certain that she would weaken in the home straight. Everybody was. But she didn't. She kept going for Chris Hayes. It was a remarkable performance. Eva messaged me straight after the race. She was thrilled. And another Irish St Leger for the boss. And for that to happen half an hour before the champions' race. It was just part of a remarkable day.

I got a bit emotional when we were walking into the parade ring. The lads went in first, AP leading them in. I was the last to go in. The crowd were brilliant, clapping and cheering. It was some atmosphere, despite the rain, or perhaps even enhanced by the rain.

That was when it hit me hardest, though, that I wasn't riding in the race.

I was supposed to ride in the race. The intention was always that I would ride. Then I had a setback a couple of weeks beforehand. We found out that the PARP inhibitor wasn't doing its job, and that the cancer had returned. It just wasn't possible. I just wasn't up to it. I needed all the energy that I could muster so that I could fight to survive. I wouldn't have had the reserves of energy that I would have needed in order to prepare to ride in the race.

We had a media day in Joseph O'Brien's, too, the week before the race. Joseph was great; he couldn't have been more helpful than he was with everything, including organising the media day at his yard with Barbara White from Horse Racing Ireland. They invited the media down to see some horses work and to interview the lads, and I wasn't well enough to go to that either. Physically and psychologically, I just couldn't face it. I concentrated on being strong enough to be able to go to the races on the day, which, thankfully, I was.

I would have loved to have been riding, though. The lads were brilliant, including me in everything, and the people were brilliant. The racegoers. It was as close as I could have got to riding in the race without actually riding in the race. In many ways, I was part of it all.

But in many other ways, I wasn't part of it at all. I wasn't competing. And it struck me there, as I stood waiting to go into the parade ring, that I wasn't riding. More than that, the realisation suddenly dawned on me that I wouldn't be riding in any race ever again, and that hit me like a hammer.

Of course, I had known for a while that I wouldn't ride again. I knew it in my guts shortly after I got sick, even though I didn't announce my retirement officially until a little while after that. But then, I was looking forward to the race, and then I was caught up in the organising and in the build-up.

It was just that moment, though, when I stood there, at the entrance to the parade ring, quiet in my head with noise all around me, and I thought, I will never ride in a race again. I would have loved to have been going out there with the nine lads, in my breeches and boots and silks. Get legged up in the parade ring and off down to the start. I knew that I would never do that again, and I got quite emotional.

It was an emotional few minutes. There was a wave of emotion in the parade ring, and I was swept away on it. Cameras and microphones everywhere, and every one of them wanted a little bit of time with me. I didn't mind. I was happy to speak to whoever wanted to speak with me.

I was nervous, though. I was nervous for the lads, nervous that something would go wrong. The last thing I wanted was for a horse to get injured or, worse, for one of the jockeys to get injured.

I was never worried about injury when I was riding. It was a part of it, we all knew that; riding horses has always been a dangerous pursuit. Ambulances follow you as you work. But I never thought of the possibility of a fall or an injury when I was riding. On that day, though, it was one of the main things on my mind.

It would have been on me. My fault. My responsibility. I had asked all the lads to ride, and they had all said yes. If anything went wrong – 'Well, Pat Smullen asked us to do it.'

Of course, none of them ever said that, or ever made me feel like that. They all wanted to ride and, unsurprisingly, they all wanted to win. All nine of them have that competitive streak, that will to win that all champions have. It wasn't just a saunter up the Curragh for a bit of a laugh.

It was a competition, make no mistake. The lads took it very seriously. People don't realise what some of them had to go through in order just to ride in the race. AP McCoy had to lose a stone to get down to his riding weight. They could have all said no, but they didn't.

It was all nice beforehand though, all great craic, all for a good cause, raising money, all for Pat, all of that – but every single one of them was desperate to win the race. Even on the day, before the race, they were in the zone. None of them relaxed until after the race.

I watched as each one of them left the parade ring. AP McCoy and Kieren Fallon and Ted Durcan and Paul Carberry and Richard Hughes and Joseph O'Brien and Charlie Swan and Johnny Murtagh and Ruby Walsh, champions all. They had won 66 championships between them. Unbelievable. And I wondered: was there ever, in the history of horse racing, a group of jockeys so talented and so accomplished, who had scaled the heights that they had scaled between them, assembled for one race?

Amazing that we had got to that stage.

I watched the race on the big screen from the parade ring. There was no point in trying to make my way back up to the box or up to the stands to watch it. And, despite my primary concern being for everybody, that everybody would come back safely, I still found myself getting involved in the race as a competition.

AP led on Quizical from the start, and he wasn't headed. Ruby challenged on the far side on Aussie Valentine at the two-furlong marker, and at first I thought that he was going to win. Then Johnny challenged him on the stands side on Red Striker, and I thought *he* was going to win. And all the while, Carberry was moving up on the fair rail on Katiymann, typical Carberry, swinging along. But AP had kept a little in reserve, and Quizical picked up again inside the final furlong when he went for him. There was no way McCoy was going to let anyone past him!

There was some cheer for them as they went to the line. There was some atmosphere. It was great that it was a close finish, because the crowd really got involved, cheering them home. And Dessie Scahill's commentary was brilliant. My first reaction was, Thank God, they're all home safely. It was only then that I thought, That was some race.

The big screen focused in on AP, and you could see the delight in his face. He waved to the stands. He was beaming. It was as if he had just won the Gold Cup. They pulled up, the lads congratulated AP, and then they all paraded back up the track, back up past the stands again, all nine of them in a line. The crowd clapped and cheered again and the lads lapped it all up.

But the highlight of the day for me was when they came back into the winner's enclosure, the reception that they got. You could see the people swarming down from the stands towards the winner's enclosure to welcome them back in, and that was an unbelievable sight. It was great to experience an atmosphere like that at the Curragh again, too.

It was a mixture of everything, the day that was in it, all the emotion, the fact that it was such a good race, such a great spectacle, a tight finish. There was the fact that all those jockeys, all of them household names, were all there in one race. And AP McCoy winning it, beating Ruby Walsh and Johnny Murtagh and Paul Carberry in the finish. You couldn't have written a better outcome. It was all of that together. All the ingredients were there.

I was quite overcome by it all. It just all caught up with me there, in the winner's enclosure, with AP doing his flying dismount and everything. (Frankie Dettori he isn't!) And I thought, How good is racing? For all these people to be here, in the rain, to come to the Curragh for starters, and then to flock to the winner's enclosure like they did.

Even people outside of racing. I saw people at the races that day, local people, people I knew, whom I had never seen at the races before. I was overwhelmed by it all, really.

I was thrilled for Sheila and John Lavery too, trainer and owner of Quizical. It meant an awful lot to them. Sheila said that she would have loved if I had ridden Quizical for her but, if I couldn't, then AP was next best. Sheila is brilliant. I rode a lot of work for her early in my career, and I became very friendly with her and John. They were always very good to me. John is a great man. He deserves all the luck he gets. He wanted to run two horses in the race. That's just the type of man he is.

A couple of weeks earlier, Lester Piggott had presented John with his prize after one of his horses had won, and he thought that it couldn't get any better in racing, Lester presenting him with his prize. And then it did: AP McCoy winning on his horse. I'd say, in years to come, he will be happier with a picture of AP on his mantelpiece than he would have been with a picture of me!

There were presentations and more interviews. Eva's children, Mischa and Chiara, made a presentation to me, just a recognition of my career, and of riding for Moyglare Stud, which was lovely.

The lads all came up to Eva's box with their wives and partners and families, and we had good craic there. I think a lot of the lads appreciated that their children were there. AP, for example, his daughter Eve would probably be old enough to remember him riding, but his son Archie was only about 18 months old when he retired. He's six now. It was great for AP that Archie could see him ride again.

And Ruby's girls and Richard's kids and Paul's kids. All of them. It was great that all the families were there to enjoy it. And all AP wanted afterwards was food!

I think that Frances got a bit emotional when the race finished. The fact that I hadn't ridden in it. She watched the race in the box with the kids. My mother got a bit emotional then too. It was an emotional day.

It was a one-off, it was always going to be a one-off, so it was great that it went as well as it did. You couldn't do it again. It would be wrong to try to do it again. You couldn't expect that the same people would be as generous again with their donations or with their time.

We all went to the Hanged Man's restaurant that evening in Milltown – Pat Keane's place, our usual haunt – all the riders and all their partners. It was a great night, and it rounded off a fantastic day.

We were late enough getting back, I'd say it was about 12 o'clock by the time we got home, and I went to bed: worn out, drained, but hugely relieved and satisfied. The day was all that I had hoped it would be.

CHAPTER 29

The 2014 season started off well and it just rolled along. I won the Park Express Stakes on Vote Often and I won the Leopardstown 2000 Guineas Trial on Go For Goal, so I had two Group races in the bag before the end of March.

I rode a filly for Eddie Lynam on her racecourse debut at the Curragh on Irish Guineas weekend, Anthem Alexander, and she ran a nice race to finish sixth. The ground was soft that day and she took a blow with me, which wasn't surprising. Eddie always liked his horses to come on for their first runs. She was a lovely filly, though, a big filly; she looked like a colt in the ring, and she showed lots of speed. I was thinking that she could do even better over five furlongs, and I told Eddie that I would like to ride her when she next ran. Noel O'Callaghan owned her, and he was happy enough to allow me to stay on her.

Her next run was over five furlongs at Tipperary two weeks later, on good to firm ground. So five furlongs on fast ground at Tipperary, totally different from six furlongs on soft ground at the Curragh. I thought that she would win, and she duly did, by seven lengths. She was electric that day – she was all speed.

The obvious race for her after that was the Queen Mary Stakes, the second race on the second day at Royal Ascot.

In the meantime, I had won the Amethyst Stakes at

Leopardstown on Mustajeeb, a really nice colt owned by Sheikh Hamdan and trained by Dermot. It was a good performance by a three-year-old, beating the older horses at that early stage of the season. He was the only three-year-old in the race. The obvious target for him after that was the Irish 2000 Guineas, and he ran well in that to finish third, but he just didn't get home over a mile on the soft ground against Kingman. Kingman was immense that day anyway – we might not have beaten him over any distance or on any ground!

I thought that Mustajeeb was a fast horse, that he would benefit from a drop down in trip, and Dermot thought similarly, so he geared Mustajeeb up for the Jersey Stakes over seven furlongs, the first race on the second day of Royal Ascot.

Sheikh Hamdan had two other horses in the Jersey Stakes that year – Muwaary and Anjaal – so I ended up wearing the third colours, the pink cap; but it didn't matter. It didn't mean that Mustajeeb was going to run any more slowly just because I was wearing the pink cap instead of the blue-and-white striped one, or even the black one. As it turned out, he ran quite quickly, he showed lots of pace and he finished off his race strongly to beat Muwaary by a length, with the two of us clear of the rest.

It was great to get another Royal Ascot winner on the board, my fifth. Great to ride another Royal Ascot winner for Dermot, and my first Royal Ascot winner for Sheikh Hamdan. Sheikh Hamdan was a massive supporter of mine all the way throughout my career and afterwards as well. Arguably, even more importantly afterwards.

When I went out to ride Anthem Alexander in the Queen Mary Stakes, just about 20 minutes after I had dismounted from Mustajeeb's back in the winner's enclosure, I was bursting with confidence. A Royal Ascot win will do that to you.

Anthem Alexander was brilliant too. She got into her racing

rhythm quite quickly, just behind the front rank. A nice gap opened up in front of me between Ryan Moore and Victor Espinoza, and I just let her move into it. Suddenly we were in the front rank and travelled well on the run to the furlong marker. We got home by a neck.

Again, that was some feeling. My sixth Royal Ascot winner, just 35 minutes after my fifth, and the first two winners on the day. I was delighted to be able to repay the faith that Noel O'Callaghan had shown in me, and I was delighted for Eddie.

I went to Gowran Park on 21 September that year with 98 winners on the board for the season. I won the two-year-olds' maiden on Intransive for the boss and Prince Khalid Abdullah and, an hour and a half later, I won the feature race on the day, the Group 3 Denny Cordell Lavarack & Lanwades Stud Stakes, on Brooch, also for the boss and Prince Khalid.

That was a big deal for me, 100 winners. I played it down in the media – I said that it was a nice thing to do, a nice achievement – but, in reality, it had been a big objective for me for a little while. I always thought that, if I could ride 100 winners in a season, that that would be good enough to win the championship. It wasn't an automatic: Joseph had ridden 126 winners in 2013, but he was the first person in a decade to ride over a hundred winners, and it had never happened that a jockey had ridden 100 winners in an Irish Flat racing season and hadn't won the championship.

It didn't happen that year either. I ended the season on 108 winners. And the 2014 champion.

My rivalry with my nephew Joseph reached a peak on British Champions' Day at Ascot in 2014. It was the first race on the day, the British Champions Long Distance Cup. I was riding

Forgotten Rules for Dermot and Moyglare. Joseph was riding the favourite, Leading Light, for Aidan.

I loved Forgotten Rules. He was so talented, but he was fragile. He was racing for just the third time in his life when we took him to Ascot for the Long Distance Cup in October, but we fancied him quite a bit; I thought that his talent would more than make up for his lack of experience. It was an ideal race for him: two miles and soft ground. That was his race.

The Long Distance Cup in 2014 was Forgotten Rules at his best. I settled him towards the back of the field early on, I allowed them at it up front, I was happy just to get him settled and get him covered up at the back. I tracked Joseph up from Swinley Bottom to the home turn. I was four wide around the home turn, but I didn't mind. On soft ground, I never minded going wide around the home turn at Ascot.

I came up on the outside of Joseph and I asked Forgotten Rules to pick up. When I did, he lugged a little to his right. That was just his inexperience, and he moved sharply to his right, into the other horses.

I had my whip in my left hand. I should have switched it into my right, but I didn't. I gave him a smack with my left hand, and he moved to his right again. At the same time, Rab Havlin's horse Marzocco moved a bit to his left, and Leading Light was the main sufferer. He was in between the two of us. Joseph had to snatch up and take his horse back. It looked bad. I shouldn't have allowed my horse to lug in like that.

That incident obviously didn't help Leading Light, but it didn't help Forgotten Rules either. By the time I got him back balanced and racing in a straight line, Pallasator and Andrea Atzeni had kicked three lengths clear. Forgotten Rules was strong and tough, though. We got up level with Pallasator as we raced inside the final furlong, and we went clear. It was a top-class performance by a top-class horse, and it was great for me to bag another big race for Dermot and for Moyglare.

The stewards suspended me for three days for the incident that occurred inside the two-furlong marker, and I didn't complain. I couldn't. I deserved every one of those days.

CHAPTER 30

I let another Cheltenham Bumper get away in 2014.

Not because Forgotten Rules didn't run in it (although I probably would have found a way to not win it on him too!), but because Vigil did.

Vigil was a nice horse. He had finished second in a bumper at Fairyhouse on New Year's Day on his racecourse debut under Derek O'Connor, and he had stepped forward from that to win a good bumper at Leopardstown on Hennessy Gold Cup day under Robbie McNamara.

I had to choose between Vigil and Silver Concorde, and there wasn't much in it. Silver Concorde was another nice young horse who had won his bumper at Leopardstown's Christmas Festival earlier that National Hunt season. Both horses had been working well in the lead-up to Cheltenham, and it was just a case of me choosing the right one.

Vigil liked soft ground, Silver Concorde liked good ground, and at the time of jockey bookings, it looked like it was going to come up on the soft side, so I chose Vigil, which meant that Robbie McNamara would ride Silver Concorde. That was me not reckoning with how quickly Cheltenham's racecourse could dry out.

I walked the track that day – I walked the track nearly every day that I was racing, but at Cheltenham I was always meticulous. Every year that I was riding there, I walked every inch of the bumper track. And that year, I couldn't believe how dry the track had become. They were calling the ground good, good to soft in places, but I couldn't find many good to soft places.

I had Vigil in a good position from early, just behind the leaders and plenty of racing room, about three or four off the inside rail. We travelled well down the hill and we moved up on the outside to join the front rank on the run to the home turn. We moved up on the outside of Patrick Mullins on the leader, Black Hercules, as we rounded the home turn, but Patrick picked up again as we straightened up, and my horse just couldn't pick up well enough on the ground to get past him.

Then I saw Robbie's yellow cap over to my left. Dr Ronan Lambe's colours. Oh no! Robbie swooped up the inside, hit the front as we raced through the wings of the final flight of hurdles, and powered up the hill in front of all of us. All I could do was keep Vigil going, and he did keep on bravely up the hill, but he kept on into fifth place, not into first place.

Robbie gave Silver Concorde a fantastic ride. He delivered him late, a typical Robbie McNamara ride, and used his turn of foot. It was a first Cheltenham Festival win for Robbie, and he rode his second the following day when, again, he was very good on Spring Heeled in the Kim Muir. Robbie had a terrible fall at Wexford just over a year later and suffered injuries that saw him paralysed from the waist down. It was horrendous. Very sad. He was a top-class jockey.

In time, I learned to be delighted for Robbie, that he had ridden his first Cheltenham Festival winner, and for Dermot, his first Champion Bumper. But that took a while. In the immediate aftermath of the race, I was only sorry for me. Even when, flying back home from Cheltenham that night, Frances and I had a glass of wine with Dermot at the airport; he was celebrating and we were celebrating with him on the outside, but on the inside I was in knots.

That was as close as I got in the Champion Bumper at Cheltenham. Silver Concorde in 2014 was up there with Rite Of Passage in 2009 for me as one that got away. They were the two that got away. I had a feeling after Silver Concorde that it just wasn't going to happen, and it didn't. I rode Vigil again in the race in 2015. We finished fifth once more, my fourth attempt, my fourth miss, and I didn't get to ride in the race again.

Hugo Palmer was very good to me too. I rode a horse for Hugo, Short Squeeze, in the Royal Hunt Cup at Royal Ascot in 2014. We finished down the field. Short Squeeze was just too keen through the early stages of the race, he used up too much energy, so he didn't give himself a chance of getting home.

Hugo fitted a tongue-tie and a set of cheekpieces for his next run, in a big one-mile handicap at York's Ebor meeting two months later, and he asked me to ride him again. The plan was to drop Short Squeeze out, get him settled and deliver him late. It was one of those races in which everything dropped right for me, and when everything dropped right for you on a hold-up horse in a competitive handicap like that, you could look like a hero!

We were drawn wide, so I got him back in the field and settled and towards the inside before we raced out of the back straight. I took my time in the home straight, too. We were well back in the field passing the three-furlong marker, but we were still travelling well, and I knew that he didn't want to be in front for too long, so I waited. I charted a path among horses, I moved to the left as we raced to the furlong pole, and he picked up. A gap developed right in front of us, and Short Squeeze had the pace to get into it. After that, it was just a case of whether or not we had enough ground to make up the two lengths or so that we needed to make up on Top Notch Tonto. And we did, just about. We got up in the final strides and we won by a head.

It looked great, as those hold-up rides often do when they work out. But actually, I was only doing what I needed to do in order to give Short Squeeze the best chance of winning that I could give him. He had to be ridden like that – he had to be dropped out and ridden cold. Even so, that ride got lots of positive comments, and it probably led to an even greater demand for my services in Britain, which was nice.

I rode Covert Love for Hugo, too, in the Irish Oaks the following season. She was owned by a good friend of mine, Mark McStay, in partnership with Hugo Merry. Dermot didn't have anything in the Irish Oaks that year, so she was a great ride to pick up, and we won well. That was fantastic, my first Irish Oaks, another Irish Classic.

I rode Covert Love in the Yorkshire Oaks at York next time, when we were just beaten by Kevin Manning on Jim Bolger's filly Pleascach, but Covert Love bounced back to form in October when she carried me to victory in the Prix de l'Opéra at Longchamp on Prix de l'Arc de Triomphe day.

CHAPTER 31

We thought that Zawraq was an exciting horse from the time that we started to get to know him. Bred and owned by Sheikh Hamdan, he was by Kildangan Stud's top-class stallion Shamardal and he was out of a half-sister to Sheikh Hamdan's 1000 Guineas winner Ghanaati, so he was bred to be a champion.

And he started showing ability from very early in his life. Even as a very young horse, he was impressive, and when he started doing a little bit more at home as the summer went on, he did everything very easily. He made his racecourse debut at Leopardstown in October 2014, and he kept on well to beat a well-bred and expensive newcomer of Aidan O'Brien's, Sir Isaac Newton.

I set out to make the running on Zawraq that day and, when Sir Isaac Newton came up on our outside a furlong out, and actually headed us, Zawraq battled back well and we got back up to win by half a length, the two of us pulling well clear of the third horse.

I loved the way that he battled. I loved the attitude that he showed, his will to win. Put that along with his obvious talent, and the sky was the limit.

Zawraq had everything that you wanted in a racehorse. He had all the attributes. He had the breeding, he had the talent, he had the attitude. He was lovely-mannered, too, a kind horse who did everything easily for you, and who had a great attitude to life.

He made his three-year-old debut in the Guineas Trial at Leopardstown in April, and won easily. The ground was very soft that day, but it didn't matter to him. He had so much talent. After that, the Epsom Derby was his only goal.

Everything went smoothly with him after the Guineas Trial. He came out of the race great and he continued to thrive and to impress in his work. His final piece of serious work was on the Tuesday before the Derby in early June, up the Old Vic gallop on the Curragh, and he was spectacular. Dermot came over to me afterwards with a big smile on his face. I probably had a big smile on my face too. We both knew how well he had worked and we both knew that he had a great chance of winning the Epsom Derby.

Before we walked off the Old Vic, though, disaster. I could feel Zawraq take a lame step, so I jumped down off him and I could see that there was a little bit of swelling in his joint. In an instant, I went from the high of a phenomenal piece of work, the rush that that gave me, to the low of knowing that something was wrong. We got him back to the yard quickly, and then he was straight over to Joe O'Donnell, Dermot's brilliant vet. Joe and Claire Hawkes had a look at him, and the prognosis was not good.

Turned out, poor Zawraq had fractured his off-fore cannon bone.

Of course, I learned later that more devastating things can happen in life, but at the time I was fairly inconsolable. I knew, at that stage of my career, how difficult it was to happen upon a good horse, a truly top-class horse who would even be deserving of his or her place in the top races. So to have a horse like Zawraq, the ability that he had, the potential that he had, and to see it all go up in smoke in an instant at the top of the Old Vic that morning, it was devastating. That morning was my worst morning ever on the gallops.

Zawraq was never the same horse again after his injury. He didn't race again that season, he didn't race again until late in 2016, when he ran well to finish second in a listed race back at Leopardstown. And he ran twice the following season, but he never came back to what he was and he never got to where he could have got to.

The 2015 season was still a very good season, though. I won the Heritage Stakes and the Mooresbridge Stakes on Fascinating Rock, and we finished second in the Group 1 Tattersalls Gold Cup – we went down by just a neck to Al Kazeem.

That was a fantastic renewal of the Tattersalls Gold Cup. Al Kazeem was an Eclipse winner who had won the Prix d'Harcourt in France earlier that season. Subsequent King George winner Postponed was also in that Tattersalls Gold Cup, as was The Grey Gatsby, who had beaten Australia in the Irish Champion Stakes at Leopardstown the previous September. That was one of the strongest renewals of the Tattersalls Gold Cup ever run, and Fascinating Rock ran a massive race to get as close as he did. And he went one better in the race the following season, when he stayed on well on soft ground to beat Found by almost four lengths.

I won the Enterprise Stakes at Leopardstown on Fascinating Rock in September 2015, and then we went to Ascot to take on Found and Jack Hobbs in the Champion Stakes. Jack Hobbs was a short-priced favourite for that race. He had won the Irish Derby by five lengths and he had warmed up for the Champion Stakes nicely by winning the September Stakes at Kempton. Found was a top-class filly of Aidan's. She had finished second to the Derby winner Golden Horn in the Irish Champion Stakes the previous month – a race in which I had finished third on Free Eagle – and the following month she got her revenge on him in the Breeders' Cup Turf.

Fascinating Rock was a 10/1 shot for the Champion Stakes, but I didn't regard him as a 10/1 shot. It was an ideal race for him, 10 furlongs on soft ground, and his work beforehand had been very good. As well as that, there was always going to be a good pace in the race. Godolphin had a pacemaker in there for Jack Hobbs, Maverick Wave, and he went fast from the outset. That was ideal for Fascinating Rock. He always wanted a good pace to aim at. Fast pace, soft ground, 10 furlongs.

It was one of those races in which everything went right for me. I just allowed my horse to settle into his race. We were well back early on, but I was happy with that; I knew that the pace was strong on the soft ground. The longer the race went on, the more my confidence grew. He travelled so well for me that it appeared as if he was getting stronger with every stride that he took.

We were still only eighth or ninth when we turned for home, but I knew that I had plenty of horse underneath me. As we turned into the straight, I had a decision to make: go outside and give away ground but ensure a clear passage up the home straight, or save ground, go inside, and try to pick my way though. Over the years, I had learned that it was difficult to go wide into the home straight at Ascot and win. That day, I would have had to go fairly wide in order to get a clear path, and on soft ground it can be easier to pick your way through than on fast ground – the gaps can open up more easily – so I went inside, and the gaps did open up. One of those races.

We closed on the leaders and I went to go inside the leader, Jack Hobbs, as we got to the furlong pole. We got a gap, clear sailing. I knew that we had the measure of Jack Hobbs as we raced inside the final furlong and, while out of the corner of my eye I could see Ryan Moore on Found closing to my right,

I knew that my horse wasn't stopping. He stayed 10 furlongs really well off a fast pace on soft ground, and he was strong all the way to the line.

That was another good day for me at Ascot. I loved Ascot; I loved riding good horses at Ascot. I always thought that I rode the track well. That made sense: if you were good at something, it usually followed that you enjoyed it, or if you enjoyed something, it usually followed that you were good at it, or that you got good at it. I put a lot of that down to Ruby Walsh. When we were living in Carlow, I had a lot of conversations with Ruby about riding, different theories, different strategies, how to ride different tracks. He was obviously a National Hunt jockey and I was a Flat jockey, but the same principles applied. And Ruby said to me one day that you couldn't go wide at Ascot, that it was very hard to win if you went wide. That always stuck with me.

I didn't go wide on Free Eagle, either, in the Prince of Wales's Stakes at Royal Ascot in 2015.

My plan was to be handy on Free Eagle that day, but not necessarily to lead. The French horse Gailo Chop went on, but his rider, Julien Augé, steadied it up as we raced out of Swinley Bottom. I didn't want to get caught too far back in the field if it developed into a sprint finish off a sedate pace, so I allowed Free Eagle to move up a little, so that we could just sit up on the outside of the leader as we raced to the home turn.

I was happy with my position there. I didn't need to go to the front; I just wanted to have a forward position so that we could start the sprint finish with a head start on most of my rivals. That was always my thinking: you didn't want to be too far back off a slow pace. A horse can only go so fast and, if a race develops into a sprint, you are usually at a disadvantage if you are starting the sprint from behind.

I sat up on the outside of Julien Augé as we rounded the home turn, and I sat for a little bit as we straightened up. I could hear all the others congregating behind me, but still I waited. With my prominent position, the longer I could delay, the shorter I could make the sprint, the better my chance was of winning.

Frankie Dettori came up on my outside on Western Hymn as we passed the two-furlong marker, and I couldn't wait any longer. I went for Free Eagle and he picked up, and we went about a length clear. I thought that that would be enough, and it was, but only just. He took a blow with me 50 yards out; he was running on empty for the last 50 yards. Everything was quickening, but we held on. Just. Jamie Spencer on The Grey Gatsby came at us. He closed and closed as we raced to the line; he got very close, but I knew that we hit the line well. I thought that we had held on and we did. By a short head.

It was another super training performance by Dermot. Free Eagle was a really talented horse, and we thought that he could have been a Derby horse too, but he was fragile. He was immature. He raced twice as a two-year-old, but he didn't make it to the track as a three-year-old until September 2014, when he returned and won the Group 3 KPMG Enterprise Stakes at Leopardstown.

He was making his debut as a four-year-old in the Prince of Wales's Stakes at Royal Ascot. That wasn't ideal – there is no substitute for match practice – but the way that the race turned out, it was more a test of speed than it was of race fitness, and that suited us well. Free Eagle had lots of speed.

I was happy with the ride that I gave him too. I was happy that I adopted tactics to suit the race as it developed. I knew that Free Eagle had a really good turn of foot, and I was happy that I was able to get into a position that would be able to use that turn of foot to best effect.

That was a very satisfying win. It was one of those rare

occasions on which you felt that the ride that you gave a horse made the difference between winning and losing. And given that it was at the highest level, in a Group 1 race at Royal Ascot, one of the biggest stages in world racing, I got a big kick out of that. I'd say that it was the best ride that I ever gave a horse in my career.

Free Eagle was also at the centre of one of the most frustrating races of my career. It was his next run after he had won the Prince of Wales's Stakes, in the Irish Champion Stakes at Leopardstown. That was some race in terms of quality, as the Irish Champion Stakes usually was. The Derby winner and Eclipse winner Golden Horn was favourite, and there was strength in depth: Cirrus Des Aigles and Found and The Grey Gatsby and Pleascach and Highland Reel.

I was very happy through the race. We got a good position from early, just behind the leaders and one off the inside rail, Kevin Manning and Pleascach on my inside, Frankie Dettori and Golden Horn and Joseph O'Brien and Highland Reel just in front of me, disputing the running. I moved up on the outside of Joseph as we rounded the home turn. It meant going three wide, but I wanted to get close to Frankie. I didn't want to be too far behind him when he kicked for home.

Frankie started to row away just before we entered the home straight, but Free Eagle was able to cover the move without me asking him for too much. We were about half a length behind him as we raced inside the final furlong when, suddenly and inexplicably, Golden Horn jinked to his right and cannoned into us. It took me completely by surprise and poor Free Eagle didn't know what was happening. He had to check his stride, he lost all momentum, and we had to start again. Frankie's horse got going again too in front, and we couldn't reel him in. To make matters worse, Seamie Heffernan sneaked up on our inside on Found, and beat us for second place by half a length.

I always had a very good relationship with Seamie, but I cursed him that day! Seamie did what Seamie always did best: got his horse up to pick up as much prize money as he could pick up. But once we hadn't finished second, the stewards couldn't award the race to us even if they decided to disqualify Golden Horn.

It was nobody's fault, it wasn't Frankie's fault, it was just one of those things. Frankie had his whip in his right hand, and still his horse moved to his right. He just shied at something. Even so, I have no doubt that, if we had finished second, if Found hadn't picked up the pieces and sneaked into second place, the stewards would have awarded us the race, and that would have been fair. But, seeing as we didn't finish second, if they had disqualified Golden Horn, they would have had to award the race to Found, and Found was probably the third best horse in the race on the day. They could have only promoted us to second place, and that would have been no good to me at the time. When we passed the winning post in third place, I didn't care if they disqualified Golden Horn or not. Second was no good. I didn't care what they did once I knew that we couldn't get the race.

It was always all about winning. It was only about winning.

I did win the championship again in 2015, and I broke through the 100-winner barrier again. I ended the season with 103 winners, 38 more than my closest pursuer, Colin Keane.

CHAPTER 32

Harzand was a nice colt as a juvenile, but he wasn't anything out of the ordinary, really. It took him a little while to come to hand, but he did get to race as a juvenile – he finished fifth in a one-mile maiden at Gowran Park in September 2015.

Things changed after that. That run seemed to transform him. It happened sometimes with young horses, after a run; when the penny started to drop with them, when they realised what they were being asked to do, they could turn inside out.

Harzand didn't race again as a juvenile, but he did do a few more pieces of work before Dermot put him away for the winter, and he improved for every piece. We knew going into the winter that he was a really, really good maiden, that he definitely had the potential to be a stakes horse. But a Derby winner? Not in my wildest dreams.

He made his debut as a three-year-old at Cork the following March. We expected him to win that day, but we didn't expect him to win it by 16 lengths.

We knew then that we had a proper racehorse on our hands, and the obvious target for him was the Ballysax Stakes, a Derby trial, a Group 3 race at Leopardstown – see if he could step forward again. He had to step forward again because he had to take on better horses in the Ballysax Stakes, including three horses of Aidan O'Brien's and two of Jim Bolger's. The ground was heavy again, but there was a different rhythm to the race, a much faster tempo.

It took him a little while to sort himself out. I had to ride him a bit passing the three-furlong marker before the home turn, and we were only sixth as we straightened up with two furlongs to run, but he got his act together when we got racing up the home straight. When we met the rising ground he showed a great turn of foot. We wore down Idaho deep inside the final furlong, and we went on to beat him by over a length, with Idaho coming over seven lengths clear of the rest.

The main talk after the Ballysax among the pundits was of the St Leger, not of the Derby, which was strange in a way. The Ballysax was a Derby trial, but people just seemed to think that Harzand's main attribute was his stamina. The St Leger is run over a mile and six and a half furlongs at Doncaster in mid-September; the Derby is run over a mile and a half at Epsom in early June. I was adamant that he had the speed to be a Derby horse.

His final piece of work was on the Tuesday before the Saturday of the Derby, and his work was very good. He pulled up sound, too – we didn't need a repeat of what happened with Zawraq – and he was really well. He was in tremendous form. I didn't know if he was going to be good enough to win the Derby, but I knew that week that he was better than he had ever been.

Everything went smoothly for the rest of the week, too, and Harzand flew out early on Saturday morning for Epsom. I followed later in the morning. I was just getting out of my car at the airport when my phone rang. Martina Dunne, Dermot's secretary. It was unlikely to be good news.

'Hi, Martina.'

Trepidation.

'Pat, there's a little bit of a problem with Harzand.'

Feeling of heart sinking down to the pit of my stomach.

'He pulled off a shoe at the airport, there's a doubt about him running.'

I couldn't believe it – the rug being pulled once again from under my hopes of winning the Derby. I went into the airport, but I didn't go through into Departures straight away. It could be a big waste of a trip, a waste of a day. There was a decent meeting at the Curragh that evening. Dermot had a couple of runners. I could have cut my losses and gone straight back home and on to the Curragh that evening instead.

Then Martina called again to tell me that Harzand was making progress, that he was 50–50 to run, so I got on the plane.

Even so, I called Frances and asked her to look up flights back to Dublin from Heathrow. If Harzand was going to be withdrawn from the Derby, I was going to do all I could to get an early flight home so that I could ride at the Curragh that evening.

I was powerless, though. There was nothing that I could do, and there was nothing that anyone could have done. When Harzand was getting off the horsebox, he pulled a shoe off and he stood on one of the nails. It happened regularly: a horse would stand one foot on the other and pull the shoe off, and then stand on the nails of the shoe that had come off. So he was extremely sore and very lame. Of all the times for something like that to happen – on Derby morning!

It was all down to the farrier and the lads after that, and they were brilliant. Jim Reilly, Jim Bolger's farrier, did a fantastic job. I tried to go through my normal routine. I got to the track early and I walked the track, came back in and checked my weight, which was good.

I stayed in my suit for a while, though. I didn't get stripped. I was still half expecting to hear that Harzand was going to be withdrawn, and if that happened, I wasn't going to lose a minute in getting back to the airport.

Dermot called me from the yard at about 12 o'clock and told me that they had got the shoe back on and that they were icing Harzand's foot. Things were looking a little better than they had looked before. So I got stripped and got into the sauna. I didn't need to lose any weight, but I always felt refreshed, ready to go, after I had had a little sweat. It was just the routine. I got out of the sauna and did my stretches, got into my gear. I only had one ride on the day, so I could focus on just one thing, one horse, one race.

After the fourth race, the Dash, Dermot came in to get the saddle.

'The situation is this,' he said to me. 'I've spoken to everyone, and the stewards understand the decision is yours now.'

Mine?

'Harzand appears to be fine, but if you canter him down to the start, and you feel that he is not right, you are to withdraw him at the start.'

That gave me great confidence going out, that they were trusting me with the decision. Dermot and Harzand's owner, His Highness the Aga Khan. I came back into the weigh room and met my valet in England, Chris Maude.

'Well?' he asked expectantly.

'Well, he's running,' I said. 'All is good at the minute, anyway.'

'That's it,' said Chris. 'You'll win.'

Everybody was a little bit nervous in the parade ring beforehand. Of course everyone was a little bit nervous – it was the Derby, one of the most important horse races in the world. His Highness was there, the Aga Khan's racing manager Pat Downes was there, Dermot was there.

'Do the right thing, Pat,' His Highness said to me. 'Whatever you feel is the right thing to do when you get to the start. Just do the right thing by the horse.'

I got on the horse, and he felt great. He felt fresh and well, jig-jogging around the paddock. Not too fresh, just in great form with himself, in good health. We got onto the track and that was a nervy time, when we broke into a canter on our way to the start. If he didn't feel right, our Derby day was over for another year. One lame step and I was going to have to withdraw him, Derby or no Derby, and that would have been heartbreaking.

It was a very anxious time for everybody, and it was a particularly anxious time for me, because the decision was on me. One bad step and he was out – but actually he was perfect. After he took two strides, I knew that we were in business because he moved beautifully; he floated to the start.

It wasn't a difficult decision, then, to let him take his chance in the race. There wasn't even a hint that there was anything wrong with his foot. He felt great on the way to the start, and he felt great through the early stages of the race. I was a little further back than ideal early on, but I wanted to track Seamie Heffernan on our old friend Idaho. I thought that he could give me a good tow into the race, so I got myself into a nice position, in about seventh or eighth place, two off the rail and tracking Idaho.

The Epsom Derby is always a rough race. The track is unusual, for starters, undulating and turning and against a camber, and stakes are high. You have to fight for every inch of ground that you get; you have to use up your horse at different stages of the race, just to get or hold a position.

Donnacha O'Brien was just on my inside on Shogun; he angled to get out as we started to head down around Tattenham Corner, but that would have forced me too wide, so I had to use up Harzand a little bit just to make sure that Donnacha stayed in there and that I didn't have to go four wide.

So we were three wide down around Tattenham Corner and into the home straight, and that was fine. I wanted to keep going forward, but I decided to stay in and follow Idaho around the home turn. That was an important part of the race, and if I had come around Idaho at that point, I would have given away too much ground.

I asked Harzand to pick up when we straightened up for home, and he did, so I was able to angle out. I got a break in traffic behind Idaho as we raced to the two-furlong marker, so I was able to take Harzand out towards the outside without breaking his momentum, and he kept going forward. Idaho hit the front at the two-furlong marker, but we made ground after him and, by the time we got to the furlong pole, we were in front.

When we hit the front, I pulled my whip through to my left hand and I thought, Here we go, all the way to the line. Then I saw the white face of US Army Ranger appearing at my right boot, Ryan Moore in all-out-drive position, and I asked Harzand for everything that he had. After running his lungs out for 11½ furlongs, I asked him to pick up again, and he did. That was his willingness for you, his positive attitude, his desire to win. He dug deeper than he had ever dug in his entire life. You could be as strong in a finish as you liked, you could switch your whip and change your hands and drive your horse forward but, in the end, inside the final 100 yards of a Derby, it was all down to the horse; he had to want to win, and Harzand was phenomenal that day. He fought off US Army Ranger's challenge, and he went on to win by a length and a half.

People asked me to describe that feeling afterwards, and I struggled. What was it like when you hit the line? How did that feel? The Derby?

I was lucky enough to win lots of big races at home and around the world during my career, but winning the Derby was different from everything else. The first thing that flashed through my mind was that I couldn't believe it. Fundamentally, I couldn't believe that we were after getting to the winning line in front in the Epsom Derby.

We went past the line and all the way to the bottom of the pull-up. We slowed to a walk and all the lads were saying well done, patting me on the back, shaking my hand. I was walking around for a second – it seemed like forever but it was only for a second or two – and it didn't feel real. I always appreciated winning big races, but I still couldn't believe that I had won the Derby.

Strangely, I didn't think that it would mean as much to me as it did in the end. Of course, you start riding as a young fellow, you have all your dreams. What race would you most like to win? The Derby. Always the Derby.

But then, when I did actually win it, it meant more to me even than I thought it would. It was like it meant even more to me in reality than it did in my childhood dreams.

And all the emotion. I felt like laughing, I felt like crying, and I did a bit of both.

It was emotional for everyone, for Dermot, his first Epsom Derby too, for all the lads. It was one of the few big races missing from his CV, and it was only right that he should tick that box. I was delighted that I was able to deliver an Epsom Derby win for him.

His Highness the Aga Khan had won the Derby before, four times, with Shergar and Shahrastani and Kahyasi and Sinndar, but it was still an emotional time for him and for his family and for his racing manager Pat Downes, probably heightened by all the doubts beforehand about whether or not Harzand would even line up in the race.

On a personal level, it was the pinnacle for me. I knew then that, no matter how many more years I rode for, no matter what else I achieved, no matter what else I won, it wouldn't get any better than that. Winning the Epsom Derby, my first Epsom Derby.

Unfortunately, the end of my career was a lot closer than I thought it was.

CHAPTER 33

I t was very nice to wake up on Sunday morning with an extra tick on my CV: Pat Smullen, Derby-winning jockey.

I wasn't riding at Listowel that day, which was unusual, so I was just around the house with Frances and the kids. I actually spent the morning putting up showjumping fences for the kids, and they spent the morning riding, so I was very happy just to be around there at home with all the family.

We had a lovely day, actually. Some of the neighbours came around just to say well done. A few had come around, too, the night before. The racing photographer Caroline Norris, a really good friend of ours, came around too and took some photographs.

Harzand was arriving back to Dermot's at three o'clock so I went up to Dermot's for that. It was good to see Harzand again, and to see Dermot and all the staff. There was a great buzz around the place, a great feeling that something significant had been achieved.

There was that sense around Rhode, too. There was a great sense of community. Rhode majored on Gaelic football, but they majored on sport and on community too, and they had a night for us later in the week in one of the local pubs. I brought the Derby trophy up and there were great celebrations.

There were banners put up around the village: 'Welcome to Rhode, home of Derby-winning jockey Pat Smullen!' I was a bit embarrassed by all the attention, and the lads, Kevin Manning and Declan McDonogh and Fran Berry, used to slag me about the signs every time they'd come and pick me up to go racing afterwards, but I really appreciated the effort that the local community made. It was all very nice. It also brought it home to me how big the Derby was, that it was a race that went beyond racing.

I went up to the local schools, too, to Ballybryan, where our kids went, and to Rhode, where I went, which was brilliant. The kids drew pictures of horses and races for me, and they asked me all sorts of questions: how did it feel, were you tired, what was it like to meet the Queen?

They put a plaque up in the hallway in the school with my name on it, and never in my wildest dreams did I ever think that that would happen. That was very special to me.

'What do you want to be when you grow up?'

'A jockey.'

'Good man, Patrick.'

Amazing the way the world goes around.

Harzand was sore when he came home. I saw him walking off the horsebox at Dermot's on his return, and I said to Frances, 'Well, he won't be running in the Irish Derby anyway,' which was disappointing. But he did.

Just shows you the horse's resolution. There were only three weeks between the Epsom Derby and the Irish Derby, and he was on a course of antibiotics for a week, so that was an easy week. Then he was doing just light work for the second week, and during the third week he did one half-speed and one proper piece of work. It was a rushed preparation, but he was such a talented racehorse that he was able to cope with it.

It was different, going to the Curragh for the Irish Derby. Harzand was favourite, the Epsom Derby winner; he was an odds-on shot. People thought that it was just a case of him going out and winning it, but it wasn't as simple as that. It was only three weeks after he had won at Epsom, 21 days, and he needed every one of those days to recover.

Consequently, there was more pressure on us during the build-up to the Irish Derby. There was more attention on us, the short-priced favourite, the Epsom Derby winner going back to our own Derby, literally across the road from Rosewell House. We were well under the radar during the lead-up to Epsom; nobody was talking about Harzand until a couple of days before the race. The absolute opposite was the case in the lead-up to the Irish Derby. All the talk was of Harzand.

The pressure that goes with expectation.

It wasn't all plain sailing, either. I thought that our main danger was Idaho, our old sparring partner Idaho, one of four horses that Aidan O'Brien ran in the race, and the choice of Ryan Moore. We were drawn on the inside in stall two, which could often be a disadvantage at the Curragh. Colm O'Donoghue was in stall three, just beside us, on Idaho's stable companion Shogun, and he raced up alongside me and got in front of me before we had gone a furlong. I was happy enough with that, I was happy with our position, until Colm decided to pull the pace up. I was in danger of being put into a pocket, so I had to get Harzand out of there and use him up a bit to get outside Shogun. Leigh Roche on Dermot's other horse Ebediyin then moved up on the outside into the lead and stretched out, so I was able to move up and tuck back in behind Ebediyin and Port Douglas and Seamie Heffernan.

I was happy that I was in the perfect position, third place behind a good pace that Ebediyin was setting. I was then in a position where I had lots of options.

I moved up on the outside as we rounded the home turn, and we easily went into the lead just over two furlongs out. We got to the front and moved over onto the inside rail, but I didn't go for him until we raced inside the two-furlong marker and I could see the familiar white face of Idaho coming up to my left under Ryan Moore. Ryan delivered him at the perfect time; this time it was Idaho coming at Harzand instead of Harzand coming at Idaho.

I wasn't certain how it would go – Idaho mounted a strong challenge up on our outside and I thought for a few strides that we might be beaten – but Harzand picked up again when I really needed him. He fought all the way to the line, and he stretched away close home to win by half a length.

In my eyes, that was a hell of a horse race. Both horses kept picking up the whole way to the line. We both galloped to the line very strongly, and it was a huge performance by Harzand.

That was another brilliant day. Another Irish Derby. It's massive, in front of your home crowd, and all my family were there this time, unlike at Epsom.

It was different from Epsom, though. There was a sense of disbelief about Epsom, especially with all the doubt that there had been in the lead-up to the race. It was winning the race that you had dreamed about winning your entire life, with the odds stacked against you. At the Curragh, we were expected to win – the market said that we were more likely to win than we were to lose – so when we did win it, it was more relief than elation.

I always felt that Harzand was not the same horse after that. I think that his Irish Derby win took a lot out of him, Idaho pushed him so hard. He had had four races in the space of a very short time, including two lung-bursting efforts to win two Derbies. He got a nice break after that, he deserved a nice break, and he was working well during the build-up to the Irish Champion Stakes. He only finished eighth in that race, behind Almanzor, and he was struck into, so he had a valid excuse, but I just never felt that he was the same horse afterwards. He ran in the Prix de l'Arc de Triomphe in October, finishing down the field behind Found, and he retired to his owner His Highness the Aga Khan's Gilltown Stud, a dual Derby winner.

I always had a good relationship with Prince Khalid Abdullah's Juddmonte team and with their chief executive, Douglas Erskine Crum. I was delighted when Prince Khalid started sending horses to Dermot. The Juddmonte breeding was top-class, and the Juddmonte horses were a massive addition to Rosewell House. And the history! As a kid I used to watch those horses in the famous colours, Danehill and Warning and Sanglamore and Zafonic, winning all those big races. Putting on Prince Khalid's silks, seeing them hanging up on your peg in the weigh room, green, pink sash, white sleeves: you'd grow a foot.

I was lucky in that I got to ride lots of good horses and win lots of good races in those silks – horses like Famous Name and Emulous and Brooch, obviously, for Dermot – but later on I got to ride some of the Juddmonte horses for British trainers, Snow Sky and Time Test and Kings Fete. Then, at the end of the 2016 season, Douglas asked me if I would take the job of retained rider for Prince Khalid.

I was blown away in the beginning. Prince Khalid asked Douglas to ask me, and Douglas and I had a few meetings at the time to discuss it. It was obviously a massive job, a massive opportunity. It was something new and fresh, a new challenge, and one of the best jobs in racing. It was a big vote of confidence in me too, it was a great fillip for me personally, that one of the biggest owner/breeders of thoroughbred horses, one of the best operations in the racing world, wanted me as their first jockey.

Of course, there were lots and lots of implications. It would have meant leaving Dermot Weld, for starters, leaving Moyglare, leaving all Dermot's owners, and all the history that went with that, all the brilliant relationships that I had formed, all the people, all the horses. It would have meant not riding for all the smaller trainers for whom I rode whenever I could, and it would have meant riding for different trainers in Britain, not being based in one yard, not being a stable jockey, but going around the different yards riding the Juddmonte horses. And it would have meant relocating to England.

That was the biggest thing for me in the end, moving to England and all that that involved. Moving my family. Moving our kids.

There were so many things to consider, and we took our time considering them. I always thought that, when you had a big decision to make, you took the time to gather all the information that you needed to gather in order to help you in making your decision. You spoke to whoever you needed to speak to, you got whatever advice you needed, you considered all that you needed to consider. Then you made your decision and, when you made it, that was it. There was no looking back. No thinking what-if.

It was a torturous time, really, the time that we spent deliberating. It was exciting, but it was torturous, trying to consider all the different implications, how our lives would be impacted. We looked into living in Newmarket. Frances looked into boarding schools for Hannah. I spoke to Dermot and told him about the offer. I had spent too much time with him, I had too deep a relationship with him, too much respect for him, to just spring something like that on him. I thought that I owed it to him to let him know that I had been offered the job, and that I was thinking about taking it.

I could have gone on my own, I could have lived in England

for six or eight months of the year, left Frances and the kids in Ireland, seen them sporadically during the year and then spent the winters together, but that was never the way we lived our lives. We were all in it together. Wherever we were, we were all there together.

Other jockeys were able to commute. Ruby Walsh and Barry Geraghty commuted between Ireland and Britain for years, but their jobs in Britain were different. Ruby was riding for Paul Nicholls in England, and Barry was riding for Nicky Henderson. One yard. All the horses were in one location. The Juddmonte horses were spread out among different trainers, so I would have had to be going around the different yards every day, riding the Juddmonte horses. I couldn't have done it while living in Ireland.

It took me over a month to decide. I spoke to Dermot, I spoke to Eva Haefner, and they were both brilliant. Dermot and Eva and the other owners in the yard came up with a package, a better retainer to keep me.

That was all very nice, it was nice to be in demand, and maybe it made the decision that I took easier than it might have been but, in the end, it came down to family. I figured that I couldn't uproot my family; I couldn't take them away from where they were. There was a part of Frances that would have been excited by a move, excited by the challenge – new job, new surroundings – but it would have been difficult for her, and it would have been very tough on the kids. They were very happy in their schools, with their friends, so to uproot them and take them to England, to Newmarket, wouldn't have been fair on them.

If I had been a single fellow, no family, no ties, no commitments, I would have been gone. I would have upped and moved myself to England. But I knew how lucky I was to have the life that I had in Ireland, I knew how happy I was and how happy our family was. To give all that up for the move to a new job, a great job but still a job, we just thought in the end that it was too big a price to pay. You look at your kids and you realise, there's more to it than just racing.

It was ironic that, the following year, one of Prince Khalid's best ever racehorses came along. Enable won the Oaks in 2017, and she won the Irish Oaks and the King George and the Yorkshire Oaks and the Arc. She was an incredible filly and, if I had taken the Juddmonte job, I would have ridden her to all those victories. Strange thing, though: I never regretted the decision that I made. I was flattered to be asked, I was humbled, and I told Douglas Erskine Crum that. It was the opportunity of a lifetime, a job that almost every jockey riding in Ireland or Britain at the time would have dreamed of. But, after over a month of deliberating, Enable or no Enable, I knew that I had made the correct decision.

My mother always said that everything happened for a reason. And when I got ill just over a year later, I was very glad that I was at home in Ireland.

CHAPTER 34

I was champion again in 2016. That was my third championship in a row and my ninth in total. It just crowned a fantastic year for me. I rode 115 winners in Ireland that season, more winners than I had ever ridden in a season in Ireland before, and 10 in Britain. And I had won the Epsom Derby on Harzand.

I didn't know it at the time, but when I rode Harzand to win the Irish Derby at the Curragh in June 2016, I was winning my last Group 1 race.

The 2017 season started off like most seasons started off, gung-ho, getting the young horses going, trying to get as many winners on the board as I could, as early as I could, building the foundations for the jockeys' championship. I had eyes on my 10th jockeys' championship, but I had a formidable opponent in Colin Keane.

Colin had been champion apprentice in 2014, and he had finished second behind me in the championship in both 2015 and 2016. Riding for Ger Lyons and with the talent that he undoubtedly had, it was only a matter of time before he would be champion. I was hoping that it might take a little more time than it did, though!

I rode Cracksman in the Irish Derby that year for Anthony Oppenheimer and John Gosden, and that was one that got away.

It wasn't my finest hour. Cracksman's regular rider, Frankie Dettori, was injured, so I was delighted to be asked to ride him in Frankie's absence. And Frankie was great with me beforehand – he told me all about the horse; he told me that he could be a bit lazy in his races sometimes and, sure enough, he never really travelled for me. On the run to the home turn, I thought we weren't going to be involved in the finish of the race at all.

He picked up, though. He was a horse who found lots for pressure. If I had been travelling better at the top of the home straight, I probably would have tried to go inside, pick my way through traffic. But that was more difficult to do when you were not travelling well. When you were not going so well, you generally wanted clear sailing so that you could keep going forward.

We moved into sixth place when we straightened up for home, and the five horses in front of us were all Ballydoyle horses, so I was certain that none of the horses' riders were going to do me any favours if I needed a bit of light as I tried to make my way through. It was always difficult to come down the outside at the Curragh and win, but I thought that, all things considered, going down the outside was the best course of action available to me at the time.

It nearly worked, too. Cracksman was tough and brave. We got the better of subsequent Arc de Triomphe winner Waldgeist, and we got past the Epsom Derby winner Wings Of Eagles and the Derrinstown winner Douglas Macarthur, but we just couldn't get past Capri, who kicked for home early close to the inside rail. We only went down by a neck, but I did feel that, if things had panned out a little differently, we could have won.

Everyone was disappointed afterwards. Nobody blamed me for the defeat, but I knew myself that if I had ridden a different race it might have made the difference of the neck by which we were beaten.

We didn't have a top-class horse that year at Rosewell House, but we had good horses. I won the Give Thanks Stakes at Cork and the Enterprise Stakes at Leopardstown on Eziyra, I won the Royal Whip Stakes and the Blandford Stakes on Shamreen, and I rode a few nice winners for Willie Mullins, Airlie Beach in the Oyster Stakes at Galway in August and Renneti in the Budweiser Race at Galway in August and in the Loughbrown Stakes at Naas in September.

Renneti was a character. He had his own ideas about the game, but he had buckets of talent. Ruby Walsh had my card well marked with him, though, about his quirks and his notions. You had to go straight down to the start with him for starters, straight into the stalls and straight back up. If you stopped on your way to the start, he could plant himself there and decide that he didn't want to go any further. And he refused to race a couple of times. But he was great that day at Galway; we won by a long way, and he was very good again at Naas.

Willie Mullins, Renneti's trainer, was always one of those trainers who, when they rang looking for you, if Dermot didn't need you, you just said yes. You just said that you would ride whatever he wanted you to ride. You wouldn't need to study the race to see if the horse had a chance or not. If Willie wanted you to ride a horse, you could be sure that the horse had a chance.

Willie had high expectations. He was a bit like Dermot like that; he didn't like to lose, but he'd leave a lot of it up to you. He'd ask you what you thought, how you thought the horse should be ridden. He wanted to know that you had thought about it and that you had a plan in your head. Then he'd give you a few pieces of information, little nuggets that would give you all the confidence that you needed before you went out to ride.

I was riding plenty for Mick Halford by then, too. Pat Downes, the Aga Khan's racing manager, had said to me that His Highness would like for me to ride his horses whenever I was available, whenever my commitments to Dermot allowed, so that was a nice position to be in. It was nice to feel wanted. His Highness had a lot of horses with Mick Halford, so I went over to ride out for Mick quite a bit, and I obviously rode the Aga Khan's horses that he had whenever I could.

I rode Riyazan, a nice two-year-old, for Mick and His Highness to win a listed race at Dundalk in early October. By then, though, I had realised that it was going to be very difficult for me to win my 10th championship. I rode three other winners at Dundalk on that Friday night, but Colin won the last on Thunder Crash for Ger Lyons. I rode Imaging to win his maiden at Limerick on the Saturday, but Colin got that back at Navan on the Sunday while I was off over at Belmont Park in New York, riding Zhukova in the Flower Bowl Stakes, in which we finished sixth of six.

That left Colin one ahead of me, 82–81, and I could see that Dermot's firepower for the remainder of the season was drying up, whereas Colin and his boss, Ger Lyons, just seemed to be getting stronger.

Colin just kept riding winners. I had a winner at Navan, and he had a winner at Navan. I had no winners at Fairyhouse, and he had one. I had no winners at Dundalk, and he had two. People said that it was going to go down to the wire, to the last meeting at Naas, to the last race at the last meeting, but it didn't. At Dundalk on 1 November, Colin had three winners and I had four seconds, and that put the final nail in it in my book.

By the time we got to the last day of the season, 5 November at Naas, Colin was in an unassailable lead: he had 98 winners to my 87. It was a lap of victory for Colin. He put the cap on it, too, by riding a double on the last day and getting to 100 winners. I rode the last winner of the day, of the season, Tocco D'Amore for Dermot in the Listed Finale Stakes, but it was scant consolation. In time, I learned to be happy for Colin – he was a worthy champion – but I was desperately disappointed at the time that I didn't win my 10th championship.

I probably wasn't at my best physically for a lot of that season. Mentally, psychologically, tactically, I thought that I was at the top of my game, but physically, I was struggling. I turned 40 in May, and it was around about then that the back pains started.

'This being forty thing is as bad as everyone told me it was.'

I kept pushing through; I thought it was a pulled muscle. I got physio constantly, but there was no easing of the pain. I was physically exhausted at the end of the season. I was usually physically exhausted at the end of the season, but the end of the 2017 season was different: it was a different kind of tiredness, an absolutely wrung-out tiredness. Completely drained. It wasn't until the following spring that I found out what was at the root of it.

BUTTERFLIES

By Frances Crowley

In his final weeks Pat said to me on a few occasions that he had a very strong feeling, a feeling that this was happening to him for a reason. He said that something was telling him that there was a purpose to his suffering and, although we never spoke of him dying, I know he meant this feeling was that there was a reason for his death.

We had a wonderful spring and early summer of 2020 on the farm. Covid-19 had struck, but we were happy to be isolated in our little piece of paradise and were gifted some glorious weather to enjoy it. Pat's chemotherapy had begun to stop being effective, so he had started a new combination of immunotherapy treatment, and for a while all appeared to be going well. In reality it was a short holiday between when he was no longer suffering from the side effects of chemo and when the cancer started to take hold again.

By early June he was starting to feel pain in his hip and so began the scans to find its source, hoping against hope that the treatment would begin to work and that maybe he had just pulled a muscle from all the physical work that he was doing on the farm. Gillian and Ruby Walsh took advantage of an easing of restrictions to have a small get-together for Royal Ascot and I remember that I doubted whether we would attend, knowing how much discomfort Pat was in. To my surprise, however, he agreed to go for a short while, and what a lovely day we had, sitting outside, catching up with everyone and enjoying the company of good friends.

I am forever grateful for that day. It was the last time his friends would see Pat and the last time I remember seeing him smile. I have a lovely photo of the two of us together from then, and it is a reminder to savour those good days and take pictures to remember them by, because you never know what is around the next corner.

At this stage we were getting increasingly worried about whether this new treatment was having any effect, but we still had to give it time to work. Unfortunately, with pancreatic cancer, time is not on your side, and we soon learned that the cancer had grown and spread again, which was a devastating blow to Pat's morale. Again, he refused to give up, and went through radiation therapy, which he found excruciating because of the position which he had to hold his body in for long periods of time.

As usual, though, he took it as a challenge, and nothing would do him but to finish the course of treatment. Another blow came when his lovely uncle Joe passed away from cancer on 13 July. His mother's only sibling, Joe had lived next door to Pat's home place. They were a tight-knit family, with Mary helping to rear her nephews, Ken and Alan, when Joe's wife, Claire, passed away at a young age – also from cancer. With Pat's own father, Paddy, also dying from cancer aged 64, it is a family which has been ravaged by the disease, and unfortunately they are not unusual in the little community of Rhode. Having buried my own father in March and again following a coffin in July, standing at Joe's graveside, I begged God to spare our family from more heartbreak, but all the time knowing deep down that more was to come.

By the end of July, I was pleading with Pat to allow himself to be admitted to hospital. More than once he said that he didn't want to go, because he was afraid that if he went into hospital he would never come out again, and this absolutely broke my heart in pieces – especially as I knew in my soul that it could be true. However, it was increasingly difficult to control his pain and we were hoping that there might be some kind of chemotherapy option to help him. So he agreed to go as soon as he had finished all of the radiotherapy sessions, because he feared that he would not be able to travel from St Vincent's to the Beacon Hospital, where he was undergoing the radiotherapy.

The effects of Covid will be long talked about. For us it meant a delay in Pat getting radiotherapy (due to the agreement where the private hospitals were made available for public use), and eventually starting it in the Beacon as this was the place where he could access it earliest. As I said before, time is not your friend with pancreatic cancer, and although I can't promise that this changed his overall outcome, it certainly didn't help his chances.

Once Pat's radiotherapy ended, we got in touch with his oncologist, Ray McDermott, and on Tuesday 4 August we travelled to St Vincent's Private Hospital together for the last time. Pat was admitted to the Hawthorn Ward, where he had spent six weeks between October and November 2018 at the time of his operation, and he was familiar with many of the staff there, including Nurse Dee Swansea, who gave him that crucial pep talk back at the start of his treatment.

He was so weak that he almost collapsed on the way to the ward but refused all help and insisted on walking to his room. It was incredibly hard to leave him there that night, but I knew that I could no longer provide at home the care and pain relief that he needed. The one thing I never had to worry about, though, was whether he would be looked after once I left the hospital. The kindness, compassion and dignity with which he was cared for in SVPH meant such comfort and peace of mind when I couldn't be there.

Pat spent the initial week or so in the Hawthorn Ward before he was moved to the Cedar Ward. He was reluctant to leave Hawthorn, but the team who needed to care for him were based in Cedar, the palliative care team. To us they were the pain relief team; we didn't speak of palliative care and, as far as we were concerned, he was there to build up his strength in order to try to get more chemotherapy.

That was the plan: get stronger, get chemo, which would kill some of the tumour and in turn lessen the pain, so he could get stronger again to get more chemo. Unfortunately, it was more like one step forward and two steps back, and although he did indeed get one small dose of chemo, this only had the result of weakening him further. He had to give it a go, though. He never wanted to give up and indeed he never gave up – the will to live never left him and, although ultimately his body gave out, his spirit was undefeatable.

Pat was almost six weeks in hospital by the time Irish Champions

Weekend came around – what a difference from the previous year, when Pat had his wonderful fundraising day in the Curragh. Because of Pat being in the palliative care ward, I was allowed to see him, so I was with him almost every day.

Unfortunately, nobody else could visit because of Covid, but we counted our blessings: most people were unable to have visitors at all, and if Pat was to contract Covid it would be disastrous. So many people were dying from Covid without their loved ones being allowed to be with them; it was absolutely horrendous to hear the stories and, although the country had the disease quite well under control in September, the fear was still very real.

I came armed with the *Racing Post* and *Irish Field* on the Saturday of Irish Champions Weekend, 12 September 2020, and Malachy Ryan had dropped in some beautiful flowers from the Moyglare garden at Eva's request for the occasion. Pat was tired but alert and looking forward to the racing. A procedure he had had the evening before helped him to feel better, and we had a nice time dissecting and analysing the racing together like we always did.

We both read a race in a very similar way and generally came to the same conclusions, but disagreements could happen just as easily! Pat was delighted to see Johnny Murtagh win the Group 1 Matron Stakes and sent him a message to congratulate him straight away. I left that evening happy enough with Pat, but a bit concerned that Ray (his oncologist) would feel that he wasn't strong enough to get more chemo when he would see him on Monday.

Pat had eaten very little on Saturday and I remember him saying on Sunday that he just didn't feel like eating at all. I was disappointed that he didn't seem as interested in the racing, even though the Moyglare-Stud-owned mare Search For A Song had a great chance in the Irish St Leger. However, he was still alert enough to spot our wonderful family doctor and former Turf Club doctor, Adrian McGoldrick, down at the start of one of the races. Adrian had been quite poorly with long Covid, so it was great to see him back racing and Pat sent him a message telling him so.

Suddenly, though, Pat got a bad pain and asked for a pain relief injection. This really knocked him out, so much so that I was unable to wake him for the Irish St Leger, which made me quite concerned. It was some time later before I was able to tell him that Search For A Song had won it again, recording a wonderful second victory in the race.

Of course, he wanted to send a message to Eva straight away, but was too tired and weak to type, so I typed the message as he dictated to me, then handed him the phone back to press 'Send' once he was happy with the message.

On the way home I was even more worried about Pat's strength, and I was apprehensive about our meeting with Ray the next day. Pat was full of hope about getting chemo, and the thought of how disappointed he would be if this did not happen was very upsetting. At this stage, the palliative care team were focusing on getting things organised at our home for Pat to be able to return and have the same level of comfort there, but Pat was determined that he would recover enough in hospital.

'A hospital bed is not entering our house,' he said.

I think he saw it as accepting defeat, accepting that he was going to die, and that he would not do.

At the hospital the next morning I was sat down and gently told that Pat was dying and that the kids should come to see him over the next few days. I knew it in my heart, but of course it was unbelievably difficult to hear the words. I resolved to get the kids and the rest of his family to see him as soon as possible without unduly upsetting Pat, but first I had to face the meeting with Ray and his team in Pat's room.

Ray explained to Pat that he wasn't strong enough to take another dose of chemo. Having to agree with him felt like an utter betrayal of my husband, knowing how much he wanted more treatment. When Pat protested that he was doing his best, it broke my heart into pieces. Of course he was doing his best, like he always did, in everything he did, he was trying so hard to get better. It was all I could do not to break down at this stage, but I really wanted to be strong for Pat.

I generally did my crying in the car: on the way up to the hospital, so that I could hold it together for Pat, and on the way home, so that I could hold it together for the kids. One day when I was with Pat in his room, gazing out the window at the gulls and the usual scene outside the hospital, the thought came to me that I might not be looking at this scene for much longer and that this long journey in our lives could be coming to an end. When Pat saw the tears streaming down my face he simply said, 'You've got to be strong, Frances.'

From then on that's what I tried to do. To this day I can hear his voice saying those words in my head.

I left the hospital early to collect Hannah from school in Newbridge and I told Pat that I might bring her up to see him. He was exhausted so I slipped away and left him to sleep. When I rang later that evening, I could get no reply from his phone, so I eventually rang the ward and the nurse woke him to take the call. He told me that he was just so tired and not to come back up; he just wanted to sleep.

I regret it now, but I didn't go back that night with Hannah. I regret not bundling his whole family into the car and getting everyone up to see him straight away. Thinking we had more time, I didn't want to frighten the kids or alarm Pat, so I decided that they should come to the hospital over the next couple of days and not in a big group. I don't know why I didn't feel more urgency and I regret it immensely. Perhaps it was an element of disbelief on my part, or some kind of denial.

When I got to the hospital myself on Tuesday morning, Pat had declined markedly but could still talk to me. Again, the nurse had to sit me down and explain that he didn't have much time, so I scrambled everyone and told them to get there as quickly as possible. Hannah was the first to arrive, brought by my sister Annemarie. Pat was able to attempt to say hello to her, but he slipped into a deep sleep after that and was unresponsive by the time Paddy and Sarah arrived, along with Pat's mother, Mary, and his two brothers Ger and Brian.

Pat's eldest brother, Seán, was still in Canada, but the boys held up a phone to Pat's ear to allow Seán to speak to him. I can't imagine how difficult this was for Seán, being so far away while this was happening. My heart also went out to Mary, who was saying goodbye to her precious son, and it made me feel guilty that I had been given the privilege of looking after him all this time while she, his mother, could not even visit him.

Everyone took turns to sit with Pat alone and have some time in private with him, and I told Hannah, Paddy and Sarah to try to say everything they wanted to him now. I reassured the kids that he could hear everything that they said, even if he couldn't respond, and I am absolutely certain that this was the case.

Over and over we all thanked him for being such a wonderful dad and husband, and hugged and kissed him again and again. Sarah, being the smallest, was able to lie on the bed with him and tenderly hold him. She surprised me with her ability to understand what was happening and give Pat as much affection as she could squeeze into such a short time. At one stage she startled us all by jumping up and screaming at the top of her voice, 'It's not fair!'

How right she was.

Hannah, as usual, showed maturity beyond her years, putting her arms around the other two and comforting them, and speaking to her dad to reassure him that we were all there and loved him so very much. Paddy, I think, was in such a state of shock and disbelief that he was even quieter than his usual quiet self and just held his father's hand in silence. My heart broke for them all, and once again I wished that I could have had them there sooner.

I had brought up the topic of trying to get the kids in to see him a few times over the six weeks he was in hospital, but he repeated that he did not want them to see him like that and to wait until he was looking a bit better. However, I also have a hunch that Pat just wasn't able for the emotion and sadness of saying goodbye to his children, and perhaps, despite all of his strength and courage throughout his ordeal, this task was just beyond him.

I had taken a quick break and was having a cup of tea downstairs that evening while one of the family had some time alone with Pat. His cousins Ken and Alan had arrived, as had Kevin O'Ryan, his brother-in-law, best friend and agent. The hospital staff were very understanding and allowed the family a corner to ourselves, the hospital being quite deserted because of Covid.

All of a sudden, I got a feeling, a feeling of dread being the only way I can describe it, and I remembered getting the same feeling just before my father died, six months previously. I quietly made my way back to Pat's room and quickly realised that it was time to call everyone together to spend his final moments with him.

We all kissed him one last time and told him how much we loved him, leaving his three children to be the last to do so. Hannah, then Sarah, and finally Paddy, kissed their father goodbye and as Paddy's lips touched Pat's forehead, he took his final breath. It was a moment not just of immense sadness, but also of absolute peace, and that was the feeling that enveloped the room. For the longest time afterwards I sat staring into his gorgeous blue eyes, knowing that I would never get the opportunity again. It felt like I could see right into his soul and I never wanted it to end.

It was a tired and numb little family that arrived back to Brickfield Stud that night. Sarah had taken to sleeping with me while Pat was in hospital and I was glad of the comfort that she gave me, too. Sarah headed off to bed while I locked up, and shortly afterwards I could hear her calling excitedly from the bedroom. I rushed up, thinking that something was wrong, and was surprised to see two butterflies fluttering above our bed. I just stared blankly at them, puzzled by their appearance, circling above the bed, and it occurred to me that a picture of a butterfly had been put on the door of Pat's hospital room earlier that evening. However, exhausted and thinking of everything that was before us over the next few days, I didn't dwell on it and hunted them out the window so that we could get some much-needed rest.

Wednesday was all about bringing Pat home. It was requested that we should drive by the Curragh Racecourse, where Pat rode so many big winners and worked for most of his career. He had died on 15 September 2020, exactly one year after his champions' race day at the Curragh, which had a poignant significance. The road leading to, and away from, the racecourse was lined with friends and colleagues of Pat. The racecourse entrance where we pulled in to receive flowers was a sea of familiar faces with eyes full of sadness above the Covid masks.

Social distancing was being adhered to, but you could sense the urge that people had to run towards you and show their love for Pat and heartbreak at his loss. Along the road home, people came out to pay their respects to Pat – crowds who would usually have cheered him home on a winner now standing in silence as he passed on his way home for the last time. I know he would have felt not just immense pride but also huge gratitude for this moving tribute, and it is something that his whole family will remember for the rest of their lives.

I awoke early on Thursday morning, my head full of things that needed to be done. I decided that I was going to attempt to do the eulogy for Pat, but I didn't know if I would be strong enough. A few weeks earlier a woman had lost her husband and children in a terrible car accident involving a flood and I remembered how she spoke at their funerals. Her words, that she had no-one left to hug, stuck in my mind. Well, I still had my kids to hug and love. I was so much more fortunate than her, and that's what convinced me that I could stand up and speak. It would not sound right coming from someone else, so I had to write the words that I knew Pat would want me to say.

The sunrise was not strong enough to pierce through the morning fog, so I turned on the lights in the kitchen before making my way to the yard to feed some horses. Being on my own in the yard where Pat and I had spent so much time together and harboured so many hopes and dreams naturally made me very sad, and by the time I got back into the house the tears were flowing. I asked Pat if he was happy. Was he at peace? Was he somewhere nice with his dad? If all these things were true then I could somehow reach peace myself.

At that moment the lights went off. Worried that we were going to have to deal with a power cut, I was relieved when the lights came back on after a few seconds. I turned to reset the time on the cooker, as you would always have to do after the electricity went off. I was puzzled to see that the time hadn't changed on the cooker and went to check the fuseboard, but no fuse had blown either. It wasn't a power cut or a blown fuse, so what was it?

Cases of Covid were low in September 2020, but funerals were still limited to very small numbers. Most of Pat's close friends and extended family had not seen him for so long that we wanted them to be able to say goodbye to him, but we also had to be prepared in case large numbers of people turned up. Thankfully, we were blessed with some beautiful September weather over those days, which enabled us to keep everyone outside as much as possible, with lots of ventilation when inside.

The room where Pat lay was our so-called 'good room' and I often complained to Pat that it was a complete white elephant, never being used save for maybe at Christmas time. The irony of it now being the perfect space for people to visit Pat occurred to me and I felt that he would definitely be saying, 'I told you so.'

All the windows were open in the room to satisfy the need for good ventilation, and a steady stream of people started turning up. Organising a funeral is a daunting prospect at the best of times, but Covid-19 added a whole other layer of sadness to everything. No hugging, no handshakes, keep apart, keep distant. Every human touch designed to comfort and heal was banned. I was terrified that Pat's funeral could be a spreading event for the disease, but found it impossible to turn away anyone who wanted to say a final goodbye to him. With the windows open, I couldn't help but notice two butterflies fluttering in and out of the room all day, flying over Pat and across our heads. Earlier in the morning Sarah had called me to show me another butterfly perched on her finger. Bemused, I said, 'What is it with all these butterflies?', recalling the two that had been in Pat's and my bedroom the night Pat died. 'Look it up,' my sister replied. 'They're a symbol for the soul, for rebirth and resurrection.'

Indeed, a quick search will tell you that in almost every culture, the butterfly does symbolise these things, and their sudden appearance became a source of wonder and comfort from then on.

Friday was the day we were all dreading. Time to say our final goodbyes to our gorgeous husband, father, brother and son – the funeral mass and burial. The road all the way to the church in Rhode was lined with people. Our friends and neighbours, the schoolchildren outside Ballybryan school where Pat had dropped off and picked up our own children countless times, so many friends dotted here and there who had travelled miles, and finally the guard of honour made up of Pat's fellow jockeys. The start time of the races that day had been pushed back to allow the jockeys time to attend the funeral and still make it to the races. I allowed myself a wry smile – it wasn't the first time that Pat managed to get the start time changed to suit him!

The church was beautifully decorated with flowers from the Moyglare Stud garden, flowers which remained there for Paddy's confirmation a week later. I spoke to Eva Haefner the day before to thank her for this lovely gesture. Although Pat was always careful to respect the boundaries between employer and employee, there was something special about their relationship and they were very close, constantly messaging each other over and back. Eva was still in a bit of shock when we spoke, as she had received a message from him on Wednesday morning when she knew he had already passed away. It was the message that Pat wanted to send Eva on Sunday evening after her Irish St Leger win. I have no idea why it only reached her then, but it must have been very emotional for her to get it at that time.

I had written everything down that I thought Pat might want me to say and was determined to deliver a eulogy that he would be proud of. I was so heartbroken for all Pat's friends who had missed out on the last months of his life, for his community who had lost their local hero and of course for his family who were now without a son, brother and father. So many cancer sufferers had taken courage from Pat's positive outlook, and I knew that Pat would not want them to lose hope. Finally, I knew he would want me to thank the wonderful doctors, nurses and caregivers in St Vincent's Private Hospital, who had looked after him with such kindness over the previous two and a half years.

I never felt as calm as I did delivering those words for him, and I can only put it down to Pat holding my hand every step of the way. Indeed, as a family, as we made our way to the graveside that day, I think the calmness and peace that surrounded us came straight from him and gave us all the strength we needed.

As for the butterflies – they became a permanent fixture in our lives. They constantly appeared in our bedrooms out of nowhere; no sooner was one put out the window than another would appear, and coming into October, generally windows were kept closed, so we were constantly amazed by the sight of them.

It was the second week of October when I had to fill out the form for Pat's death cert. An advantage of Covid was that you no longer had to make a sad and lonely trek to council offices for this, but could fill out the form in the privacy of your home and post it. Nevertheless, it was still an upsetting job and I sat on my own at the kitchen island in tears afterwards.

A sudden noise startled me, and there on the kitchen window, a butterfly had appeared, flapping like crazy. Maybe just a coincidence, but I can't explain how comforted I felt in that moment and the peace that came over me.

Another one appeared on 13 November as we sat, feet up, watching *The Late Late Show* in the living room. Again, out of nowhere it flew in from the adjoining kitchen and fluttered above us around the room. Maybe another coincidence, but 13 November is our wedding anniversary.

Christmas approached and there was no sign of the butterflies disappearing. The day before Christmas Eve, I couldn't stop thinking of how I would have to take the presents in from where we usually hid them in the sauna room on my own that year. I crept in under the cover of darkness to hide a newly wrapped present, and what was waiting for me there? A butterfly.

Not long after the funeral, I was in bed one night, just drifting off to sleep, when Hannah came in to wake me. She is a bit of a night owl and had been lying on her bed thinking of her dad and crying.

'You know that light in my bathroom that hasn't worked for years?' she asked. Indeed I did: despite the electrician's best efforts, it never really worked.

'Well,' Hannah said, 'as I was crying on my bed it just came on.'

That light had never worked before or since. Actually, I have had to add a correction to the previous sentence. The light did come on again. The morning of Hannah's first Leaving Cert exam, nervous and emotional after strapping her dad's watch on her wrist, she was finishing getting ready and was about to leave her bathroom when on popped the light again. Probably just a coincidence, but she left for her exams that morning feeling that her dad was right there with her.

After Hannah woke me up that night to tell me about her light, it got me thinking about the time the lights went off in the kitchen at the time of the funeral. All of the strange little coincidences had led us all to believe that Pat was sending us signs that he was okay.

Now, I also have two lights, either side of my mirror, which have not worked for some time. One night as I was getting ready for bed I said to Pat, 'I know that you're happy, at peace and in a wonderful place.' Just as the thought was in my head, one of the little lights popped on and flashed three times. Maybe just a coincidence, but to me that night it was absolute confirmation of the message that we think Pat was trying to give us.

I had never heard of this type of thing before save for the odd mention of a robin appearing, which didn't really resonate with me at the time, so when these things started happening, I was absolutely dumbfounded. It wasn't that I either believed or disbelieved in these things before, but honestly my rational mind would have dismissed as utter nonsense what is basically a form of communication from beyond the grave. If Santa Claus and the Tooth Fairy had both appeared and sat down for a cup of tea, I don't think I would have been more surprised than I was by all of these things.

I had been telling our family of all these strange little things that had happened and they were fascinated. Taking a walk on the farm one day, I was chatting to my sister on the phone, and she confided to me that she was finding white feathers and was convinced that they were little signs from our dad, with whom she was very close. After the phone call I thought to myself how Pat had always hated the pigeons that nested in the barn and made a terrible mess.

'Well, you won't be sending me dirty old pigeon feathers anyway, Pat,' I thought. Instantly, I was stopped in my tracks by the most beautiful big feather, right there at my feet. I had never come across a feather like it on the farm and was dumbfounded that it should appear just as I was thinking those thoughts. I've kept that feather (probably a buzzard's), and I will always treasure it.

One other strange thing happened to me involving a feather. Lily, one of our terriers, is allowed to sleep in the back hall as she rarely barks. One night, however, at around 3.30 a.m., she was making a terrible fuss, so I went down to let her out. Shivering, I closed the back door and stood looking out, hoping she wasn't going to be too long and silently cursing her for waking me up. As I stared out, something caught my eye, floating down out of the sky. It was a tiny feather and as it reached the ground, I ran out to pick it up. I have no idea what bird could have been flying by at that hour, but I thought it pretty strange that it lost a feather right then and I just happened to be standing there to catch it!

If just one of these things had happened, and to be honest there were plenty of others, we would have shrugged and passed it off as a coincidence. However, when you are in the moment and these things occur, it is the strangest feeling of elation mixed with utter disbelief. It was as if Pat had reached out and touched us with a little sense of the intense love and peace that he himself was experiencing. I truly believe that Pat was somehow able to send us signs to let us know that he was okay and was there with us when we needed him. The comfort this brought us helped us get through an unbelievably difficult period in our lives and, although the void that Pat has left is almost unbearable at times, my children and I believe that we have the most amazing guardian angel looking after us now. I myself no longer fear death; I know where I am going, and I know that Pat will be there to meet me.

Pat has shown us that there is so much more to life, and we are extremely grateful to him for this gift. He said to me before he died that he had a very strong feeling that this was happening for a reason. Maybe that reason was to help his family find this peace; and maybe by sharing these things in his book then Pat can help others find peace. If you have been diagnosed with a terminal illness, if you have lost someone you love or if you simply recognise that life itself is eventually terminal for us all, then it might be of comfort to be reminded that there is somewhere else. Pat is there, he has shown us, and if there was a reason for his death, as he so strongly felt, then maybe this is it.